Voices of Historical and Contemporary Black American Pioneers

VOLUME 2: LAW AND GOVERNMENT

Edited by Vernon L. Farmer
and Evelyn Shepherd-Wynn

Foreword
Benjamin S. Carson, Sr.

Afterword
Guion S. "Guy" Bluford, Jr.

AN IMPRINT OF ABC-CLIO, LLC
Santa Barbara, California • Denver, Colorado • Oxford, England

Voices of Historical and Contemporary Black American Pioneers

Volume 1

Medicine and Science

Volume 2

Law and Government

Volume 3

Aviation, Armed Forces, and Astronautics

Volume 4

Education, Social Sciences, and Humanities

Voices of Historical and Contemporary Black American Pioneers

VOLUME 2: LAW AND GOVERNMENT

Vernon L. Farmer
Editor-in-Chief

Evelyn Shepherd-Wynn
Associate Editor

In Collaboration with
Lisa Pertillar Brevard
and
In Consultation with
Ernesta Pendleton Williams

Farmer's Research Group
Evelyn Shepherd-Wynn • Lisa Pertillar Brevard
Ernesta Pendleton Williams • Clovis Jones, Jr.
Ralph Ferguson • Emily M. Birch
Neari F. Warner • Joy A. Jordan
Frances S. Conley • Peggy Porter
Brittany Hoskins • Stacy Cassius
Jordan A. Wynn

Foreword
Benjamin S. Carson, Sr.

Afterword
Guion S. "Guy" Bluford, Jr.

PRAEGER

AN IMPRINT OF ABC-CLIO, LLC
Santa Barbara, California • Denver, Colorado • Oxford, England

Library of Congress Cataloging-in-Publication Data

Voices of historical and contemporary Black American pioneers / edited by Vernon L. Farmer and Evelyn Shepherd-Wynn ; foreword, Benjamin S. Carson, Sr. ; afterword, Guion S. "Guy" Bluford, Jr.
    v. ; cm.
  Includes bibliographical references and index.
  ISBN 978-0-313-39224-5 (hard back : alk. paper) —
  ISBN 978-0-313-39225-2 (ebook)
  1. African Americans—Biography.   I. Farmer, Vernon L.   II. Shepherd-Wynn, Evelyn.
  E185.96.V65 2012
  920.0092'96073—dc23
  [B]

                                                           2011053511

ISBN: 978-0-313-39224-5
EISBN: 978-0-313-39225-2

16 15 14 13 12   1 2 3 4 5

This book is also available on the World Wide Web as an eBook.
Visit www.abc-clio.com for details.

Praeger
An Imprint of ABC-CLIO, LLC

ABC-CLIO, LLC
130 Cremona Drive, P.O. Box 1911
Santa Barbara, California 93116-1911

This book is printed on acid-free paper ∞
Manufactured in the United States of America

Dedication

*To Vernyatta Lee Farmer and Joshua Lee Farmer, my sons,
and Jacob Lee and Gabriel Adam, my grandsons, whose very
existence inspired me to take on the daunting challenge
of producing this scholarly multivolume set.*
—*Vernon Lee Farmer*

*To my daughter, Jordan Alexis Wynn, whom I invited to travel with
us on this journey through Black American history, I hope that the
journey will help her embrace her heritage and understand that
education is the great equalizer, if she is to claim her rightful place
in the world; and to my mother, Lavern D. Shepherd, for her
steadfast love and support during this daunting research effort.*
—*Evelyn Shepherd-Wynn*

*To all Black people, young and old, and other people of color,
we hope that by reading this multivolume set, you will gain
a greater sense of self, a greater sense of belonging, and a
greater sense of urgency about your own profession and career
and the contributions you hope to make in strengthening
the Black community and edifying America and the world.*
—*Vernon Lee Farmer and Evelyn Shepherd-Wynn*

Volume 2 Contents

Foreword

BENJAMIN S. CARSON, SR.

Pediatric Neurosurgeon,
Johns Hopkins Hospital,
Baltimore, Maryland

You could probably ask a hundred successful people "what is the key to career success," and you would probably get close to a hundred different answers, but there would be some commonalities. I think one of the things most people would agree on is that there is no point in reinventing the wheel. By learning from the triumphs and the mistakes others have made along the way, it is possible to achieve success more rapidly than if all the lessons have to be learned personally. Fortunately, we can learn from not only contemporaries but also from people who are historical figures. One of the historical figures that inspired me was Booker T. Washington when I read his book *Up from Slavery*. He was born a slave, and it was illegal for slaves to read; however, he not only taught himself to read but also read every book he could get his hands on and became an adviser to presidents. It taught me that one has to take initiative and sometimes, perhaps, even take a few risks in order to achieve success.

I vividly remember being a high school student in inner-city Detroit and feeling sorry for so many of my teachers who truly wanted to teach the children but had to spend an inordinate amount of time handling discipline problems. It was not infrequent that the entire hour would go by with nothing being taught because of discipline problems. That was obviously going to have a negative impact on my education; therefore, I made a conscious decision to go back and see all of my teachers after school and ask them, "What did you intend to teach today?" They would be very happy to see me, and they would know that they would at least be able to get important information across to one student. I eventually became the person who set up many of the science laboratory experiments for my classmates, and, of course, I had to learn from the teachers what the points of the experiments were, and even if the class was not concluded successfully, I still had the benefit of learning what the lesson had been. It was this type of initiative that allowed me to go to Yale University despite graduating from an inner-city high school in Detroit with a poor academic teaching record.

In addition to getting a handle on my academic subjects, I took initiative in supplementing my cultural education and would travel downtown to the Detroit Institute of Art on many occasions until I knew virtually every painting there—who had painted them, when the artists were born, when the artists died, and what period the paintings represented. I also taught myself classical music in addition to being quite familiar with all the Motown favorites.

The bottom line is this: If you want to be successful, it is necessary to take the initiative and not simply wait for someone else to provide the road map to your success. It should also be pointed out that there are likely to be some roadblocks on the way to success. I vividly remember being told by my medical school adviser to drop out of medical school six weeks into my first semester because I had done poorly on the first comprehensive set of examinations. He was kind enough to offer to help get me into another discipline at the university, but he really had no helpful suggestions about how I might succeed in medicine. Because medicine had been my only dream, I could not accept his advice and went back to my apartment and started thinking and realized that I did not learn much from boring lectures, but I learned a great deal from reading. I, therefore, decided to skip the boring lectures, which took six to eight hours of my day, and to spend that time reading. That resulted in a dramatic improvement in my academic performance. Years later, when I returned to my medical school as the commencement speaker, I was looking for that adviser so I could tell him that he was not really cut out to be an adviser.

I think you will find that many of the people you will read about in *Voices of Historical and Contemporary Black American Pioneers* will have had similar experiences, but the one thing they all refused to do was to become a victim. If you think you are a victim, then you *are* one, and that will negatively impact whatever career you decide to pursue. The human brain is an incredible organ, capable of remembering everything that you have ever seen or heard and is able to process more than two million bits of information per second. With that type of ammunition, none of us ever need to consider ourselves as victims. The persons who have the most to do with what happens to us is us, and unlike animals, we have the ability to extract information from the past and the present and to project it into a plan for the future. It is that ability to plan and strategize that gives us control of our environment and our destiny.

Finally, when you do achieve success, please remember to utilize the platform that you are afforded to encourage others to use their God-given talents not only to create success in their own lives but also in the lives of all of those who fall within their sphere of influence.

A Tribute to Mrs. Rosa Parks

JOHN CONYERS, JR.

United States Congressman,
14th Congressional District,
Detroit, Michigan

Rosa Parks was a matriarch of extraordinary courage and grace. And she was my friend. I knew her for more than four decades, and upon her passing in 2005 it was my honor to introduce the resolution in Congress to allow her to lie in state at the U.S. Capitol Rotunda, the first woman and the second African American to lie at the same exalted place as presidents and war heroes. It was a long road from the Montgomery bus seat she refused to give up to being among only 30 Americans ever honored in this way, but no one ever deserved it more.

She risked death when she quietly refused to give up her seat on that fateful day, but her resolve lit a fire under the Civil Rights Movement and ignited Americans to end racial discrimination. It was Rosa who gave the NAACP the much-needed momentum to endure a yearlong boycott that ultimately led the Supreme Court to hold segregated buses unconstitutional. It was her graceful determination that inspired the passage of the 1964 Voting Rights Act, and in 2006, it was her shoulders on which I stood as I led the Congress in passing the reauthorization of the Voting Rights Act, extending its protections to language and physical barriers as well.

I will never forget the day I met Rosa Parks. She walked into my first campaign office, having recently moved to Detroit from Alabama, and offered to help, completely unsolicited. She was there "to help me win," she said, and I was flattered beyond words that she even knew who I was. Many believed that Dr. Martin Luther King, Jr. had sent her, but she never said. Following my election to Congress, she honored me further by working in my congressional office for 24 years, advocating for my constituents in Detroit and speaking out against injustice, poverty, and inhumanity everywhere.

Her death inspired tens of thousands of Americans to travel to Washington, D.C. Most of them were too young to have marched in the 1960s, but all of them were inspired by her willingness to be used by history to move a nation. Her legacy, the gift she left for all of us, is that even ordinary people can make a difference if they are committed to their ideals.

A Tribute to the Tuskegee Airmen

CHARLES B. RANGEL

United States Congressman,
5th Congressional District,
New York, New York

Black Americans have been on the front lines of every one of America's major conflicts, lending their livelihoods for the good of their country. It has not always been easy. Over the years, the pall of discrimination, at times ill treatment, and segregation hung as terribly sad albatrosses around their necks. But their service was, nevertheless, a source of inordinate pride for them, and now, for us and our communities.

The Tuskegee Airmen of World War II laid life and limb on the line, leaving the confines of Tuskegee, Alabama, to head to Europe in defense of a country that routinely and systematically left them on the outskirts. They were fighting not in support of the Jim Crow system that awaited them at home, but in support of a steadfast belief in how great America could become. Those men showed remarkable foresight, limitless bravery, and a commendable regard for country above self. The first African American pilots to be trained as military aviators in the Army Air Corps, the Tuskegee Airmen were viewed as an experiment by skeptics who doubted that Blacks had the requisite skill to man airplanes. But after completing 15,500 missions, destroying 260 enemy aircrafts, and earning a historic 150 Distinguished Flying Crosses, 744 Air Medals, 8 Purple Hearts, and 14 Bronze Stars, it was clear: they not only did their jobs but also did them superbly well.

Two years ago, the surviving airmen stood in the Capitol Rotunda—some in wheelchairs—before a crowd of 700 to accept the Congressional Gold Medal, the highest civilian honor awarded by Congress. That joyous occasion finally brought these courageous men the long overdue glory and recognition they deserve. I led the effort to award them those medals because theirs is a quintessentially American story of struggle and triumph. Those men tore down the racial barriers in the Armed Forces that had held back generations of Black Americans. While Blacks were historically disregarded in most accounts of American heroism and achievement and were left out of textbooks, these airmen served as unsung trailblazers who made their own history. Their feats were more than just military accomplishments; they fueled social change in the desegregation of the military and the recognition of civil rights.

Our community should feel moved and motivated by their incredible sacrifices. It should lend inspiration to all young Black Americans that hard work and determination can lead to illustrious careers. Many of the Tuskegee Airmen served their country ably and admirably, and then went on to further their formal education and to continue serving their country in various fields, like Percy Sutton, Roscoe Brown, and Lee Archer. Today's youth stand on their shoulders, enjoying rights and opportunities that were unimaginable to these men at the time. May we channel that pioneering spirit in all of our endeavors, and work toward a better America for our families and our communities.

A Tribute to Barack H. Obama

VERNON L. FARMER

Professor of Educational Leadership,
College of Education,
Grambling State University,
Grambling, Louisiana

The world witnessed a watershed event in America on January 20, 2009, when Barack H. Obama made history, becoming the first Black American to ascend to the presidency of the United States. American citizens throughout the country banded together and spoke with one voice to help him make history. In fact, some of the very citizens whose lives and contributions are profiled in *Voices of Historical and Contemporary Black American Pioneers* helped pave the way for Obama's singular achievement. Obama's voice of change rallied voices of people from all races and ethnic groups to join him in his fervent campaign for a better world, beginning with a better America. He called upon all Americans to band together, to work collaboratively under his leadership, and to help bring change to America, making America a better place for all of its citizens: me, you, and us. As President Obama reminds us, "There is not a Black America and a White America and Latino America and Asian America, there's the United States of America!" (2004 Democratic National Convention Keynote Address). United we stand, determined to fight oppression and enlarge the vision of freedom for which our ancestors fought and died, a vision that we have the power to manifest today in ways in which previous generations could only dream.

What surprise and honor President Obama must have felt to have been awarded the Nobel Peace Prize during his first year as president, "for his extraordinary efforts to strengthen international diplomacy and cooperation between peoples" ("The Nobel Peace Prize 2009"). Obama became the third Black American to receive this honor, following Ralph H. Bunche and Martin Luther King, Jr. Obama did not rise to prominence alone; however, as is true of many of the pioneers profiled in this book, Obama worked diligently and was inspired by others: prominent activists, past and present; his mother; his wife, First Lady Michelle Obama; and his children, Malia and Sasha. The First Family continues to inspire the nation and the world.

Voices of Historical and Contemporary Black American Pioneers is a tribute to Barack Obama's ascension to the position of commander-in-chief of the United States of America.

References

2004 Democratic National Convention Keynote Address. July 27, 2004. Boston, Massachusetts.

"The Nobel Peace Prize 2009." Press Release. Nobelprize.org. http://www.nobelprize.org/nobel_prizes/peace/laureates/2009/press.html.

A Tribute to Martin Luther King, Jr.

EVELYN SHEPHERD-WYNN

Assistant Professor of English,
College of Arts and Sciences,
Grambling State University,
Grambling, Louisiana

Martin Luther King, Jr. lived for only 39 years, yet he became America's foremost civil rights leader and is regarded as the greatest American leader of his era. Because King was a moral leader, in addition to studying the Gospel, he also studied Mohandas Gandhi's nonviolence strategy, successfully adapting it in the civil rights struggle, resulting in his resounding speech "I Have a Dream," which was given during the historic March on Washington in 1963. "I Have a Dream" propelled the passage of the Civil Rights Act of 1964 and the Voting Rights Act of 1965. It also laid the foundation for King to receive the Nobel Peace Prize in 1964, making him the youngest person in America and the second Black American (after Ralph Bunche) to receive the award. In 1983, largely through the efforts of his wife, Coretta Scott King, musician/activist Stevie Wonder, and a groundswell of ardent supporters, King's birthday was declared a national holiday, and the first official recognition of this day took place in 1986. To this day, King remains the only American civilian so honored.

King's use of nonviolent protest accelerated social and political change in America. The powerful voice of this one man calmed the outcries of citizens across the country, particularly in the state of Alabama and its cities of Selma, Montgomery, Anniston, and Birmingham, where, during the struggle for civil rights, Black and White Americans had suffered for justice, callously firehosed, viciously attacked by dogs, and brutally beaten by police—denied not only their citizenship rights but also their very right to exist. With *Voices of Historical and Contemporary Black American Pioneers*, we pay tribute to pioneer Dr. Martin Luther King, Jr. His nonviolent protests and words of hope echoed throughout the land, allowing the world to see the racism and bigotry in the United States. In the process, he became a champion of change for all. He is one of the world's most revered Americans, and a Washington, D.C., monument honoring his life and legacy has been constructed. It stands as the only monument of an American citizen erected among the monuments of former U.S. presidents.

The measure of a man is determined by the positive changes that he effects upon himself, his family, and the family of humankind. The Rev. Dr. Martin Luther King, Jr.'s nonviolent efforts helped to bring about positive effectual changes ranging from the era of Jim Crow to the Civil Rights Act of 1964, the Voting Rights Act of 1965, and the election of President Barack Obama in 2008. King's voice was the voice of one man, but its truth resounds in the minds and hearts of many.

Acknowledgments

When pursuing a scholarly work of this magnitude (a multivolume set), it is inevitable that it will take a collective effort of many individuals. With this in mind, the editors acknowledge those who played a role, both small and large, in helping to bring this five-year research project to fruition. However, there is one individual, Lisa Pertillar Brevard, who played an immeasurable role in the making of this multivolume set. The editors wish to extend their everlasting gratitude to the following individuals.

Contributors: Clara L. Adams-Ender, James H. Ammons, Keith D. Amos, Glenn B. Anderson, Lauren Anderson, Hilary Hurd Anyaso, Lee A. "Buddy" Archer, Jr., Bob Ashby, Joe N. Ballard, Mary L. Balthazar, Jill E. Bargonetti, Wilton A. Barham, Gregory Battle, Denise L. Bean, Paul E. Bibbins, Jr., Barry C. Black, Guion S. "Guy" Bluford, Jr., Charles F. Bolden, Jr., Darien Bradford, Carol Moseley Braun, Donna L. Brazile, Lisa Pertillar Brevard, Carl Brooks, Roscoe C. Brown, Jr., Steve A. Buddington, Arthur L. Burnett, Sr., Arthur L. Burnett II, Yvonne D. Cagle, Lisa D. Cain, Alexa I. Canady, Benjamin S. Carson Sr., Joye M. Carter, William Lacy Clay, Jr., George Cliette, Kelvin Cochran, James Pierpont Comer, Frances S. Conley, John Conyers, Jr., LaDoris J. Cordell, Comer Cottrell, Jr., Marcus S. Cox, Robert Crear, Robert L. Curbeam, Jr., Daryl Cumber Dance, Scott Jackson Dantley, Elizabeth K. Davenport, Lawrence F. Davenport, Henry V. Davis, Wilbert Ellis, Noel Leo Erskine, Charlene T. Evans, Keith C. Ferdinand, Ralph Ferguson, Robin L. Ferguson, Bill Fletcher, Jr., Elson S. Floyd, Rebera Elliot Foston, Mary H. Futrell, Thurston Gaines, Richard "Rick" Gallot, Antoine M. Garibaldi, Myra Gordon, Joseph L. Graves, Jr., Frederick D. Gregory, Ervin V. Griffin, Sr., Lani Guinier, S. Keith Hargrove, Bernard A. Harris, Jr., JoAnn W. Haysbert, Allan D. Headley, Asa Herring, Joan E. Higginbotham, Paul B.

Higginbotham, Frederick C. Hobdy, Edward Honor, Russel L. Honoré, Freeman A. Hrabowski, III, Heather McTeer Hudson, Alexander Jefferson, Bernette Joshua Johnson, James H. Johnson, Jr., Michael P. Johnson, Jr., William A. Johnson Jr., Clovis Jones, Jr., Emil Jones, Jr., Joy A. Jordan, Kim M. Keenan, Damon J. Keith, Joyce E. King, Otis J. Latin Sr., Rita Jo Lewis, William A. Massey, Gary S. May, John McCray, Jr., Jimmie McJamerson, Ronald E. Mickens, Karl Minter, Yolanda T. Moses, Kenneth A. Murphy, Clarence Ray Nagin, Jr., Lloyd W. "Fig" Newton, Levi A. Nwachuku, Major R. Owens, David Parks, Elisabeth Ann Petry, Lloyd G. Phillips, Belinda Pinckney, Peggy Porter, Colin Luther Powell, Winston S. Price, Peggy A. Quince, Charles B. Rangel, J. Paul Reason, Teresa L. Reed, Pamela Trotman Reid, Velma Richardson, Eddie G. Robinson, Sr., Victor G. J. Rodgers, Vincent G. J. Rodgers, William M. Rodgers III, John W. Rogers, Jr., Robert L. Satcher, Winston E. Scott, Leah Ward Sears, Abdulalim A. Shabazz, Brett A. Sims, William Spriggs, James H. Stith, Melvin T. Stith, Maurice C. Taylor, Kyle Turner, Neil deGrasse Tyson, Diallo S. Wallace, Isiah M. Warner, Neari F. Warner, James C. Warren, Diane E. Watson, Luke J. Weathers, E. Carol Webster, Belle S. Wheelan, Jesse White, Bennie E. Williams, Ernesta Pendleton Williams, Scott W. Williams, Johnnie E. Wilson, and Stephanie D. Wilson.

A great deal of appreciation is owed to ABC-CLIO editors: Emily M. Birch (former editor), Vicki Moran, Beth Ptalis, Valentina Tursini, Robin Tutt, and Betsy Crist.

Gratitude is extended to supporters from the private sector for their invaluable assistance: Christine Biggers, park ranger for the Tuskegee Airmen National Historic Site at Moten Field in Tuskegee, Alabama; Gayle Frere, public relations liaison at the National Aeronautics and Space Administration (NASA); Chris Heartman, manager of the JW Marriott Desert Ridge Resort and Spa, Phoenix, Arizona; and John Miller, vice president of public relations at US Airways.

A special note of appreciation is extended to the individuals who provided technical and library assistance: Catherine Bonner, Brenda Cooper, Shannon Davis, Bernie Evans, Maraine Hall, Mechelle Hall, Mable Houston, Uju Ifeanyi, Patricia Johnson, Audrey Jones, Linda Jones,

Jennifer McMullen, Carolyn McNeal, Rosemary Mokia, Melanie Monroe, Gloria Moore, Gaylon Murray, Pamela Payne, and Uranda Siad.

We are no less indebted to the student participants: Minelva Arlette, Lissa Baptiste, Stacy Cassius, Ferney Detouche, Fiona Francis, Andryne M. Henderson, Latosha Henry, Brittany Hoskin, DoKeitra Mayweather, Nikema Smith, and Jordan A. Wynn.

A heartfelt thanks to the staff at the following libraries: A. C. Lewis Memorial Library at Grambling State University, Grambling, Louisiana; Fintel Library at Roanoke College, Salem, Virginia; Fondren Library at Rice University, Dallas, Texas; Ford Motor Co. Library at Tuskegee University, Tuskegee, Alabama; Founders Library and the Moorland-Springarn Research Center at Howard University, Washington, D.C.; M. D. Anderson Library at the University of Houston, Houston, Texas; Noel Memorial Library at Louisiana State University, Shreveport, Louisiana; Prescott Memorial Library at Louisiana Tech University, Ruston, Louisiana; Robert J. Terry and Thurgood Marshall Law Libraries at Texas Southern University, Houston, Texas; The Savery Library at Talladega College, Talladega, Alabama; Thomas Cole Winston, Sr. Library at Wiley College, Marshall, Texas; ULM Library at the University of Louisiana, Monroe, Louisiana; and the University Library at Southern University in Shreveport, Louisiana.

Finally, a heartfelt appreciation goes to Ruby Lewis for her superb editing skills and substantive proofreading of the document and to Karla L. Williams for her proofreading ability and excellent tracking skills on the galley of this manuscript.

Introduction

Dear Reader:

You are cordially invited to travel with us through Black American history to learn more about the lives and careers of Black American pioneers. Our vehicle is *Voices of Historical and Contemporary Black American Pioneers*—the very book you are holding. Our destination is empowerment and self-actualization. As you travel with us, we hope you will gain a sense of belonging and a sense of what it must have been like to travel the paths of pioneers. We hope that as you gain a greater sense of self, you will also gain a sense of urgency about your own profession and career and the contributions you hope to make in strengthening the Black community and edifying America and the world.

But first, let us tell you about *our* journey so far. The groundbreaking *Voices of Historical and Contemporary Black American Pioneers* will introduce you to Black American pioneers from the distant and recent past, describing their extraordinary accomplishments and phenomenal contributions. We focus on the pioneers' beginnings and trace their development. We explore the lives and careers of historical Black American pioneers in different fields, including the armed forces, astronautics, aviation, education, government, humanities, law, medicine, science, and social science. We validate the pioneers' accomplishments and contributions as they struggled with violence, racism, discrimination, and bigotry in America. We invited a cadre of contemporary Black American scholars and professionals from these different professions and career fields to also make their voices heard.

Voices of Historical and Contemporary Black American Pioneers is organized into four volumes, mapped along three genres: biographies, autobiographies, and original interviews. Each volume begins with a two-page introduction, followed by the life stories and career histories of Black

American figures, poignantly told, recounting victories in the face of often painful experiences. These life stories resonate within human hearts. The criteria for selecting the pioneers were simple but stringent: each person profiled in this book had to have made a unique contribution to the world that not only advanced his or her field of work but also made a positive impact on society, serving as an example for others to follow. First and foremost, they are family members, professionals, and social activists, and they call themselves Americans, or African Americans, or Black Americans. As editors, we decided to use the term "Black American," because it reflects not only pan-African heritage but also American identity and global citizenship.

Farmer's Research Group provided cross-checking to determine the accuracy of entries whenever sources gave conflicting information. Whenever possible, we located at least three reputable sources to confirm background information of all the entries which is a strong feature of this multivolume set. Although we spent thousands of hours cross-checking entries in this multivolume set, we encourage readers to notify the publisher or the editors if inaccuracies are found.

By compiling this rare multivolume set, we hope to connect the current generation with past generations of knowledge and wisdom. Although most previous books in this area often provide deep accounts, they typically focus only on historical figures or contemporary figures, rarely both. *Voices of Historical and Contemporary Black American Pioneers* bridges the two, covering the period beginning with the immediate postcolonial period and continuing into the 21st century. In our efforts to tie together threads of history and culture, we visited places that helped us crystallize the life stories and career histories of Black American pioneers.

In 2005, we began our journey to a number of libraries, archives, museums, exhibits, and institutes, commencing what was to become a five-year research period that ended in 2010, and the sixth year was spent finalizing the writing of the four-volume set. As we traveled to the various sites, different modes of transportation (car, bus, train, and airplane) allowed us to engage in conversation with various audiences in the hopes that the information gleaned would help set the tone for the collection's unifying narratives—its unifying "voice." This "voice," threaded throughout the collection, educates and inspires by amplifying, underscoring, and extending the lessons of the pioneers.

During the five-year research period, we visited a number of libraries and archives to examine the lives and careers of Black American figures. We began our research at Grambling State University's A. C. Lewis Memorial Library. We spent many hours conducting research in the Mary Watson Hymon Afro-American Center, studying its collection of books, journals, magazines, periodicals, newspapers, artifacts, and other documents representing Black Americans and their heritage, culture, and history. Much of the early writing for the biographies took place in the Charles P. Adams and Carter G. Woodson buildings, which housed our respective offices. These historic buildings were named in honor of Charles P. Adams, founder of Grambling State University, and Carter G. Woodson, who was credited with founding Negro History Week (now called Black History Month). The images of these historical pioneers served as a daily stimulus as the narratives took shape.

The pioneers' voices led us to Houston, Texas, to study the extensive special collections of African American history at Texas Southern University's Robert James Terry Library, namely the Barbara Jordan Archives, the Freedmen Bureau Records, and the Heartman Collection. Although many of the artifacts in the collections have been carefully preserved, they nevertheless showed wear and tear; yet the voices of the pioneers, as heard through the Freedmen Papers, carried a freshness and contemporary relevance that remains engraved upon our minds and souls. We also reviewed a collection of legal documents at the Thurgood Marshall Law School Library at Texas Southern University concerning Charles Hamilton Houston, Thurgood Marshall, William Hastie, Jr., Robert Carter, Oliver Hill, Spottswood W. Robinson III, and other legal scholars. These legal geniuses fought steadfastly so that Black Americans could have the right to sit at the welcome table.

We traveled to Washington, D.C., to examine resources at Howard University's Moorland-Spingarn Research Center, housing one of the widest-ranging collections of manuscripts, periodicals, newspapers, microfiche, microforms, rare books, and other artifacts concerned with Black American ancestry, history, and culture, which is located in historic Founders Library. This library, with its clock tower, stands in prominent view on the campus and has been central to the lives of Howard students since its dedication in 1939. Visitors to the undergraduate library cannot fail to feel the importance of the five original oak-paneled reading rooms, the high ceilings, and the long hallways with glass-encased displays of Harlem Renaissance book jackets, distinguished faculty publications, and Howard University history. The importance and rarity of some of the documents housed within these walls are legendary. For example, the Moorland-Spingarn Research Center is the repository for correspondence between Langston Hughes and Zora Neale Hurston, and the original manuscripts of Dr. Ralph J. Bunche and other notable Blacks are found here. Departments include oral histories, music, photographs, and manuscripts. In addition, one can trace the history of the Black press; Blacks in the military, including the Tuskeegee Airmen; and the struggle through the years for voting rights. The library, when it opened, rivaled those of the Ivy League schools in technical and modern conveniences and today continues to stand as a monument from slavery to freedom chronicling the Black American experience worldwide.

We also visited the Howard University Law School Library on the Dumbarton Oaks campus. Here we again reviewed legal documents about the Civil Rights Movement, as well as papers written by and about such legal scholars as Charles Hamilton Houston, Thurgood Marshall, William Hastie, Jr., Constance Baker Motley, and other distinguished legal scholars who fought for parity for Black Americans. Their voices showed us the power of Black literacy in harnessing the letter of the law for the betterment of society. Judge Damon J. Keith perhaps best described the value of Howard University Law School Library when he said, "Through Howard University Law School, we came to know these lawyers who are legends today in African American legal history. . . .They taught us that the Constitution was our best hope, that equality would come through the law" (The Damon J. Keith Law Collection of African American Legal History).

Another library we consulted took the form of a fellow scholar: Lisa Pertillar Brevard, whom we visited on three occasions. (Brevard is a contributing author for this collection; a Hurricane Katrina survivor and former Dillard University professor and resident of the City of New Orleans. After the hurricane, she obtained visiting faculty status at Roanoke College in Salem, Virginia. She is currently Core Faculty for Humanities at Walden University.) During our first visit, we bused from Louisiana to southwestern Virginia to meet with her at Roanoke College's Fintel Library to flesh out the overall structure, themes, tone, and timbre of the narratives connecting *Voices of Historical and Contemporary Black American Pioneers*. Surrounded by books and other media representing the knowledge of many generations and many peoples from around the world, we focused our efforts on unifying the varied voices of this manuscript, preparing them for the world to hear.

Our second visit to Roanoke Valley entailed an airplane ride. After several days of working with Brevard on the narrative, we boarded our flight to return home. While en route from Virginia to Louisiana, the airplane encountered a tumultuous storm. As we left Virginia, the pilot advised all passengers and flight attendants to remain seated, as he guided the aircraft through the storm. Meanwhile, the quiet, prayerful energy of everyone onboard seemed to balance the jarring turbulence of the flight. Only after we made a safe landing in Atlanta did we realize that our pilot was a Black American. How ironic when we were writing about the Tuskegee Airmen who recalled how, in the early days, Black Americans were not allowed to fly, and about Bessie Coleman, a pioneering Black American pilot who overcame racism and sexism to first earn her wings in France. Yet our very lives seemed to depend on our faith in the Almighty and the superb abilities of a Black American pilot.

Our third visit to the Roanoke Valley entailed driving from Louisiana to Virginia, this time for a meeting with Brevard in the relaxed atmosphere of a local coffee house. Taking in hot coffee, fruit teas, and pastries at the Daily Grind, we also took time to reaffirm our commitment to this project and renew our strength and focus, completing multiple drafts of the narratives over several days. The journey was far from over, however. Across the ensuing years, as the manuscript took shape, telephones and computer technologies continued to connect us to Brevard, while the voices of the early pioneers led us to explore many other places.

As we traveled to Tuskegee, Alabama, to study the resources at Tuskegee University's Ford Motor Company Library, we had an informative sojourn. As we approached the Tuskegee University campus, we were reminded of our rich history, realizing that history abounds on this campus and in this small town. And rightfully so, for Tuskegee is the home of Booker T. Washington, the educator, orator, and the first president of Tuskegee Institute; George Washington Carver, the scientist and agriculturalist; and the Tuskegee Airmen, the first Black American unit to fly in the U.S. military. Continuing our research at the Tuskegee University library, one of the first displays we observed was a commemorative exhibition of works where Tuskegee's first-year student body compared Booker T. Washington and Barack Obama. The comparisons drawn between the two specifically focused on each man's leadership and oratorical style, expressed via the students' informative exhibits and related research papers. While visiting Tuskegee, we also reviewed several unique collections housed in the Washington Room and the Rare Book Room. In the Washington Room, appropriately named after Booker T. Washington, we reviewed materials authored by and written about the Black American experience; the largest collections focused on the history and literature of African Americans, Africa, and the Black diaspora. An air of nostalgia and high expectations held us aloft as we entered the Rare Book Room adjacent to the Washington Room. The Rare Book Room houses papers by and about George Washington Carver and the presidents of Tuskegee University.

The rich resources of the libraries of Grambling State University, Texas Southern University, Howard University, and Tuskegee University were invaluable to us in writing the narrative for *Voices of Historical and Contemporary Black American Pioneers*. These vehicles, libraries and archives, constitute key repositories in the preservation of Black American history and culture as they house some of the most valuable information concerning the legacies of many historical Black American pioneers, upon whose shoulders contemporary Black American pioneers stand.

Our five-year scholarly sojourn also took us to museums and exhibits throughout the United States. In fact, while attending the 39th Annual Conference of the Research Association of Minority Professors in Montgomery, Alabama, we had occasion to revisit Tuskegee University, where we toured the George Washington Carver Museum, which houses George Washington Carver's educational exhibits, laboratory equipment, many of his peanut and sweet potato products, and his original works of art. One of the key attractions of the museum is an audio recording of Carver's voice. We heard the voice of the pioneer lecturing to his students! Hearing his gentle, melodious voice brought his legacy to life, deeply moving us and inspiring pride deep within. Carver's voice was not the only pioneer voice resounding in the hallowed halls of Tuskegee, however.

Through the magic of early audio recording technology, we also heard the commanding voice of Booker T. Washington, orating his Exposition Speech—one of the first audio recordings made by a Black American. Hearing Washington's voice helped us put his perspective into historical context; his very voice transported us to *his* time and circumstances. Symbolically underscoring and extending the pioneer's voice is an honored statue of Washington, elegant and resolute, standing tall and aptly occupying the focal point of the Tuskegee University campus. Booker T. Washington's statue keeps watch over his beloved university, reminding everyone of its history and purpose. Washington's wise gaze also approvingly looked upon us during our research in Virginia.

At the close of a day-long research and writing session, we thought we had lost a major portion of the book manuscript due to a computer glitch. Exhausted, disappointed, and overwhelmed, we decided to take a break from work and get a bite to eat. As we sat silently in O'Charley's restaurant, we both acknowledged a strange, eerie feeling, but didn't know why. Moments later, we looked up and realized that a large oil-on-canvas portrait of Booker T. Washington, part of the restaurant's decor honoring the Virginia native, hung on the wall, serendipitously giving us hope. Booker T. Washington's presence also reminded us of our history and purpose—why we were visiting with Lisa Brevard in Salem, Virginia. We returned to Grambling, Louisiana, recharged with our mission to tell stories of Black American success.

Continuing our research, we visited the Rosa Parks Museum at Troy University in Montgomery, Alabama. The museum is a must-see for all, but especially for children. The exhibit offers opportunities for visitors to witness, through a time machine and an interactive reenactment, Rosa Parks's refusal to take a back seat in a Montgomery, Alabama, public bus, along with other Civil Rights Movement events. Having an opportunity to see this reenactment gave us a greater sense of appreciation for Parks and her pivotal role as Mother of the Civil Rights Movement. Fortunately, we had the prime opportunity earlier in our careers to have visited Mrs. Parks when she worked in the office of Congressman John Conyers, Jr.

While in Montgomery, we also visited the Civil Rights Memorial Center. As we approached the entrance to the museum, our attention was quickly drawn to a Civil Rights Memorial, an enthralling symbol of the Civil Rights Movement, in which the names of 40 martyrs are carved into a granite table, recording their deaths in relation to the Civil Rights Movement's historical timeline. As water emerges and flows from the center of the monument, it runs across the historical timeline in a clockwise motion, slowly traveling across the names of martyrs who lost their lives during the movement: Louis Allen, Willie Brewster, Benjamin Brown, James Earl Chaney, Johnnie Mae Chappell, Addie Mae Collins, Vernon Ferdinand Dahmer, Jonathan Myrick Daniels, Henry Hezekiah Dee, Cpl. Roman Ducksworth, Jr., Willie Edwards, Jr., Medgar Evers, Andrew Goodman, Paul Guihard, Samuel Ephesians Hammond, Jr., Jimmie Lee Jackson, Wharlest Jackson, the Rev. Martin Luther King, Jr., the Rev. Bruce Klunder, the Rev. George Lee, Herbert Lee, Viola Gregg Liuzzo, Denise McNair, Delano Herman Middleton, Charles Eddie Moore, Oneal Moore, William Lewis Moore, Mack Charles Parker, Lt. Col. Lemuel Penn, the Rev. James Reeb, John Earl Reese, Carole Robertson, Michael Henry Schwerner, Henry Ezekial Smith, Lamar Smith, Emmett Louis Till, Clarence Triggs, Virgil Lamar Ware, Cynthia Wesley, Ben Chester White. and Samuel Leamon Younge, Jr.

These martyrs gave their lives to the struggle; recalling their names reminded us of what the Civil Rights struggle really stood for: a fight against social injustices so that, like the flowing water, the scales of justice would be *even* for *all*. Standing beside other visitors, we all seemed to have found ourselves in an inspired, yet somber, trance. Even more breathtaking, behind the monument stands a granite wall with water streaming continuously down one side and glistening and gliding over Dr. Martin Luther King, Jr.'s famous paraphrase of Amos 5:24: "We will not be satisfied until justice rolls down like water and righteousness like a mighty stream." With a "mighty stream" of purpose resounding in our souls, we pledged ourselves anew to the *Voices of Historical and Contemporary Black American Pioneers.*

Once inside the Civil Rights Memorial Center, we viewed a short film that invited visitors to continue the fight for social justice. As we exited the museum, like thousands before us, we added our names to the Wall of Tolerance using an interactive touch screen. Standing silently, we watched our names, Vernon L. Farmer and Evelyn Shepherd-Wynn, gradually appear among the stars, in concert with the names of others, gradually increasing in size, and, just as slowly as the names appeared, they disappeared. What a powerful experience! How comforting to know that our names had joined the names of hundreds of thousands of others in the fight for social justice.

The Southern Poverty Law Center (SPLC), known for ensuring justice and equality for all people, was our next stop. The civil rights lawyers at the center have defended many victims of hate groups. Our tour of the center commenced with a film featuring the life of Black American pioneers. After the film, Morris Dees, noted civil rights attorney and founding member of the SPLC, gave an inspiring talk about the nonprofit organization's role in helping to ensure justice for all. Dees' presence and message reminded us all of the legacy of many activists, from many backgrounds, engaged in the fight for civil rights.

Our scholarly sojourn took us to the Birmingham Civil Rights Institute (BCRI), a thoroughly enlightening experience. Strategically located at the heart of the city, where many acts of violence, bigotry, and racism occurred during the Civil Rights Movement, the BCRI's historical reenactments symbolically made us eyewitnesses to key historical events. Among its many exhibits is a portrayal of education during the early 1960s. The sharp visual contrast between the inadequate classrooms of Black children and the well-stocked, well-maintained classrooms of White children was clear. Young viewers, seeing the worn, outdated textbooks, dilapidated desks, and chalkless chalk boards—all remnants of "separate but equal" education for Black children during the 1960s—marveled at their forebears' thirst for knowledge and resilience in the face of overt racism. The stark scene reminded us that even though Black American children lacked top-notch (or even average) educational facilities, they excelled anyway.

Also among the exhibits at the BCRI is the Movement Gallery, which successfully achieved its goal: it "moved" us through a journey of segregation, racism, and related antics of the 1960s South, unfolding critical events of the time period along the way. Included in the moving exhibit is an authentic firebombed Freedom Riders' bus, standing as a representative of all such buses that carried Black and White civil rights activists en route to New Orleans; although the bus showed all the signs of having been badly burned, somehow it was strategically positioned as if ready to continue its journey at any moment. Another striking exhibit depicts the visage of Dr. Martin Luther King, Jr. seated behind the actual door of the jail cell where he penned the famous "Letter from Birmingham Jail." All we could do was stand and observe, our emotions running from awe to hurt, from hurt to solitude, and from solitude to pride. The video of Dr. Martin Luther King, Jr. giving his profound "I Have a Dream" speech also left its indelible mark on our emotions. It's one of those speeches that you can hear a thousand times, and each time it draws you in and takes you back to the time period, sending chills down the spine. Two segregated public washing sinks on display, one for "whites" and one for "blacks," symbolically washed away any bitterness of past pains, bolstering the resolve of all in attendance to never again allow segregation to rule. In addition, the exhibit containing the speeches, desk, and photos of Mayor Richard Arrington, the first Black American mayor of Birmingham, Alabama, were powerful historical reminders of the time period.

The BCRI is the focal point of the historic district, surrounded by key historical Civil Rights Movement monuments. Opposite the institute stands the Sixteenth Street Baptist Church, where four young Black American girls were killed in a church bombing. Also across the street is the Kelly Ingram Park, which houses various commemorative sculptures, one depicting police dogs lashing out at visitors and baring their teeth and another of a young Black American boy and girl being attacked by water hoses—a visceral, interactive view of the everyday fight for civil rights. From start to finish, the institute related the civil rights struggle in the most segregated city in the South and then its turnaround.

After touring the BCRI, we drove to Atlanta, Georgia, to visit the Martin Luther King, Jr. National Historic Site, currently one of the most visited historic sites in America. Its comprehensiveness provides a wide range of activities and exhibits that give visitors opportunities to learn more about King's family, vision, and voice. We began our tour at the Ebenezer Baptist Church, but it was under construction, so we immediately picked up our tour in front of Freedom Hall, adjacent to the church. Upon entering Freedom Hall, visitors encounter a memorial tomb encasing the remains of Dr. Martin Luther King, Jr. and his wife, Coretta Scott King, which serves as a beacon of hope. Behind the tomb shines a reflecting pool. All of these sights gently command respect and pride. We stood spellbound, watching over the two who gave their all to America and the world. Upon paying our respects, we walked the expanse of the International Civil Rights Hall of Fame, our footsteps echoing the marches for freedom as we read about key proponents of the Civil Rights Movement. We then entered the Freedom Hall and went to the second floor. There we saw on exhibit cherished treasures of King's career, including his pastoral robe and Bible, his Nobel Peace Prize, and a large statue of Mohandas Gandhi.

Opposite the Freedom Hall and the Ebenezer Baptist Church stands the Martin Luther King Center. Again, Gandhi's influence upon King is evident, as visitors encounter a commanding statue, donated in 1998 by the Indian Council of Cultural Relations, in tribute to Gandhi. King studied and adapted Gandhi's nonviolent strategies, successfully applying them during the Civil Rights Movement. The King Center offers interactive games and activities for people of all ages to learn about King's life and legacy. Amplifying the experience, videos show pivotal reenactments of cruelty and the inhumanness of racist police officers and members of the Klu Klux Klan. Although the Martin Luther King, Jr. National Historic

Site in Atlanta gives a tremendous tribute to King's life and career, the development of the Martin Luther King, Jr. National Memorial in Washington, D.C., serves as a fitting counterpoint. The national memorial is the first featuring a Black American and the first of an American citizen who has not served as president of the United States. The official dedication ceremony for the memorial, originally scheduled for August 28, 2011, the anniversary of King's "I Have a Dream" speech, had to be rescheduled for October 16, 2011, because of Hurricane Irene.

Detroit was also a locus of the Civil Rights Movement. Visiting the Charles H. Wright Museum of African American History in Detroit, Michigan, helped us to immerse ourselves into the lives and careers of some of the early Black American pioneers. Among the museum's many attractions are *And Still We Rise*, *'A' Is for Africa*, *Detroit Performs*, *Ring of Genealogy*, and *Stories in Stained Glass*. Of all the exhibits that we toured, *And Still We Rise* left us spellbound. It covers a wide range of Black experiences through time, highlights the origin of our civilization to the present day, and crosses geographic boundaries. Traveling through the times and themes of *And Still We Rise*, we found ourselves on a riveting journey, witnessing some of the more shocking, dehumanizing abuses our ancestors suffered. Perhaps the most transformative experience was reliving the Middle Passage. We traversed the 70-foot replica of a transatlantic slave ship that housed 40 life-sized, human-like bodies cramped in fetal positions, which symbolically brought us back to the depths of slavery, evoking sincere sorrows. Lifelike murals of such historical figures as Frederick Douglass, Martin Luther King, Jr., Malcolm X, Harriet Tubman, and other extraordinary Black Americans were at once larger than life and inspiringly real.

Physically tired, our spirits buoyed, we returned to Tuskegee. Our destination this time was the new, cutting-edge Tuskegee Airmen National Historic Site and Museum at Moton Field. As the park ranger shuttled us to the museum, we observed that the main street to the site is called Chappie James Avenue, in honor of General Daniel "Chappie" James, Jr., a Tuskegee Institute graduate, a Tuskegee Airman, and the first Black American to become a four-star general in the U.S. Air Force. We found another street on the site, Chief Anderson Drive, honoring Charles Alfred "Chief" Anderson, the Father of Black Aviation, the flight instructor for more than 1,000 Tuskegee Airmen and the pilot who had once flown Eleanor Roosevelt. In order to counter the view that African Americans were not capable of flying, Mrs. Roosevelt toured Tuskegee in 1941, and Anderson gave her a plane ride that was headlined in newspapers across the country. And still another street was named in honor of yet another military giant: B. O. Davis, Jr. Avenue, for General Benjamin O. Davis, Jr., the first commander and fighter of the 332nd Fighter Group of the Tuskegee Airmen and the first Black American to become a general in the U.S. Air Force. Our tour included the new terminal, which houses several P-5 Mustangs, the Tuskegee Airmen's signature vehicle, aloft in Hangar 1. Moreover, the museum includes model airplanes, parachutes, pilots' uniforms, and the Tuskegee Airmen's iconic leather bomber jackets, complete with white scarves. We had an opportunity to sit in an interactive cockpit, simulating some of the many training exercises the Airmen executed. Plans are underfoot to render Hangar 2 into an IMAX Theater, where a P-5 Mustang will "fly," suspended from the ceiling. The historic museum site will be a terrific tribute to the Tuskegee Airmen and a symbol of their history.

US Airways shuttled us from Dallas, Texas, to Phoenix, Arizona, as friends of the Tuskegee Airmen, where we participated in the Congressional Gold Medal Award ceremony. During that ceremony, Governor Janet Napolitano honored the Tuskegee Airmen by issuing a proclamation and presenting replicas of the Congressional Gold Medal that the Tuskegee Airmen had received from President George Bush in 2007, highlighting their influence on education. Vernon L. Farmer, chief editor of this book, spoke briefly on education, and Evelyn Shepherd-Wynn, associate editor, graciously hosted Lieutenant Colonel Luke Weathers, a Tuskegee Airman and World War II veteran who shot down two German planes. As Weathers explained, "I wasn't planning on shooting down the enemy; I was afraid" (L. Weathers, personal communication, May 24, 2007). Weathers's frank explanation of his fear in the face of heroism grounded all of us in the realities of humanity.

In August 2007, we drove to Gaylord, Texas, to attend the 36th Annual Tuskegee Airmen National Conference with the purpose of meeting as many airmen as we could, gathering additional information, and scheduling interviews for this book. In October 2007, we flew from Dallas, Texas, to Scottsdale, Arizona, where we proudly interviewed original Tuskegee Airmen Robert Ashby, Thurston Gaines, and Asa Herring. Their voices, along with the voices of many others, held our spirits aloft as we continued our research and writing.

Visits to selected libraries and archives, museums, exhibits, hospitals, and law schools enriched our sojourn, helping us delve deeply into the lives and careers of historical and contemporary Black pioneers. As a result, we became not only emotionally stirred and encouraged by their accomplishments and contributions but also keenly aware of hallmarks of their success. In addition to exemplifying great intelligence and insight, many of them were highly gifted, often becoming the first in varied professions and career fields.

Despite a dominant society that encouraged Black American failure, our research reveals that strong parental encouragement and support bolstered the efforts and successes of many Black men and women. Not surprisingly, many of the aforementioned were in the vanguard of the Civil Rights Movement; their successes against the odds continue to inspire. The overriding goal of these courageous Black American pioneers was not only to open doors and to advance the varied professions and career fields for Blacks but also to do so for the benefit of all humankind. May their lives and legacies inspire us all to reach higher.

Engineered with love and fueled with a passion for Black American history and culture, *Voices of Historical and Contemporary Black American Pioneers* is ready to take us far and wide to meet the pioneers, past and present, and to help us explore and be inspired.

All aboard!

Vernon L. Farmer
Evelyn Shepherd-Wynn

VOLUME 2
Law and Government

The welcome table means much in Black American culture. It means family, belonging, and community. It means conversation, debate, and purposeful social engagement. It means reaching across the generations and across the globe. Tables are used to chart progress. Tables are where arguments are raised and settled. Tables are where bodies and souls are nourished. Tables are where decisions, large and small, are made and manifested.

In Volume 2, we introduce you to historical and contemporary Black Americans in law and government who have fought to bring justice and equality to all at the welcome table. From the era predating *Brown v. Board of Education*, you will meet individuals whose lives were consumed by their diligent work on behalf of ordinary citizens, many of whom were voiceless and left out of the democratic promise of "life, liberty and the pursuit of happiness."

Volume 2 probes the concept of America as a country of laws with stated values of freedom and equality for all of its citizens. As a result, pioneering Black American lawyers, men and women, positioned themselves as leaders and used the judicial system to fight racism and discrimination in education, employment, transportation, voting, housing, and other areas where civil rights had been denied. Many were both scholars and practitioners, pressing for legislative action that would eliminate unfair treatment in the everyday lives of minority citizens. This struggle for due process and civil rights has occupied the attention of the largest number of Black American lawyers and judges even while some have made great strides in corporate law, criminal procedures, and other areas of jurisprudence.

Covering the progress of Black American citizens, Volume 2 shows the advancement of a people who moved from being considered second-class citizens to being respected colleagues working within the system to advance the rights and interests of Black Americans. It demonstrates the concentrated determination and selflessness of these pioneers to spend hours and resources to advance the cause of equality and social justice. American voters have elected Black American candidates at all levels of government from mayors of small and large cities, to governors of states, congressional representatives, and heads of states.

Finally, Volume 2 demonstrates Dr. Martin Luther King, Jr.'s powerful thought, which has often been restated by others, that "the arc of the moral universe is long, but it bends toward justice. It bends towards justice, but here is the thing: it does not bend on its own. It bends because each of us in our own ways put our hand on that arc and we bend it in the direction of justice" (Obama 2008). No longer is race an accepted basis for policy decisions in the American legal and political system. Today, we are witnesses to the culmination of the efforts and struggles of Black American pioneers in law and government: the election of Barack Hussein Obama, the nation's first Black American president. The climb of Black Americans from disenfranchisement to the Supreme Court to the highest office of president has been an arduous process by any measurement, but this rich legacy of work will continue until all Black Americans and other minority citizens receive the full promise of America. Consequently, any American alive today should appreciate and celebrate the historical and contemporary Black American pioneers mentioned in this volume as being instrumental in their own ways, however large or small, in advancing the rights and responsibilities of true American citizenship.

Reference

Obama, Barack. (April 4, 2008). "The Arc of the Universe is Long But It Bends Towards Justice." Speech on Remembering Dr. Martin Luther King, Jr., Fort Wayne, Indiana.

CHAPTER 1

The Welcome Table

**VERNON L. FARMER, EVELYN SHEPHERD-WYNN,
AND LISA PERTILLAR BREVARD**

I'm gonna sit at the welcome table
I'm gonna sit at the welcome table
Some of these days, hallelujah!
I'm gonna sit at the welcome table
Some of these days

—African American spiritual

Sitting at the table doesn't make you a diner,
unless you eat some of what's on that plate.
—Malcolm X, "The Ballot or the Bullet," April 3, 1964, p. 26

Black American pioneers have worked tirelessly to change the social injustices in the American judicial and political system that have negatively affected Black people for more than a century. As late as 2009, Congress made a public apology for the 400 years of Black enslavement:

(A) Acknowledg[ing] the fundamental injustice, cruelty, brutality, and inhumanity of slavery and Jim Crow laws;

(B) Apologiz[ing] to African-Americans on behalf of the people of the United States, for the wrongs committed against them and their ancestors who suffered under slavery and Jim Crow laws; and

(C) Express[ing] its recommitment to the principle that all people are created equal and endowed with inalienable rights to life, liberty, and the pursuit of happiness, and call[ing] on all people of the United States to work toward eliminating racial prejudices, injustices, and discrimination from our society. (S.CON.RES.26 June 18, 2009)

Although Congress apologized for the atrocities imposed on Black people during slavery, many Black American lawyers and politicians did not and could not wait for an apology; rather, they fought to sit at the welcome table, invited and uninvited, and to make decisions, large and small, to alleviate some of the social and political injustices.

Law

Perhaps no area of American culture illuminates the power and possibility of Black Americans sitting at the welcome table better than the field of jurisprudence. Before the establishment of the National Association for the Advancement of Colored People (NAACP) in 1909, there were a number of Black lawyers who received their licenses through apprenticeships. Robert Morris, William Henry Johnson, and Edward Garrison Draper were among the first lawyers to be trained through apprenticeships. However, Moses Wenslydale Moore (Howard University Law School), John P. Green (Ohio Union Law School), and Wathal G. Wynn (Howard University Law School) were the first formally trained Black lawyers who graduated in 1871 (Smith 1993), all of whom had to appear before a judge to be examined before they could practice law. After Moore had been scrutinized before Judge John Elliott, the local newspaper, *Mobile Daily Register,* reported:

> Moses Wenslydale Moore, a Negro as black as the ace of spades . . . presented himself for [an] examination, stating that he had been admitted to the bar in the District of Columbia. The court requested Judge Gibbons to examine him, and [an] examination was conducted in open court. A great deal of interest was manifested on the part of the bar . . . from the fact of the applicant's color. He passed a very satisfactory examination, and an order was made by the Court admitting him to the bar. This is the first Negro ever admitted to the bar in Mobile. (quoted in Smith 1993, 271)

Under the same type of scrutiny, Green was admitted to the bar in 1871 in Cleveland, Ohio. In similar fashion, Smith recorded that "Wynn was admitted to the bar on the motion of Judge Alfred Mortan, becoming Virginia's first black American lawyer" (225). Although there are many Black American lawyers worthy of inclusion in this volume, we introduce and reacquaint you with some of those that helped the NAACP reverse the landmark Supreme Court case, *Plessy v. Ferguson* (1896).

We begin with Charles Hamilton Houston, one of the foremost legal scholars during the period. The NAACP solicited the help of Charles Hamilton Houston to serve as special counsel to the civic organization. Born in 1895 in Washington, D.C., Houston was an only child whose father was a professor at Howard University Law School and whose mother was a cosmetologist who serviced the elite in Washington, D.C. At the age of 15, Houston enrolled in Amherst College in Massachusetts, graduating at age 19 with a major in history and a minor in English. In *Groundwork: Charles Hamilton Houston and the Struggle for Civil Rights* (1983), McNeil explains that Houston's father's ultimate dream was to share a law firm with his son titled "Houston & Houston, Attorneys at Law" (47).

Although Houston applied to Harvard, he wanted to explore other career interests. Therefore, he taught English for a brief period at Dunbar High School in Washington, D.C.; however, when he found out that he had a hernia and chronic rhinitis, he stopped teaching. During this time he was accepted to Harvard and began law school. He taught at Howard University and then entered the U.S. Army. After serving in World War I in a segregated environment, Houston vowed to work for equality for all. Consequently, he earned his law degrees, the bachelor of laws in 1922 and the doctorate in 1923, from Harvard University. During his tenure at Harvard, he served on the editorial board of Harvard's *Law Review*, becoming the first Black American to serve in this prestigious position. Houston served as editor from 1921 to 1922, editing volume 35. While at Harvard, Houston was also responsible for establishing the Dunbar Law Club for students who were excluded from the White law clubs. This was an important feat as it allowed Blacks to have a direct line to law firms and attorneys in the Boston-Cambridge area (McNeil 1983, 52).

Houston went on to become a part-time instructor at Howard's Law School, where he convinced Howard's Board of Trustees to make the law school full time; the school would go on to train one-fourth of the nation's civil rights lawyers (McNeil 1983). Houston believed Howard Law School should "make itself a more efficient training school" in order to prepare "capable and socially alert Negro lawyers" to serve the Black community (McNeil 1983, 71). Houston argued that Black lawyers should meet both the legal and personal needs of his clients:

[The] Negro lawyer must be trained as a social engineer and group interpreter. Due to the Negro's social and political condition . . . the Negro lawyer must be prepared to anticipate, guide and interpret his group advancement . . . [Moreover, he must act as] business adviser . . . for the protection of the scattered resources possessed or controlled by the group. . . . He must provide more ways and means for holding within the group the income now flowing through it. (quoted in McNeil 1983, 71)

Before the *Brown v. Board of Education* case (1954), Houston argued and won the *Gaines v. Canada* case in 1938 before the U.S. Supreme Court, making him the first Black American to win a case before this august body. John Swett Rock was "the first black [American] to be admitted to practice before the United States Supreme Court" in 1865 (Segal 1983, 127), and Violette Neatly Anderson was the first Black American woman to be admitted to practice before the U.S. Supreme Court in 1926 (Hine 1993).

As special counsel to the NAACP, Houston pulled together a group of young Black American legal architects who shared a common goal; all specialized in civil rights law so they could position themselves to fight against racism in education, transportation, housing, government, and other areas that affected the lives of Black people. As lead strategist, Houston, along with his young architects, drew the blueprint for the legal team so they could begin undoing some of the wrongs in America's judicial system on the local, state, and national levels. As they argued cases throughout the United States, many wrongs were overturned on the local level. Houston had indeed begun to change the American judicial system, such that its design and application would foster equality for all, and in the process, ensure citizenship rights and responsibilities for Black Americans and all humankind.

As his health gradually failed him, Houston sent his family to Louisiana because he wanted his son, Charlie, Jr., to remember him as "vigorous, impressive, and strong" (McNeil 1983, 209). Initially hospitalized in Bethesda Naval Hospital, he was later transferred to Freedman's Hospital so his friends could visit him without difficulty. In 1950, Houston died of acute coronary thrombosis. Among his many friends and constituents who attended his funeral, Thurgood Marshall, Oliver W. Hill, Benjamin F. Amos, George Marion Johnson, Edward P. Lovett, Phineas Indritz, and Joseph Waddy served as pallberarers (McNeil 1983, 211).

Houston worked closely with a number of Black American legal scholars, including his cousin William H. Hastie, Jr., who was born in Knoxville, Tennessee, in 1904 to William Henry Hastie, Sr. and Roberta Childs. Hastie's mother, a teacher, was a graduate of Fisk University and Talladega College, and Hastie's father had studied math and pharmacy at Ohio Wesleyan Academy and Howard University, respectively. Both of them fought fervently against racism. Hastie's parents were staunch disciplinarians, as Ware writes, "Sometimes his parents folded young Bill across their knees—he was no angel" (1984, 5). It was because of their loving discipline that Hastie stayed on course.

Many successful Black Americans attended Dunbar High School in Washington, D.C., so it was no surprise that Hastie's parents enrolled him in the college preparatory school, too. Hastie followed the same path as Houston, attending the same high school, Dunbar, where he graduated in 1921; attending the same college, Amherst, where he earned an AB in 1925; and earning his LLB degree from the same university, Harvard, in 1930. While attending Harvard, like Houston, Hastie served on the editorial board of the *Law Review*, making him the second Black to serve in the position (Ware 1984). As a member of Houston's law firm and a professor of law at Howard, Hastie helped Houston outline the strategy for the *Brown v. Board of Education* case. He went on to become the first Black to sit on a federal appellate court, the U.S. Court of Appeals for the Third Circuit, from 1949 to 1971. According to Wade's *Black Men of Amherst* (1976), Judge Hastie "was rarely if ever overruled on a decision" (75). Before this appointment, Hastie had won a number of civil rights cases before the U.S. Supreme Court and supported efforts to desegregate the U.S. military during World War II. Hastie's mother played a major role in his life, and although his father died during Hastie's senior year in high school, he was very influential in his life. When Hastie died in Philadelphia in 1976 at age 71, he had in his possession a "black tin box containing three letters that he had received from his father when he was eight years old" (Wade 1976, 4). In one of the letters, his father told him that his cousin William L. Houston, an attorney, and his son, Charles Hamilton

Houston, would play significant roles in his life. The history books can attest that his father's advice indeed came true.

While at Howard University, Houston groomed many young legal minds who joined in the effort to eradicate social injustices against Blacks. Another Black American among those legal minds was Thurgood Marshall. Marshall was born in Baltimore, Maryland, in 1908 to mulatto parents. His mother, Norma, an elementary school teacher, wanted Marshall to pursue a career in dentistry. Though he spent the first two years of college studying dentistry, he found himself leaning toward the profession of law. Marshall explained that his father "never told me to become a lawyer, but he turned me into one. He did it by teaching me to argue, by challenging my logic on every point, by making me prove every statement I made" (Goldman 1992, 23). Marshall went on to pursue an AB degree in humanities from Lincoln University in 1930. He later pursued a law degree at Howard University after he received a rejection letter from the University of Maryland. Under Houston's guidance, Marshall graduated in 1933.

Marshall called Houston "Iron Shoe" because he was known for his staunch work ethics and demanded the same from his students and colleagues (Goldman 1992, 82). Upon graduation, Marshall began his law practice but soon found that his clients were few and money was scarce. He went so far as to offer free services to gain experience, and, according to Marshall, "It was all those freebees that finally sent me to the NAACP" (27). It was Houston and Marshall's work at the NAACP that helped to strengthen their mentor-mentee relationship. Having assisted Houston in drawing the blueprint for *Brown v. Board of Education* and being one of Houston's favorite pupils, it seemed only fitting that Marshall should serve as lead counsel for the NAACP and the lead attorney for the *Brown* case after Houston's death.

Before Houston's death, Marshall had strategically selected five cases representative of the type of social injustices that had been imposed upon Black American citizens throughout the United States: *Briggs v. Elliot* (1951), *Davis v. Board of Education of Prince Edward County* (1951), *Boling v. Sharpe* (1951), *Belton v. Gebhart* (1951), and *Oliver L. Brown et al. v. Board of Education of Topeka* (1951). These cases were combined to become *Brown v. Board of Education* (1954). Marshall served as lead attorney for *Briggs v. Elliott*, the first of the five cases to be argued. As his legal career flourished, Marshall won Supreme Court cases that overturned laws concerning the unfair treatment of Blacks in regards to housing, transportation, and voting.

These accomplishments were recognized by President Lyndon Johnson, who nominated Marshall to the Supreme Court in 1967. Facing strong opposition from four southern senators on the Judiciary Committee, Marshall was asked "60 questions on constitutional history and the meaning of the 13th, 14th and 15th amendments" (Goldman 1992, 154), all of which he answered proficiently, thereby earning him confirmation by the Senate by 69 to 11. On the day of his confirmation, Marshall recalls a conversation he had with President Johnson: "Johnson said: 'Well, congratulations, but the hell you caused me. Goddammit, I never went through so much hell'" (154). Marshall went on to achieve an exemplary career. He was one of the most prominent Black American civil rights legal scholars of his time and the nation's first Black American to serve as a U.S. Supreme Court justice, serving 24 years on the high court. One of his landmark decisions was about discriminatory practices and affirmative action, in particular during the *University of California Regents v. Bakke* case, which prompted Marshall to write:

> [T]he racism of our society has been so pervasive that none, regardless of wealth or position, has managed to escape its impact. The experience of Negroes in America has been different in kind, not just in degree, from that of other ethnic groups. It is not merely the history of slavery alone but also that a whole people were marked as inferior by the law. And that mark has endured. The dream of America as the great melting pot has not been realized for the Negro; because of his skin color he never even made it into the pot. (260)

After his retirement in 1991, Marshall's health gradually deteriorated; he was slightly overweight and suffered from glaucoma and heart problems. In 1993, at the age of 85, Marshall died of heart failure at Bethesda Naval Medical Center.

In addition to Marshall, Houston mentored other young Black American legal architects, among whom were James M. Nabrit, Jr., Spottswood W. Robinson III, Robert Carter, Oliver Hill, and Constance Baker Motley. The careers of these young legal scholars skyrocketed after *Brown*. One of these scholars, James M. Nabrit, Jr. was born in 1900 in Atlanta, Georgia, to James M. Nabrit, Sr., a baker and Baptist minister, and Norma Walton. He graduated from Morehouse College in 1923. He went on to earn a JD degree from Yale University in 1927. Nabrit taught the first formal course on civil rights in the country while serving as a professor, dean of the law school, and president of Howard University for two terms from 1960 to 1965 and from 1968 to 1969 (Smith 1993). Nabrit argued that the civil rights course should

> discover what the law was in respect to minorities in this area of civil rights; second, to develop techniques for raising constitutional questions in respect to disabilities affecting minorities . . . and third, to separate those disabilities for which legislative action would be required for their elimination. (quoted in Smith 1993, 51)

Nabrit was also one of the attorneys on *Boling v. Sharpe*, one of the cases later used with *Brown v. Board of Education*. However, *Boling v. Sharpe* was decided under the Due Process Clause of the Fifth Amendment instead of the 14th Amendment Equal Protection Clause, which decided the *Brown* case. In 1997, Nabrit, a resident of Washington, D.C., was pronounced dead upon arrival at the Walter Reed Army Medical Center.

Other young Black American lawyers advanced their careers after *Brown* as well. Spottswood W. Robinson III and Robert L. Carter were at Howard University when they witnessed the first time a lawyer, in this case Charles Hamilton Houston, rehearsed his oral argument for *Missouri ex rel. Gaines v. Canada* (1938) before faculty and students at Howard's Law School. What an awesome training ground for young budding Black American lawyers. The case was later won before the U.S. Supreme Court, which ruled that the Missouri Supreme Court had made a mistake and that the petitioner should not have been denied admission to the University of Missouri (Smith 1993, 150). Spottswood W. Robinson III stood tall among the Black American young lawyers trained by Houston. He went on to become the first Black on the U.S. District Court in Washington and the first Black to be named judge and chief judge on the U.S. Court of Appeals for the District of Columbia, where he served from 1981 until 1986. Robinson was born in Richmond, Virginia, in 1916. His parents were Spottswood William Robinson, Jr. and Inez Clements Robinson. Robinson graduated from Armstrong High School and earned a bachelor's degree at Virginia Union University in 1936. In the same year, he enrolled at Howard University Law School, where his father had also matriculated. Robinson graduated at the top of his class in 1939 and thus was invited to serve as a faculty member at Howard; his tenure lasted for 18 years.

Fresh out of graduate school and having done research on restrictive covenant cases, Spottswood was asked by Houston to help him prepare for a restrictive covenant case. Working from lunch until 4:00 a.m., Robinson recalled:

> They [Robinson and Houston] ate lunch and went back to the room at the end of the hall of the Houston firm offices. At 2:00 p.m. Houston gathered several large crayonlike black pencils, placed a green eyeshade around his forehead, and began to read the draft line by line. They took a dinner break—ordering sandwiches from a takeout restaurant—and continued until 1:00 a.m. Houston looked up and asked Robinson if he wanted to take a break and start again at about 7:00 a.m. This being a rather unattractive offer to Robinson, he insisted that they go on with the review. At 4:00 a.m. Houston completed reading the brief and making his notes and returned it to Robinson for a rewrite. (Smith 1993, 177)

This experience remained branded in Robinson's mind until his death, and he referred to Charles Hamilton Houston as "Thoroughness was Charlie" (177). While residing in Richmond, Virginia, Robinson died of heart failure after a lengthy illness in 1998.

Robert L. Carter was another one of the lawyers who helped Houston and Marshall with the civil rights cases. Carter was born in Careyville, Florida, in 1917. He earned his BA degree in political science from Lincoln University in Pennsylvania. He went on to earn his JD degree from Howard University in 1940 and his LLM degree at Columbia University in 1941. Carter, an enlisted man in the U.S. Army, faced overt racism, experiences that seemed to ignite his professional career. After the war, he became Marshall's assistant at the NAACP, helping to prepare for and argue the *Brown* case. Before Houston's death, he wrote to Carter, "These education cases are now tight sufficiently so that anyone familiar with the course of the decisions should be able to guide the cases through. You and Thurgood can proceed without any fear of crossing any plans I might have" (McNeil 1983, 200). Upon Marshall's death in 1993, Carter was named the Legal Defense Fund's (LDF) general counsel. During his 24-year tenure, Carter won 22 of 23 cases before the Supreme Court. One of the cases he is most noted for, other than *Brown*, was the *NAACP v. Alabama* case (1958). A number of southern states, particularly Alabama, tried to strike back after *Brown* by passing legislation mandating the

NAACP to reveal its members. Carter won the case before the Supreme Court, which ruled that the NAACP did not have to make public its membership ("Robert L. Carter" n.d.).

Among Oliver W. Hill's many contributions during the *Brown* era was his service as lead attorney, along with Spottswood W. Robinson III, in *Davis v. County School Board of Prince Edward County.* Born in 1907 in Richmond, Virginia, Oliver W. Hill was raised by his mother and stepfather in Washington, D.C. He earned an LLB degree from Howard University School of Law in 1993. After *Brown*, Hill became known for the case *Alston v. School Board of Norfolk, Virginia* (1940), which gave Black teachers the right to receive the same pay as their White counterparts in the state of Virginia. As lead attorney for the *Alston* case, Hill, along with Thurgood Marshall, William Hastie, and Leon A. Ransom, won the case on the fundamental premise "that the fixing of salary schedules for the teachers is action by the state which is subject to the limitations prescribed by the Fourteenth Amendment" (Smith 1993, 236). He later argued that Black American children should have the same access to transportation as White children ("Oliver White Hill" n.d.). In 2007, at the age of 100, Hill died of heart failure at his home in Richmond, Virginia.

Constance Baker Motley was the only woman lawyer on the litigation team for *Brown v. Board of Education.* Motley was born in New Haven, Connecticut, in 1921. Motley set her eyes on becoming a lawyer when she was 15 years old. "No one thought that was a good idea, and I received no encouragement. My mother thought I should be a hairdresser; my father had no thoughts on the subject," explained Motley (Motley 1998, 44). Just think, had Motley not pursued her career goal, she would not have been the only woman serving on the litigation team for *Brown v. Board of Education.* Motley is credited with preparing the draft complaint for the case. Interestingly, she had not met any women lawyers during her childhood. Motley had not heard of Charlotte E. Ray, the first Black woman lawyer in the country and the first university-trained woman lawyer. It was while Motley was in high school that she learned of Jane Matilda Bolin, who became the nation's first Black woman judge in 1939. These female pioneers paved the way for Motley and other Black female attorneys.

After *Brown,* Motley's most memorable case was *Meredith v. Fair* (1962), where, as the lead attorney, she argued and won the case before the U.S. Supreme Court. The court ordered the University of Mississippi to integrate. Motley wrote in her autobiography that the state thought that by examining Meredith's military record it would provide reason for disqualifying him. Motley wrote, "The state of Mississippi attempted to find some ground on which Meredith could be disqualified. If he [Meredith] had been convicted of a felony, or even some lesser crime, the university could have seized on that as reason for denying his admission" (Motley 1998, 168–169). She later stated:

> I read into the trial record the part of his service records that noted he [Meredith] was the thriftiest man in the service in terms of "the conversation of men and materials." His records also noted that he had pursued education, not only for himself, but had urged other servicemen to do likewise. It further revealed that he had saved his own money as well as money for the Air Force through self-sacrifice. (173)

Motley would become the first Black American woman federal judge. "When I was called to the White House in January 1966, I did not know that the date on which I was told to appear would be the date on which Johnson would announce my appointment to the federal bench" (Motley 1998, 212). Motley earned a BA degree in economics from New York University's Washington Square College in 1943 and an LLB degree from Columbia University in 1946. Motley died of congestive heart failure in 2005 at the age of 84.

To the Charles Hamilton Houston alignment with Thurgood Marshall, which we consider the Houston–Marshall era, was added A. Leon Higginbotham Jr., a foremost Black American judge who spent more than four decades (1952 to 1996) examining the law from a theoretical and practical perspective. Higginbotham was born in Trenton, New Jersey, in 1928, and was raised there during the Great Depression. Higginbotham's parents were hard workers; his mother was a maid and his father a factory worker.

Higginbotham earned a BA degree in sociology from Antioch College in 1949 and a bachelor of laws degree from Yale University Law School in 1952. He spent 29 years serving as an appellate judge and the remainder of his career teaching about the theory and philosophy of the law at Harvard University (Higginbotham 1978). Higginbotham, a great intellectual who fought against civil injustices, authored many articles and several books, including *In the Matter of Color: The Colonial Period* (1978) and *Shades of Freedom: Racial Politics and Presumptions of the American Legal Process* (1996), which are required reading in many legal courses across the country. At the close of his career, he drafted one of the most prolific arguments during President Bill Clinton's impeachment hearing, using the theme "thought comes before speech." Higginbotham argued that there are various degrees of perjury, pointing out reasons why President Clinton should not be impeached. As history would have it, President Clinton was not impeached. In 1998, while residing in Boston, Higginbotham died of a stroke at age 70.

The Houston–Marshall era produced many contemporary Black American lawyers and judges who made their mark in the legal system. In 1991, a year after Supreme Court Justice Thurgood Marshall's retirement, President George Bush nominated Clarence Thomas to become an associate justice for the U.S. Supreme Court, making him the second Black American to serve on the highest court in 1991.

Thomas was born in Pinpoint, Georgia, in 1948. In his memoir, *My Grandfather's Son* (2007), Thomas describes Pinpoint as "a heavily wooded twenty-five-acre peninsula on Shipyard Creek, a tidal salt creek ten miles southeast of Savannah. . . . too small to be properly called a town" (3). Thomas's birthplace was founded by freed slaves; however, it is ironic that his conservative views on race and affirmative action were strikingly different from those of his ancestors and his predecessor, Thurgood Marshall. Their views were so strikingly different that the distinguished Judge A. Leon Higginbotham, who had also been considered for the U.S. Supreme Court, wrote these words to Justice Thomas:

> I suggest, Justice Thomas, that you should ask yourself every day what would have happened to you if there had never been a Charles Hamilton Houston, a William Henry Hastie, a Thurgood Marshall, and that small cadre of other lawyers associated with them. (quoted in Ogletree 2005, 218)

Thomas earned his BA degree from Holy Cross College in 1971 and his JD degree from Yale University in 1974.

Since the Higginbotham era, there continues to be a growing number of successful Black American lawyers, and we can gauge how they have affected the evolution of the role of Black Americans in the legal profession. Drew S. Days, III is one of those successful lawyers. Days is the leading Black attorney to appear before the U.S. Supreme Court; he has argued more cases before the Supreme Court than any other Black American lawyer. Days was born in Atlanta, Georgia, in 1941 to Drew Saunders Days, Jr. and Dorethea Days. He earned a BA degree in English literature in 1963 from Hamilton College and an LLB in 1966 from Yale University. When Days is not practicing law, he is the Alfred M. Rankin Professor of Law at Yale Law School. Days lectures on constitutional litigation and employment discrimination law and political and civil rights. He has written two books, *Moore's Federal Practice* (1948) and *Feedback Loop: The Civil Rights Act of 1964 and Progeny* (2005), in which he discusses the ins and outs of the U.S. Supreme Court.

The Houston–Marshall era paved the way for a generation of Black American lawyers and judges who continue to fight for social justice in America's judicial system. As illustrated by the historic Black American men and women in this volume, the decisions of lawyers and judges clearly affect the course of our lives in America. Likewise, the contemporary Black American men and women in the field continue to do the same. Judges such as Damon J. Keith, Bernette Joshua Johnson, Leah Ward Sears, Paul Higginbotham, and Arthur L. Burnett, Sr. are making their mark in the history books. **Damon J. Keith** is best known for his landmark rulings as chief judge in civil rights and civil liberties cases on school desegregation, affirmative action, and housing discrimination. Keith was born in Detroit, Michigan, in 1922. Son of an autoworker, Keith learned early the value of education. This led to his earning a BA degree from West Virginia State College in 1943, an LLB degree from Howard University Law School in 1949, and a JD degree from Wayne State University Law School in 1956.

While matriculating at Howard University, Keith was taught by some of the brightest legal minds of that time period: Charles Hamilton Houston, Thurgood Marshall, William H. Hastie, Jr., and others. These civil rights attorneys helped Keith to become a legal champion in his own right. His training helped to prepare him for one of the landmark cases in America, the *United States v Sinclair* (1974) case. Keith ruled that wiretapping was unconstitutional without a court order, a ruling upheld by the U.S. Supreme Court. In this volume, Keith writes about how "this was a violation of the fundamental right guaranteed to all Americans in the Fourth Amendment of the United States Constitution: to be free from warrantless searches and seizures" (see Chapter 17 in this volume).

Bernette Joshua Johnson is the first Black American woman to serve on the Louisiana Supreme Court. She was born in Ascension Parish, Louisiana, along with three brothers. When her father returned from the Navy, the family moved to New Orleans because there were no jobs in

Ascension. It was in New Orleans that Johnson received an education that prepared her for law school. Johnson received a BA degree from Spelman College in 1964 and was one of the first Black American women to attend law school at Louisiana State University, where she received her JD degree in 1969. She received an honorary doctorate of laws from Spelman College in 2001.

Leah Ward Sears, Johnson's colleague, is the youngest person and the first Black American woman to serve on the Supreme Court of Georgia and the first Black woman chief justice of a state supreme court in the United States. Sears was born in Heidelberg, Germany, in 1955. She received a BS degree in human development and family studies from Cornell University in 1976, a JD degree from Emory University School of Law in 1980, and an LLM degree from the University of Virginia School of Law in 1995.

Also included in this group are Arthur L. Burnett, Sr. and Paul B. Higginbotham. Among the many positions he has held in the legal career field, **Arthur L. Burnett, Sr.** currently holds senior judge status in the Superior Court of the District of Columbia. He is also the national executive director of the National African American Drug Policy. In this volume, Burnett acknowledges:

> When I entered Howard University in September 1952 as a 17-year-old teenager, I had not had algebra and my entrance exams showed that my English skills were still deficient, even though I had graduated as the valedictorian of my high school class. Thus, in my first semester, I only took 11 hours of college-level courses as I had to take an additional six hours of remedial high school courses. I made all As, and at the end of the semester, I went to Dean Miller of the School of Liberal Arts and urged him to give me approval to take the normal load of courses plus 6 additional hours for a total of 23 semester hours of work so that I would be even with my classmates. After a lengthy conversation, he approved my request. I again made all As and finished first in my class with a 4.0 average.

Burnett Sr.'s willingness to share problems he encountered when he first began his undergraduate studies is an excellent example for young aspiring legal scholars.

Paul B. Higginbotham is the first Black to sit on the appellate court in Wisconsin's history. An alumnus of the University of Wisconsin at

Madison, Higginbotham earned BA and JD degrees in 1981 and 1985, respectively. Higginbotham and his twin brother, Stephen, were born in Philadelphia, Pennsylvania, in 1954. Born in a family that fought against social injustices, Higginbotham is committed to helping to continue the fight for justice for all. As he states later in this volume:

> I paid my way through law school and for everything over and above the grants that I received from the Legal Education Opportunities (LEO) program at the University of Wisconsin Law School. . . . I have been working since I was 11 years old and always had to fight for myself— so it was nice to get that support from LEO; it was wonderful not to work through the law school process alone. There was a point, however, when I was ready to ditch it all. I was struggling in law school and my personal life. The support system the LEO program provided was critical to my decision to persevere and finish law school. The LEO program is all about helping students move through law school so they come out knowing "I can do this."

Many civil rights lawyers also specialize in other areas, including family, criminal, corporate, bankruptcy, accident and personal injury, immigration, patents and other areas of law. Charles J. Ogletree, Jr. and Derrick Bell are among many civil rights lawyers who practice their craft in academia and in the courts. Charles J. Ogletree, Jr. is a legal theorist who is well respected in the profession for bringing race and civil rights issues to the forefront. Ogletree, the son of migrant farm workers, Charles, Sr. and Willie Mae Ogletree, was born in Merced, California, in 1952. He earned his undergraduate and graduate degrees in political science from Stanford University in 1974 and 1975, respectively. He later earned a JD degree from Harvard Law School in 1978. Ogletree is the Harvard Law School Jesse Climenko Professor of Law and founder and executive director of the Charles Hamilton Houston Institute for Race and Justice. Ogletree's major research interest is criminal justice with varying aspects including administration and race (Ogletree 2005).

In academia is Derrick A. Bell, an outspoken civil rights advocate who was the first tenured Black American professor at Harvard Law School. Bell was born and raised in the renowned Hill District of Pittsburgh in 1930. He earned an AB degree from Duquesne University in 1952. He also earned an LLB from the University of Pittsburgh Law School in 1957. His lectures address civil rights and the law. Coming from a family that was poor, Bell was the first to attend college and graduate. As a member of the ROTC (Reserve Officers' Training Corps), upon graduation Bell was transferred to Korea. When observing that Harvard, unlike other prestigious institutions, was unwilling to award tenure to a qualified Black female law professor, Bell, in protest, took a leave of absence from Harvard and later resigned when the administration refused to hire a minority woman. In *Faces at the Bottom of the Well: The Permanence of Race*, Bell writes:

> I did what I felt was appropriate and within my power to protest injustices after analysis and reasoning failed to convince my colleagues they were wrong. No one has to tell me how deeply invested law teachers are in their stellar grades and law review editorship standards. Even so, I keep trying new ways to make them see what they clearly do not want to see, what perhaps they're incapable of seeing. And not only at Harvard, I use these arguments at law schools across the country. (142)

He later joined the law faculty at New York University as a visiting professor. Bell has authored numerous books, including *Race, Racism, and American Law* (1973), which is used as a textbook in law schools around the country. In 2005, Richard Delgado and Jean Stefanic edited *The Derrick Bell Reader*, a compilation of Bell's writings on legal issues concerning affirmative action, legal education, ethics, and other key topics related to the law.

The efforts of these contemporary pioneers continue to open doors for other legal scholars. In particular, Bell's protest helped to pave the way for **Lani Guinier**, who in 1998 became the first Black American woman to receive tenure at the Harvard Law School and is now the Bennett Boskey Professor of Law. Guinier earned her BA degree from Radcliffe College in 1971 and a JD degree from Yale Law School in 1974. In this volume, Guinier shares her life and career story in an excerpt from her book, *Lift Every Voice: Turning a Civil Rights Setback into a New Vision of Social Justice* (1998). Guinier recalls being inspired to become a lawyer when she watched Constance Baker Motley on television during the James Meredith case. Guinier was born in New York in 1950 to an interracial couple; her father, Ewart, was a Black American and her mother, Eugenia, was a Jew. In *Lift Every Voice*, Guinier explains, "I may have been taught by my parents that I was interracial, but in junior high school, I became black" (Guinier 1998, 66). Guinier's career has spanned positions at the Civil Rights Division of the U.S. Department of Justice, as head of the Voting Rights project at the NAACP Legal Defense Fund, and as a tenured professor at the University of Pennsylvania Law School. One of Guinier's most pivotal and public moments in her career was in 1993, when President Clinton nominated her to head the Civil Rights Division of the Department of Justice. Although she had served in the Civil Rights Division as special assistant to Assistant Attorney General Drew S. Days under Carter's administration without scrutiny, her nomination was met with much opposition because of her misinterpreted views on voting and democracy. Consequently, Clinton withdrew his nomination. In *Lift Every Voice*, Guinier writes about the many lessons she learned from her parents about how to deal with adversity, and this was one of them:

> My father taught me to be dignified in the face of great adversity. He had become a U.S. citizen, fought a war on behalf of his adopted country, and yet never felt fully acknowledged or respected, as even a human being. He suffered so many more profound indignities than I, and yet managed to step above them. He was never bitter. I could not be bitter, either. My father was shunned by his classmates at Harvard. I was shunned by my law school friends in the White House. . . . Just as my father, during his two years at Harvard College, felt invisible, I too found myself disappearing in Washington, D.C., in the spring of 1993. But having been "invisible" as a college undergraduate, Ewart Guinier never again let himself be silenced. (62–63) [See chapter 11]

Guinier has received several awards for her excellence in teaching, including the 1994 Harvey Levin Teaching Award from the University of Pennsylvania Law School and the 2002 Sacks-Freund Award for Teaching Excellence from Harvard Law School. Her scholarly contribution to academia is beyond compare, and her work addresses such critical topics as affirmative action, race, and gender. She has published numerous articles and has authored and coauthored books including *Becoming Gentlemen: Women, Law School, and Institutional Change* (1997) and *The Miner's Canary: Enlisting Race, Resisting Power, Transforming Democracy* (2002).

A native of Los Angeles, California, John A. Payton was born in 1946. He is a highly successful litigation lawyer with the Wilmer Cutler Pickering Hale and Dorr law firm; he specializes in civil rights, education, government, and entertainment. As president of the NAACP Legal Defense Fund in 2008, Payton was hired by the University of Michigan to defend its rights to use race in its undergraduate and law school admission processes. Payton won the case when the U.S. Supreme Court ruled that the institution could use race in its undergraduate and law school admission processes. The University of Michigan's affirmative action admissions case is among many of Payton's success stories.

Payton has been a visiting professor at Harvard Law School and Georgetown Law Center. He earned a BA degree from Pomona College in 1973. He later earned a JD degree from Harvard School of Law in 1977. While at Harvard, Payton served as a member of the editorial board for Harvard's *Civil Rights and Civil Liberties Law Review*.

Jock M. Smith, a distinguished trial lawyer, was born in New York City in 1948. He is among the new generation of lawyers and is one of America's top civil litigators. In the case of *Whittaker v. Southwestern Life Insurance Company, et al.* (2004), he was responsible for winning the largest verdict ever awarded in the United States. Smith's parents were Jacob Smith and Betty Lou Bowers Nance Smith. Inspired by his father, who was also a successful lawyer, Smith earned a BS degree in history from Tuskegee University in 1970 and a law degree from the University of Notre Dame Law School in 1973. Smith's autobiography, *Climbing Jacob's Ladder: A Trial Lawyer's Journey on Behalf of the Least of These* (2002), recounts many memories of his father and how he was influenced by him. One day Jock's dad did not go to work because he wanted to visit his son's school. While at Jock's school, his dad noticed that Jock did not have stars behind his name. When he asked Jock what the stars represented, Jock said, "I don't know, good work, attendance, stuff like that" (24–25). Jock explains, "He [his father] looked me right in the eye and said, grimly, 'From now on, I want to see stars behind your name'" (25). He further writes, "All I knew was that my daddy was about the best a boy could ask for: a pal, a firm hand, a counselor" (24).

This small cadre of contemporary Black American pioneers, like Jock Smith, is still facing some of the same obstacles that confronted early Black American legal pioneers as they ascend Jacob's ladder; nevertheless, they continue to press onward as they sit at the welcome table, promoting fundamental social change in America.

Finally, the Black American men and women discussed in this volume are high achievers by America's standards. These stalwart warriors remain steadfastly on the battlefield. The history of Black legal and ethical thought in America chronicles the progress of a race of people who rose against the odds to not only sit at the welcome table but also to partake of the bounty that is there. In every instance, they challenged America to live up to its creed and promise of freedom and equality for all its citizens.

Government

The government is another area of American culture that illuminates the power and possibility of Black American people sitting at the welcome table. When President Lyndon B. Johnson signed the Voting Rights Act in 1965, America slowly and reluctantly became more tolerant of Blacks in elected positions. The passing of the Voting Rights Act was aligned with the prevailing philosophy of the NAACP, which sought to change American law to ensure citizenship rights and responsibilities for Black Americans, so all could have an opportunity to sit at the welcome table.

We begin this section of Volume 2 with a discussion of some of the prominent Black Americans who have served as mayors in the United States, primarily because American voters have been more tolerant when electing Black Americans in mayoral positions, making the integration of Blacks into America's political system on the local scene more possible. It wasn't until the late 1960s that America elected its first Black American as mayor of a major city. By 2009, more than 641 Blacks were serving in mayoral positions in major cities throughout the United States (National Conference of Black Mayors 2009). Among the first to be elected mayor of major cities in the United States are Carl Burton Stokes, Richard Hatcher, Maynard Jackson, Coleman Young, Tom Bradley, Richard Arrington, Jr., and Harold Washington. Many times their tenure focused on pivotal issues such as high poverty rates, ineffective social services programs, Black-on-Black crime, budgeting problems, and high unemployment rates, some of which came about because of dramatic demographic changes.

The citizens of Cleveland, Ohio, and Gary, Indiana, were the first to elect a Black American to serve as mayor of their cities. Carl Burton Stokes (D) and Richard Hatcher (D) were both elected mayors of these respective cities on November 7, 1967. Because Stokes took the oath on November 13, 1967, two months earlier than Hatcher, he should be recognized as the first Black mayor; Hatcher should be considered the second Black mayor because he was sworn in on January 1, 1968. There is some controversy about who is technically the first because they both won on the same day.

It is our resolve that both should be considered the first Black American mayor of a major city as they were elected on the same day.

Carl Burton Stokes was born in Cleveland, Ohio, in 1927. Stokes and his older brother, Louis Stokes, were raised in one of the first federally funded housing projects in the country, known as Outhwaite Homes. They lived in dire poverty after their father's death as their mother, a house-keeper, struggled to provide for the two boys. Stokes dropped out of high school and joined the army. After his two-year tenure in the army, he completed his high school requirements and earned his BS degree from the University of Minnesota in 1954. He went on to earn his JD degree from Cleveland Marshall Law School in 1956.

Louis Stokes and Carl Burton Stokes were both interested in politics. Louis served as Cleveland's congressman for 28 years. Carl Stokes fol-lowed in his brother's footsteps. Before running for mayor, Stokes was elected to Ohio's House of Representatives in 1962, making him the first Black American to serve in this capacity. He first ran for mayor of Cleve-land in 1965, but lost by a narrow margin. He ran again and won in 1967, becoming the first Black mayor of Cleveland.

Inheriting a city with its share of poverty and crime, Stokes used his intellect and political know-how to reduce the crime rate dramatically by hiring additional police and insisting that they treat citizens with respect. Stokes was reelected to a second term in 1969, receiving practically all of the Black votes and the majority of votes in 8 of the 11 all-White districts. After his second term, he was elected general counsel to the United Auto Workers (UAW) in 1980, and from 1983 to 1994, he served as munici-pal court judge. After his retirement, Stokes served as ambassador to the Seychelles under Clinton's administration from 1994 to 1995. In 1996, he succumbed to cancer of the esophagus while residing in Cleveland.

Richard Hatcher (D) was the first Black American elected mayor of Gary, Indiana. He served five terms. The youngest of Carlton and Cath-erine Hatcher's 13 children, Hatcher was born in Michigan City, Indiana, in 1933. Hatcher's father worked for Pullman Standard Manufacturing Railroad Cars, and his mother worked in a factory. He went on to earn his BS degree in business and government from Indiana University in 1956 and a JD degree from Valparaiso University in 1959. Hatcher's interest was sparked while at Valparaiso. He became an active participant in the Civil Rights Movement in an effort to stamp out segregation. His political interest heightened when he was elected a councilman in Gary, Indiana, in 1963 and Gary's mayor in 1967. As mayor, Hatcher was met with a city in turmoil—tuberculosis was at an all-time high due to U.S. Steel pollutants, syndicated crime was on the increase, and the unemployment rate was escalating, among many other woes (Poinsett 1970). Having inherited a poverty-stricken city, Hatcher acquired more than $300 million in federal funds to revitalize Gary's housing and social services programs. During his five terms, Hatcher's administration worked tirelessly to combat the extreme unemployment rates in the city. When he retired as mayor in 1987, Hatcher began R. Gordon Hatcher and Associates, a consulting firm. Hatcher has also served as adjunct professor of African American studies at Indiana University Northwest.

The accomplishments of Stokes and Hatcher made the integration of Blacks into America's political system more possible on the local scene. Consequently, other major cities began to follow suit.

In 1973, Maynard H. Jackson, Jr. (D) became the first Black American mayor of Atlanta, Georgia. He was reelected to a second term in 1977 but was ineligible to run for a third consecutive term because of state law. However, he later served a third term from 1990 to 1994. Jackson's father was a Baptist minister and his mother was a French professor at Spelman College. Jackson was born in Dallas, Texas, in 1938; however, he and his five siblings were raised in Atlanta, where his father served as pastor of Friendship Baptist Church. After his father's death, his grandfather, John Wesley Dobbs, the founder of the Georgia Voters League, played a significant role in molding Jackson's life. Jackson did his undergraduate studies at Morehouse College in Atlanta and earned a BA degree in political science and history in 1956. He received a JD degree from North Carolina Central University School of Law in 1964.

During his two terms as mayor of Atlanta, one of Jackson's major contributions was galvanizing the economic growth of the city when he created affirmative action programs that ensured that minority-owned businesses would receive their share of city contracts. He was also responsible for the expansion of the Hartsfield-Jackson Atlanta International Airport, which remains a major transportation hub today. After his last term as mayor in 1994, Jackson began the Atlanta Business Chronicle, a bond and security firm. Having undergone heart surgery in 1992, Jackson died of heart failure in 2003 while he was in Washington, D.C. Because of his major contributions to the city of Atlanta, Jackson's body lay in state at city hall and at Morehouse College; his funeral was held at the Atlanta Civic Center.

Meanwhile, on the West Coast, the citizens of Los Angeles elected Tom Bradley (D) as its first Black American mayor in 1973 and reelected him for four additional terms. Bradley, the son of a sharecropper and the grandson of a slave, was born in Calvert, Texas, in 1917. His father, Lee Thomas Bradley, was a porter for the Santa Fe railroad, and his mother, Crenner, was a maid. Bradley's father moved him and his four siblings to Los Angeles in 1924. He attended UCLA for three years but dropped out after passing the Los Angeles Police Department recruitment exam. While on the force, he served as a juvenile officer, a detective, and a community relations person. He later earned his JD degree from Southwestern University Law School in 1956.

Bradley held the mayoral position for 20 years, longer than any other mayor of Los Angeles. Having inherited the city after the Watts Riot, Bradley is credited with calming the city after the five-day turbulence. Among his many other achievements, Bradley was responsible for the $200 million surplus profits from the 1984 Summer Olympics hosted in Los Angeles.

Before becoming the city's first Black American mayor, Bradley was the first Black on the Los Angeles City Council, the first to run for governor of California in 1982, and the first to earn the rank of lieutenant in the Los Angeles Police Department. Having suffered a heart attack in 1996, Bradley underwent a triple bypass that resulted in a stroke. From that point on Bradley was partially paralyzed and unable to speak. Two years later, while in a Los Angeles hospital, Bradley died of a second heart attack at age 80.

During the same year Bradley was elected mayor of Los Angeles, Coleman A. Young (D) was elected the first Black American mayor of Detroit. A Tuskegee Airman, Young served an unparalleled 20 years as mayor of Detroit. Young was born in Tuscaloosa, Alabama, in 1918 to Coleman and Ida Reese Jones. Coleman's family migrated to Detroit, where they found a city in racial uproar. Young learned about politics from his father, who was a postal service worker and the owner of a tailor shop; he learned the importance of giving to the underprivileged from his mother, who was a teacher. Although Young was a very intelligent young man, he was denied access to several leading high schools in Detroit, including Detroit High School and LaSalle High School. He went on to attend Detroit's public school system. After high school he entered an electrician's apprentice school at Ford Motor Company, where he was met with much racism. He was later hired to work on the assembly line and became instrumental in the underground union activities. While working for the U.S. Postal Service, Young joined the U.S. Army in 1942, becoming one of the famed Tuskegee Airmen. After the war he became a social and civil rights activist as a result of his father's teachings.

In 1993, Young retired after serving five terms as mayor of Detroit. During his tenure Young fought against corruption in all levels of city government, from the streets to city hall. Among his many accomplishments, he made the police department more representative of the city's population, which was becoming more heavily populated by Blacks at the time. After his retirement in 1993, Young fought a long battle with poor health and died of emphysema in 1997.

In 1979, the citizens of Birmingham, Alabama, a city that was known for its racial turmoil during the 1950s, elected its first Black American mayor, Richard Arrington, Jr. (D). Arrington was born in Livingston, Alabama, in 1934. His parents, who were sharecroppers, migrated to Fairfield, Alabama, a small steel town, so his father could provide a more financially stable life for the family. But that wasn't enough. Arrington's father worked a second job as a brick mason to help meet the needs of his family. His parents instilled in all of their children that education was important to their livelihoods, so Arrington earned a BA degree in biology from Miles College and an MS degree in biology from the University of Detroit in 1957. He went on to earn a PhD degree in zoology and biochemistry from the University of Oklahoma in 1963.

Arrington began his political career in 1971 when he ran against five opponents for city councilman and won overwhelmingly. During his tenure as councilman, he exposed police brutality cases and implemented affirmative action proposals for hiring practices in the city. In *Back to Birmingham: Richard Arrington, Jr., and His Times* (1989), Franklin writes:

Arrington had recognized the ineffectiveness of Birmingham's voluntary hiring plan for blacks. Therefore, he had introduced a council resolution reaffirming the city's commitment to fair employment. When Siebels's administration continued to drag its feet on the hiring of blacks for city jobs, the young councilman wrote the mayor in July 1972, requesting information on employment. Arrington applauded the appointment of a few blacks to important positions, such as attorney Peter Hall, the first black to serve in a city judgeship. . . . As significant as these appointments may have been, they had not seriously addressed the fundamental question of affirmative action in employment for a city fast approaching 50 percent black population. (71)

Arrington's legacy was reducing the crime and unemployment rates in the city of Birmingham. He earned the confidence of Birmingham's citizens and was reelected in the mayoral position for five terms. At the close of his tenure, he left Birmingham with a $100 million endowment fund and a financially sound city. Although Arrington is retired, today at age 77, he remains politically active.

Major U.S. cities such as Chicago, Trenton, New York, and New Orleans continued to elect Black Americans to mayoral positions. Harold Lee Washington (D) became Chicago's first Black American mayor in 1983. A native of Chicago, Washington was born in 1922 to Roy and Bertha Washington. As a single parent, Washington's father, a preacher and precinct captain, raised Washington and his three siblings after his mother left the family. During Washington's young years, his father was instrumental in building his strong leadership skills. During his high school years, Washington did not feel challenged; therefore, he ran away from one school, Milwaukee's St. Benedict the Moor Catholic School, and later dropped out of another, DuSable High School. He did, however, earn his high school equivalency diploma while in the army. He went on to earn a BA degree from Roosevelt University in 1949 and a JD degree from Northwestern University School of Law in 1952.

Capitalizing upon his strong leadership skills and his love for politics, Washington was elected as a representative to the Illinois House of Representatives from 1965 to 1973. He was later elected to Congress in 1980 and served until he was elected Chicago's first Black American mayor in 1983. Washington inherited a city that was low in spirits due to financial turmoils and redistricting. In *Harold Washington: The Mayor, the Man*, Miller (1989) explains, "In April 1983 Harold Washington had inherited a city deficit in excess of $100 million, a projected 1983 shortfall estimated variously at another $60 million or so, and a bond rating that was about to slip down a notch, costing the city additional millions in debt service every year" (21). During his tenure as mayor, Washington was met with a great deal of opposition from the city council from the onset. The council wanted to prohibit him from moving forward on implementing new programs. However, as fate would have it, The "Council Wars" ended in 1986 when the courts reversed the recent ward redistricting, thereby shifting the council in his favor. Therefore, Washington was able to later implement many of his programs. In 1987, one year after winning his second term as mayor, Washington died of a heart attack.

David Norman Dinkins (D), a native of Trenton, New Jersey, was born in 1927. Dinkins's parents divorced when he was seven, and he was raised by his mother and grandmother. They relocated to Harlem, New York, for a time but later moved back to New Jersey. Dinkins attended Trenton Central High School, where he graduated near the top of his class in 1945. He then enrolled at Howard University, but his college tenure was disrupted by World War II, during which he served in the U.S. Marines. After his stint in the Marines, he returned to Howard University, graduating magna cum laude with a BS degree in mathematics. He later earned his LLB degree from Brooklyn Law School in New York.

Dinkins maintained a law practice in New York City for nearly 20 years before he began his gradual involvement in politics. Dinkins ascended through the Democratic Party organization in Harlem and joined an influential cadre of Black American politicians that included Denny Terrell, Percy Sutton, Basil Paterson, and Charles Rangel. This group, often referred to as the "Gang of Four," helped to pave the way for Dinkins to become president of Manhattan Borough.

In addition, Dinkins became the first Black American mayor of New York City in 1989 by first beating incumbent Mayor Ed Koch, who had served as mayor for 12 years, to win the Democratic nomination. He then went on to beat Rudy Giuliani, the Republican candidate for mayor. However, Dinkins lost to Giuliani in his reelection efforts in 1993 by a slight margin; he did not seek a comeback but nevertheless remains active in New York politics and the National Democratic Party.

David Dinkins later joined the faculty at Columbia University as professor of practice in public affairs in the School of International and Public Affairs. The David N. Dinkins Professorship and the Dinkins Archives and Oral History Project were established at Columbia University to recognize his extraordinary accomplishments. Columbia University Libraries acquired the papers of Dinkins, which are now accessible for research.

A new crop of Black American mayors, both men and women, and from varying age groups and cross-sections of America continue to pursue mayoral positions. In Washington, D.C., and Newark, Adrian Fenty and Cory A. Booker are two young Black Americans who have been elected mayors of major metropolitan cities.

At age 35, Adrian Fenty (D) became the youngest mayor in Washington, D.C.'s history in 2006. He earned a BA degree in English and economics from Oberlin College in 1992. In 1996, he graduated from Howard University Law School with a JD degree. In 2010, Fenty lost his bid for mayor by a margin of 53 to 46.

At age 37, Cory A. Booker (D) won an overwhelming victory to become the 36th mayor of Newark, New Jersey, in 2006. He earned a BA degree in political science in 1991 and an MA degree in sociology in 1992 from Stanford University. As a Rhodes Scholar, Booker earned a BS degree in modern history from the Queen's College in Oxford in 1994. He went on to earn a JD degree from Yale Law School in 1997.

Shirley Franklin (D) became the first woman and the first Black American woman to be elected mayor of Atlanta, serving a maximum of two consecutive six-year terms (2002, 2008). Franklin earned a BA degree in sociology from Howard University in 1968 and an MA degree in sociology from the University of Pennsylvania in 1969.

Heather McTeer Hudson (D) is serving her second term as mayor of Greenville, Mississippi (2003, 2007). Hudson is the first Black American and the first woman to be elected as mayor of Greenville. Hudson earned a BA degree in sociology from Spelman College and a JD degree from Tulane Law School in 2001.

Cedric B. Glover (D) is serving his second term as mayor of Shreveport, Louisiana (2006, 2010). He is the first Black American to be elected mayor of Shreveport. Glover attended public and private schools in the Caddo Public School system in Shreveport.

It seems only appropriate to end the discussion on Black American mayors with the city of Grambling, Louisiana. Most recently, in 2010, Edward Jones (D) was elected mayor of the city. Jones earned a BS degree in speech and drama in 1974 and an MA degree in liberal arts in 1984 from Grambling State University.

The integration of these Black American mayors, men and women, into the political arena has helped to break down political barriers as they have skillfully woven themselves into the fabric of the American political system. It is evident Black Americans have made their mark in mayoral seats in major cities throughout the country. Collectively, these mayors have used their leadership skills to bring about progressive changes in America.

Four Black Americans have served in gubernatorial positions in the history of the United States: Pinckney Benton Stewart Pinchback, Lawrence Douglas Wilder, Deval L. Patrick, and David A. Paterson. Pinchback was the only one who was appointed, and the other three Black American governors were elected.

Before Reconstruction, Pinckney Benton Stewart Pinchback (R) became the first Black governor in Louisiana (appointed) and the first in the United States. During the impeachment proceedings of Governor Henry Clay Warmoth, Pinchback served as governor of Louisiana for 35 days from December 9, 1872, to January 13, 1873 (Haskins 1973). Born the son of a former Virginia slave master and a former slave in Macon, Georgia, in 1837, Pinchback, who often passed for White, was raised in a home in Mississippi with all the benefits of a prosperous family. He attended school for a short period in Ohio at Cincinnati Gilmore School. While away at school, Pinchback's father died and his mother was denounced by his family. Fearing that they would become enslaved, Pinchback's mother and his siblings moved to Cincinnati also.

Before he became governor, Pinchback was appointed lieutenant governor when Oscar Dunn died in office, serving in that role from January 1872 to December 8, 1872. Pinchback's political career continued when he was elected to the House of Representatives in 1872 and to the U.S. Senate in 1873. Because of racism, White southerners challenged the results, and he was never allowed to assume either seat. Perhaps Pinchback's most important contribution is that he helped to establish Southern University and A&M College, a college for Blacks in Louisiana. In *The First Black Governor: Pinckney Benton Stewart Pinchback* (1973), Haskins records:

> The first major service Pinchback did for the black people of Louisiana was done at a convention; the last major service he rendered took place at another. He successfully fought on behalf of a provision for a state-supported "university for the education of persons of color," and by an act of the legislature of 1880, Southern University would be established. (241)

At age 50 Pinchback enrolled in law school at New Orleans Straight College (later Dillard University), where he graduated in 1889. Years later he moved to New York City and then Washington where he practiced law. He died in 1921.

When the Voting Rights Act of 1965 was passed, a slow but steadily increasing number of Black elected officials emerged. However, there were few in state government. In 1990, a little over a hundred years after Pinchback served his brief stint as governor, Lawrence Douglas Wilder (D) was elected the governor of Virginia, making him the first Black governor in America since Reconstruction. The grandson of a slave, Wilder was born in 1931 in Richmond, Virginia. He and his seven siblings were raised in Church Hill, one of the poorest neighborhoods in Richmond. His father, a salesman and supervisor of agents for a Black-owned insurance company, and his mother, homemaker, promoted the importance of education. Consequently, Wilder earned his BS degree in chemistry from Virginia Union University in 1951. Afterward he was drafted into the army, earning a Bronze Star for his service in the Korean War. After the war, Wilder went on to earn his JD degree from Howard University Law School in 1959.

Wilder's interest in politics was sparked early as he listened to political debates as a waiter and at the local barbershop. During Wilder's tenure as governor, he was praised by financial analysts for his expertise in bringing the state out of its economic difficulty. Wilder was not eligible to seek reelection because Virginia state law does not allow governors to serve more than one consecutive term. Continuing his political career, Wilder was elected mayor of Richmond by a landslide victory in 2004 ("L. Douglas Wilder" n.d.).

Sixteen years after Douglas Wilder's governorship, Deval L. Patrick (D) was elected governor of Massachusetts (winning elections in 2006 and 2010), making him the third Black American to serve as governor in U.S. history and the first Black American to be elected to a second term as governor. Patrick was born on the South Side of Chicago, Illinois, in 1956 to Laurdine Patrick and Emily Patrick. Patrick's father, a jazz musician, deserted his mother, leaving her to raise Patrick and his sister, Rhonda. Because he was a bright student, one of his middle-school teachers referred him to a nonprofit organization that financially supported Black American students who exhibited strong academic and leadership skills. Consequently, Patrick enrolled in Milton Academy in Milton, Massachusetts, graduating in 1974. Patrick, a first-generation college student, went on to earn his BS degree in English and American literature in 1978 and a JD degree in 1982 from Harvard University.

Before running for governor, Patrick held a number of positions, including law clerk for Judge Stephen Reinhardt, attorney for the NAACP Legal

Defense and Educational Fund in New York City, and assistant attorney general under President Bill Clinton's administration. Among his many contributions, Patrick has made Massachusetts a leader on clean energy and health care reform.

Last, after Governor Eliot Spitzer resigned because of a prostitution scandal, David A. Paterson (D) was appointed governor of New York in March 2008 to carry out Spitzer's term, making him the first Black American to serve as governor of New York, the fourth Black American to serve as governor in the United States, and the first legally blind person to serve as governor of any state. Paterson was born in Brooklyn, New York, in 1954 to Basil and Portia Paterson. His father was a labor law attorney who later became a New York state senator, secretary of state, and deputy mayor of New York City, and his mom was a homemaker. David A. Paterson contracted an ear infection when he was three months old, which damaged his optic nerve, leaving him completely blind in his left eye and with restricted vision in his right eye. Because the New York public school system would not allow Paterson to be mainstreamed into classrooms, his family relocated to Long Island so he could attend public school in a mainstream environment.

Paterson earned his BA degree in history from Columbia University in 1977 and his JD degree from Hofstra Law School in 1982. Before becoming governor, Paterson had been elected the first Black American lieutenant governor of New York in 2007, and earlier he had become New York's first Black minority leader in the state senate in 2003. The governor's role is a critical one as it helps to bridge the gap among local, state, and national governments, meeting the needs of all citizens in various ways.

It has been more than 140 years since the first Black Americans served in Congress. According to *Black Americans in Congress 1870–2007*, Joseph H. Rainey of South Carolina was the first Black American to serve in the House of Representatives in 1870 (Ragsdale and Treese 1990). The son of slaves, Rainey was born in Georgetown, South Carolina, in 1832. His father, Edward L. Rainey, bought his family's freedom from his savings as a barber, which enabled the family to move to Charleston, South Carolina. Because it was illegal to teach Black Americans to read and write, Rainey's father taught him the livelihood of barbering. Rainey went on to serve in the Confederate Army, and afterward, he and his family moved to St. George and Hamilton, Bermuda, where he supported his family as a barber.

Upon his return to the states, Rainey's acquired wealth from his time in Bermuda made him more visible and a prime candidate for the political scene. Before becoming a member of the House of Representatives, Rainey was an agent for the state land commission and a census taker. When Benjamin F. Whittemore resigned his congressional seat, the Republican Party nominated Rainey for the remainder of his term in the 41st Congress. He later ran and won a full term in the 42nd Congress. Perhaps, his greatest accomplishment was his contribution to the Committee on Freedmen's Affairs.

Since Rainey, Black Americans have continued to play significant roles in the House of Representatives. In 1941, Adam Clayton Powell Jr. (D) became the first Black American elected to the New York City Council, and this paved the way for his election to Congress from Harlem in New York. Adam Clayton Powell, Jr. was born in New Haven, Connecticut, in 1908 to Adam Clayton Powell, Sr., a Baptist minister, and Mattie Fletcher Schaffer, a homemaker. His family moved to New York when his father was assigned to Abyssinian Baptist Church, which later became one of the largest congregations in the country. Powell earned his BS degree from Colgate University in 1930 and an MA degree in religious education from Columbia University Teachers' College in 1932. When Powell became minister of his father's church in 1937, his leadership role in the Black community heightened. His organized boycott against the Transport Workers Union in 1940 was one of the first of its kind. Black Americans refused to use transportation services, which forced the union to negotiate (Hamilton 1991). Among Powell's many noteworthy accomplishments, he organized relief programs of meals for the poor. Thus, he became one of the most popular congressman among Black Americans across the country. Powell made his mark in the House of Representative while serving 12 terms in Congress. He confronted discrimination and racism wherever it raised its ugly head. Although Powell fought tirelessly for Blacks and other people of color, his legal problems and unpredictable behavior eventually undermined his influential but controversial political career. After Powell left Congress in 1969, he was diagnosed with cancer and died in Miami, Florida, in 1972.

Shirley Chisholm (D) was born in 1924 to Charles St. Hill and Ruby Seale, both native Barbadians who met and married in Brooklyn, New York. Chisholm, her two sisters, and her four cousins, were taken to Barbados to be raised by her maternal grandmother, Emily Seale, because of financial hardships. For seven years, they lived on a farm with goats, ducks, sheep, and other animals. They were educated under the British system. When Chisholm returned to America, she was in sixth grade but because she knew little about American history, she was assigned two grades behind. She was later reassigned when she demonstrated her knowledge of American history.

Although Chisholm was accepted to Vassar and Oberlin College when she graduated from high school in 1942, her parents could not afford sending her out of state. Therefore, she enrolled in Brooklyn College, where she became interested in politics, became a member of the NAACP, and worked for the Urban League. She majored in teaching and later earned her master's in early childhood education at Columbia University in 1952. In 1969, Chisholm, a Democrat from Harlem, New York, became the first Black American to win a seat in the U.S. Congress. In 1972, she became the first Black American of either gender to campaign for a major party's presidential nomination, an effort that is poignantly described in *Unbought and Unbossed* (1970). During her career in Congress, Chisholm was a foremost fighter for the civil rights of Black Americans and women. In *Unbought and Unbossed* (1970), she writes:

> There are 435 members of the House of Representatives and 417 are white males. Ten of the others are women and nine are black. I belong to both of these minorities, which makes it add up right. That makes me a celebrity, a kind of side show attraction. I was the first American citizen to be elected to Congress in spite of the double drawbacks of being female and having skin darkened by melanin. (xi)

Barbara Charline Jordan (D) made history by becoming the first Black American woman and the first Black elected to the Texas Senate since 1883. Jordan was born in Houston in 1936 in the Fourth Ward, which at one time was the economic and cultural center of Houston's Black American population. Jordan's father, Benjamin, a Baptist minister and warehouse clerk, and Arlyne, her mother, were heavily involved in the lives of Jordan and her two sisters. Jordan earned a BS degree from Texas Southern University in 1956 and a law degree from the Boston University Law School in 1959. After graduating from law school, Jordan taught briefly at Tuskegee University and then moved to Houston, where she practiced law from her parents' home for three years until she had saved enough money to open her own practice in the mid-1960s.

In 1972, Jordan became the first Black woman from the South to be elected to the United States Congress, serving as a member of the House of Representatives until 1979. One of the highlights of her illustrious career was presenting the keynote address for the Democratic National Convention in 1976. In 1994, President Clinton awarded Jordan the Presidential Medal of Freedom, the nation's highest honor for a civilian. As a congresswoman, Jordan sponsored bills that championed those in poverty, the disadvantaged, and people of color. She also sponsored legislation to expand the Voting Rights Act of 1965 to include Mexican Americans in the southwestern part of the United States and in those states where minorities had been denied the right to vote or had had their rights restricted by unfair voter registration practices. After retirement, she taught in the Lyndon B. Johnson School of Public Affairs at the University of Texas. A multiple sclerosis patient for more than 20 years, Jordan died of pneumonia in 1979. Because of her tremendous contributions to this country and to the state of Texas, she lay in state at the University of Texas at Austin for public viewing.

Finally, two of the most powerful and respected Black men currently serving in the House of Representatives are Congressmen John Conyers, Jr. (D) and Charles B. Rangel (D). As the second-longest serving member of the House, John Conyers, Jr. has been reelected 20 times by the voters in Michigan's 14th Congressional District. Conyers was born in Detroit in 1929 and was educated by the Detroit Public School System. He received his BA and JD degrees from Wayne State University and Wayne State Law School in 1957 and 1958, respectively.

Conyers is also the fifth-longest serving member of Congress. He has served on numerous committees and has had the distinct pleasure of serving as the chairman of the Judiciary Committee from 2007–2011. Conyers has authored numerous bills, including the bill establishing the Martin Luther King holiday in particular. Other bills concern violence against women, the Motor Voter Act, and the Alcohol Warning Label Act. Conyers, a long-time friend, colleague, and employer of Rosa Parks, the mother of the Civil Rights Movement, wrote a tribute to Mrs. Parks that appears in each volume of this multivolume set.

In Charles B. Rangel's autobiography, *And I Haven't Had a Bad Day Since* (2007), he wrote about the day he was appointed to the House Ways and Means Committee:

My appointment [to the House Ways and Means Committee], in December 1974, capped an incredible year for the House Democrats in general and for me as a black member in particular. The post-Watergate midterm election delivered a Democratic landslide—a 289 to 145 majority in the House—that, combined with major reforms in the seniority system and the rules, promised to break the hold of conservative Southern Democrats and moderate Republicans and clear the way for bringing truly progressive legislation to the floor. (197–198)

During his 19 years of service, Rangel has authored bills concerning housing and urban neighborhoods. He also cosponsored the long overdue bill in the House of Representatives that awarded the Tuskegee Airmen the Congressional Gold Medal of Honor for their heroism in World War II. It is only fitting that Representative Rangel would write a tribute to the Tuskegee Airmen for this multivolume set. Rangel was born in New York in 1930. He went on to earn his BS degree from York University in 1957 and his law degree from St. John's University Law School in 1960. Both Conyers and Rangel have garnered support to ensure the passage of bills that have enhanced the lives of Black Americans and other people of color.

Since 2000, **William Lacy Clay, Jr.** (D) has been a congressman from St. Louis, Missouri. Clay has been seated on a number of key committees, serving as chairman of the House Subcommittee on Information Policy and the Census and National Archives. Born in St. Louis in 1956, Clay followed in his father's footsteps. Clay's father, William Lacy Clay, Sr., was a former Missouri congressman who was also a mentor to his son. In this volume, Clay writes:

As a profession, politics chose me more than I chose politics. Growing up in St. Louis, it seems I had little choice but to go into government service. You see, I came from a family of politicians, activists, and community leaders, and my father, former Congressman William L. "Bill" Clay, Sr., was probably the most prominent among them, known nationally for his historic election in 1968 as the first African American sent to Congress from the state of Missouri.

Clay received his BA degree in government and politics from the University of Maryland in 1983 and he later attended the John F. Kennedy School of Government at Harvard University. During his tenure in the House of Representatives, Clay has been a strong advocate for the economically disadvantaged families, and he has supported legislation that prohibits unfair lending practices to homebuyers. Before he was elected to the U.S. House of Representatives, Clay served eight years as a member of the Missouri House of Representatives.

According to *Black Americans in Congress 1870–2007*, Hiram Rhodes Revels (R) served as America's first Black American senator from 1870 to 1871. Although there is ambiguity around Revel's birthdate, Thompson reports that Revels, in his "Autobiography," reported that he was born in Fayetteville, North Carolina in 1827 (Thompson 1982). His father was a Baptist preacher and his mother was of Scottish descent; both were free, and Revels was born a free man. Revels attended the Beech Grove Quaker Seminary in Liberty, Indiana, and the Darke County Seminary for Black American students in Ohio. Under the influence of his brother Willis, Revels sought religious instruction in the teachings of the church and to become a minister himself (Thompson 1982, 25). After he became an ordained pastor, Revels spent much of his time traveling throughout the country educating Black Americans. In 1857, he graduated from Knox College in Galesburg, Illinois. Encouraged to run for public office by a friend, Revels won a seat in the Mississippi State Senate. At the same time, the Mississippi State Senate also wanted to fill the U.S. Senate seats vacated by Jefferson Davis and Albert Brown in 1861; their seats had not been filled since their expiration in 1863 and 1865, respectively. Revels was a strong opponent of racial discrimination and broke new ground for Black Americans in Congress.

After his one-year tenure as senator, Revels became the first president of Alcorn University, the first land-grant school in the country. Serving in this capacity from 1871 to 1874, Revels resigned and returned to the ministry. However, two years later, in 1876, Revels regained his position as president of Alcorn University. He also remained active in the ministry, dying of a stroke while attending a religious conference in 1901.

Since Reconstruction, only four Blacks have served as senators: three were elected and one was appointed. Edward William Brooke III (R), from the state of Massachusetts, was the first Black American to be elected and then reelected to the U.S. Senate. He served as a U.S. senator for two terms, from 1967 to 1979. Brooke was born in Washington, D.C., in 1919 to Edward Brooke, Jr., an attorney, and Edna, a homemaker and a strong campaign supporter for Brooke. Brooke was raised by his father, a Howard University Law School graduate. At age 16, he enrolled in Howard University and earned a BA in sociology in 1941. He earned LLB and LLM degrees from Boston University Law School in 1948 and 1949, respectively. Before being elected senator, Brooke was elected Massachusetts attorney general, which made him the first Black American to serve in this position. Brooke was also the first Black American elected state attorney general in 1962, a major statewide office in Massachusetts. During his two terms as senator, Brooke fought to improve low-income housing, increase the minimum wage, and improve mass transit. After his tenure as senator ended in 1979, Brooke spent several years in private practice. Brooke was diagnosed with breast cancer in 2002; he currently resides on his farm in Warrenton, Virginia. In 2007, Brooke wrote his autobiography, *Bridging the Divide*.

After Brooke, Carol Moseley Braun (D) was elected senator in 1993, making her the second Black American U.S. Senator since Reconstruction. Braun was born in Chicago, Illinois, in 1947. Her father, a police officer, and her mom, a medical technician, were strong advocates of education. A product of the Chicago public school system, Braun went on to earn her BA degree from the University of Illinois at Chicago in 1969 and a JD degree from the University of Chicago in 1972. Before being elected senator, Braun served in a number of public offices, including prosecutor in Chicago's U.S. attorney's office, a member of the Illinois House of Representatives, and recorder of deeds for Cook County, Illinois. While in the Senate, Braun was a strong advocate for education, civil liberties, the war on terror, and the economy.

When asked what her career-defining moment was, Braun responded:

Winning the primary for the United States Senate was a major, major step because that was the one that I think changed expectations. When we first started out with the campaign for the Senate, the response I got, even from a lot of African Americans, was that I couldn't win—people's vision and aspirations just did not go there. When I won the primary there was almost a sense of the inexplicable, and then I went on and won the general. I had two back-to-back, hard-fought elections. The problem was that I had beaten an incumbent Democratic senator in the primary, and the political establishment made me pay. I wound up getting it from both my own party as well as from the Republicans. That was the bad news. The good news was that it raised expectations, and a record number of Black people, male and female, have stood for the United States Senate since then. You've had people running in the primaries; unfortunately, the only ones to get through to the general election have been Harold Ford, Jr. and Barack Obama; Barack is the only one to actually make it to the Senate. (C. M. Braun, personal communication, January 12, 2007).

Closing the gap in only 12 years after Braun, Barack H. Obama, Jr. (D) was elected senator for Illinois in 2005, making him the third elected Black American senator since Reconstruction. After a short stint in the Senate, Obama vied for the U.S. presidency and in 2008 became the first Black American elected president of the United States; consequently, his seat as senator was vacated. The governor appointed Roland Wallace Burris (D) to fill Obama's vacated seat in 2009, making him the fourth Black American to serve since Reconstruction.

Burris was born in Centralia, Illinois, in 1937 to Earl and Emma Burris. He earned a BA degree in political science from Southern Illinois University at Carbondale in 1959. He went on to earn his JD degree from Howard University School of Law in 1963. During his political career, Burris has served as the national bank examiner for the Office of the Comptroller of the Currency for the U.S. Treasury Department, director of the Department of Central Management Services, Illinois comptroller, and attorney general for the state of Illinois. Burris, at age 72, completed Obama's term but did not seek reelection in 2010.

On November 4, 2008, Barack H. Obama, Jr. became the first Black American president, beating his opponent, the senator from Arizona, John McCain, with 349 to 189 of the electoral votes, respectively. According to *Time* magazine's "President Obama: The Path to the White House":

> Obama won more votes than anyone else in U.S. history, the biggest Democratic victory since Lyndon Johnson crushed another Arizona Senator 44 years ago. Obama won men, which no Democrat had managed since Bill Clinton. He won 54% of Catholics, 66% of Latinos, 68% of new voters—a multicultural, multigenerational movement that shatters the old political ice pack. (Gibbs 2009, 92)

Consequently, in 2009, Barack H. Obama, Jr. became the first Black American to be sworn in as the president of the United States.

Obama was born in Honolulu, Hawaii, in 1961. His father, Barack Obama, Sr. was from Kenya, and his mother, Stanley Ann Dunham, was from Kansas City, Missouri; they met while attending the University of Hawaii. Briefly married for three years (Gibbs 2009; Ripley 2008), the two divorced, and Obama, Sr. later pursued a doctorate at Harvard University while Dunham continued her education in Honolulu. After his mother remarried in 1967, Obama's family moved to Indonesia, where he attended Catholic school until he was 10 years old. Returning to Honolulu, Obama lived with his grandparents while attending Punahou, an Ivy League preparatory school. Obama went on to attend Occidental College in Los Angeles for two years, later transferring to Columbia University in New York, where he majored in political science with specialization in international relations. Following in his father's footsteps, Obama attended Harvard University, earning a degree from Harvard Law School in 1991.

Obama's journey would not have been what it is today had it not been for the countless other historical and contemporary Black American pioneers who fought, who died, and who are fighting against social and political injustices in America even today. Recognizing the Black American pioneers who have gone before him, Obama acknowledged, "I'm very humbled by the fact that I stand on the shoulders of all the people that made all these incredible contributions to lift this country up" (Monroe 2009, 16). In particular, Black Americans Shirley A. Chisholm, Jesse L. Jackson, Lenora Fulani, Alan Keyes, Carol Moseley-Braun, and Alfred "Al" Sharpton, Jr. all competed for the office of the president of the United States, and each helped to pave the way for Obama.

Shirley Chisholm (D) was the first Black woman to run for president of the United States in 1972. She "campaigned extensively and entered primaries in twelve states, winning twenty-eight delegates and receiving 152 first ballot votes at the convention" (Ragsdale and Treese 1990, 18). Twelve years after Chisholm, Jesse Jackson ran for the office of president of the United States. He first ran for president in 1984, winning 3.5 million votes, and he ran again in 1988, nearly doubling his votes to 6.9 million. Jackson's ability to garner such a large number of votes made America and Black voters, in particular, take Black candidates more seriously.

Likewise, Lenora Fulani (I) ran for president as an independent in 1988; she was the first woman and the first Black whose name appeared on the ballot for president in all 50 states. Fulani ran again in 1992. Two years after Fulani, in 1995, Alan Keyes became the first Black American Republican presidential candidate, making him the first Black American to run for the presidency in the 21st century. Keyes was also a candidate for president in 1996 and 2000.

Both Carol Moseley Braun and Al Sharpton, Jr. ran for U.S. president in 2004. Before her campaign for the U.S. presidency, Braun, who granted the editors an interview for inclusion in this volume, was the second Black American elected to serve as a U.S. senator. Consequently, Braun's run for the presidency was no surprise. A native of Chicago, Braun is a strong supporter of minority rights and education. Although Sharpton did not become a presidential candidate for the Democratic Party in 2004, he remains at the forefront of issues that are critical to humankind.

Before Obama's run for the presidency, he was a community organizer and a U.S. senator from Illinois. Using his experiences as a community organizer and a politician, Obama stimulated a grassroot movement to ensure that all Americans, regardless of race, creed, or religion, had an opportunity to truly participate in the political process. As President Obama prepared for the Oval Office, he strategically set out to appoint Black Americans to key positions, including Eric H. Holder, Jr., U.S. attorney general; Susan E. Rice, U.S. permanent representative to the United Nations; Lisa Perez Jackson, administrator for the Environmental Protection Agency; Regina M. Benjamin, surgeon general; and Ron Kirk, U.S. trade representative. Obama has also made numerous appointments of Black Americans to the federal bench and law enforcement, including Tanya Walton Pratt, U.S. District Court for the Southern District of Indiana; Stephanie A. Finley, U.S. attorney for Louisiana's Western District; Henry Whitehorn, U.S. marshal for the Western Division; Kelvin Washington, U.S. marshal for the District of South Carolina; and numerous other Black Americans.

With Barack Obama's ascension as the 44th president of the United States and his vie for the presidency for a second term, more Black Americans are being provided opportunities to sit at the welcome table, invited and uninvited, and making decisions large and small. They have and are using their political positions to introduce bills for the betterment of all Americans.

References

Bell, D. 1993. *Faces at the Bottom of the Well: The Permanence of Racism.* New York: Basic Books.

Brooke, E. 2007. *Bridging the Divide: My Divide.* New Brunswick, NJ: Rutgers University Press.

Chisholm, S. 1970. *Unbought and Unbossed.* Boston, MA: Houghton Mifflin Co.

Franklin, J. L. 1989. *Back to Birmingham: Richard Arrington, Jr., and His Times.* Tuscaloosa: University of Alabama Press.

Gallot, M. B. G. 1985. *A History of Grambling State University.* Lanham, MD: University Press of America, Inc.

Gibbs, N. 2009. "The People's Choice." *Time: Expanded Inauguration Edition: President Obama: The Path to the White House*, 90–95.

Goldman, R. 1992. *Thurgood Marshall: Justice for All.* New York: Carroll & Graf Publishers.

Guinier, L. 1998. *Lift Every Voice: Turning a Civil Rights Setback into a New Vision of Social Justice.* New York: Simon & Schuster.

Hamilton, C. V. 1991. *Adam Clayton Powell, Jr.: The Political Biography of an American Dilemma.* New York: Macmillan Publishing Company.

Haskins, J. 1973. *The First Black Governor: Pinkney Benton Stewart Pinchback.* Trenton, NJ: Africa World Press.

Higginbotham, A. L. 1978. *In the Matter of Color: Race and the American Legal Process: The Colonial Period.* New York: Oxford University Press.

Higginbotham, A. L. 1996. *Shades of Freedom: Racial Politics and Presumptions of the American Legal Process.* New York: Oxford University Press.

Hine, D. C. 1993. *Black Women in America: An Historical Encyclopedia.* Vol. 1. Brooklyn, NY: Carlson Publishing.

"L. Douglas Wilder." n.d. Virginia Historical Society. http://www.vahistorical.org/index.htm.

McNeil, G. R. 1983. *Groundwork: Charles Hamilton Houston and the Struggle for Civil Rights.* Philadelphia: University of Pennsylvania Press.

Miller, A. 1989. *Harold Washington: The Mayor, the Man.* Chicago, IL: Bonus Books.

Monroe, B. 2009. "The Audacity of Victory: Barack Obama: Ebony's Person of the Year." *Ebony Magazine*, January, 16–26.

Motley, C. B. 1998. *Equal Justice Under Law: An Autobiography by Constance Baker Motley*. New York: Farrar, Straus and Giroux.

National Conference of Black Mayors. 2009. http://ncbm.org/.

Ogletree, C. J., Jr. 2005. *All Deliberate Speed: Reflections on the First Half Century of* Brown v. Board of Education. New York: W. W. Norton & Company.

"Oliver White Hill." n.d. Howard University School of Law. *Brown@50: Fulfilling the Promise*. http://www.brownat50.org.

Poinsett, A. 1970. *Black Power Gary Style: The Making of Mayor Richard Gordon Hatcher*. Chicago, IL: Johnson Publishing Company.

Ragsdale, B. A., and J. D. Treese. 1990. *Black Americans in Congress, 1970–1989*. Office of the Historian, U.S. House of Representatives. Washington, D.C.: U.S. Government Printing Office.

Rangel, C. B. 2007. *And I Haven't Had a Bad Day Since: From the Streets of Harlem to the Halls of Congress*. New York: Thomas Dunne Books/St. Martin's Press.

Ripley, A. 2008. "A Mother's Story." *Time Magazine*, April 21, 20–25.

"Robert L. Carter." n.d. Howard University School of Law. *Brown@50: Fulfilling the Promise*. http://www.brownat50.org.

Segal, G. R. 1983. *Blacks in the Law: Philadelphia and the Nation*. Philadelphia: University of Pennsylvania Press.

Smith, J. C. 1993. *Emancipation: The Making of the Black Lawyer 1844–1944*. Philadelphia: University of Pennsylvania Press.

Smith, J. M. 2002. *Climbing Jacob's Ladder: A Trial Lawyer's Journey on Behalf of the Least of These*. Atlanta, GA: New South Publishing.

Thomas, C. 2007. *My Grandfather's Son: A Memoir*. New York: HarperCollins Publishers.

Thompson, J. E. 1982. *Hiram R. Revels 1827–1901*. New York: Arno Press.

Wade, H., Jr. 1976. *Black Men of Amherst*. Amherst, MA: Amherst College Press.

Ware, G. 1984. *William Hastie: Grace Under Pressure*. New York: Oxford University Press.

CHAPTER 2

Dream No Small Dreams

CAROL MOSELEY BRAUN

Former U.S. Senator, D-Illinois;
Former American Ambassador
to New Zealand and Samoa;
Former U.S. Presidential Candidate;
Founder, Ambassador Organics,
Chicago, Illinois

Ambassador Carol Moseley Braun was the first female senator from Illinois and the first African American woman or Democrat to be elected to the U.S. Senate. She was an ambassador to New Zealand and Samoa (1999) and a Democratic presidential candidate in 2004. Moseley Braun received her bachelor's degree from the University of Illinois in 1969. In 1972, she earned a law degree from the University of Chicago, and the next year she joined the U.S. attorney's office in Chicago. Moseley Braun served in the Illinois state legislature (House) from 1979 to 1987. In 1992, she won a primary election against the incumbent Democratic senator and was elected to the U.S. Senate after a general election contest against a Republican candidate. After serving one term she was defeated by a Republican in 1998. She was then confirmed by the Senate as the U.S. ambassador to New Zealand from 1999 to 2001 upon appointment by President Bill Clinton. In 2010, Moseley Braun ran an unsuccessful campaign for mayor of Chicago. Moseley Braun is the founder of Good Food Organics, a company dedicated to providing high-quality organic food to the American people. The Ambassador Organics brand is reserved for biodynamic organic products. These products are triply certified, as USDA Organic, Demeter Biodynamic and Fair Trade.

Wynn and Farmer: Would you describe your early background, including information about your parents, your siblings, and overall childhood experiences?

Ambassador Braun: I was very blessed to have a family with deep roots in the community. We were given an opportunity to have a quality education, both in the public and private schools—Catholic schools specifically. My father was a dreamer and my mother had both feet on the ground, but together they provided us with an upbringing that on hindsight we were very fortunate to have. We went to good schools, we lived in good neighborhoods, and we didn't have any real fear of crime growing up. We had some dysfunction in the family, but I think all families these days are dysfunctional in one way or another. I had three siblings: two younger brothers and one younger sister. Our parents did their best to give us a family life that was encouraging, nurturing, and supportive of our growth and development.

Wynn and Farmer: Would you discuss your school experiences—elementary and high school—recounting any issues and how you went about resolving those issues?

Ambassador Braun: I had a childhood that was a combination of an urban and a rural childhood. I grew up in the city but spent a good deal of time on a farm. I still call myself a farm girl at heart. The farm gave me a slightly different approach to what school was about as opposed to other kids my age who grew up entirely in the city. I think that made a big difference. I was interested in nature, the natural sciences, agriculture, and what is now called cultural anthropology—those kinds of things.

Wynn and Farmer: What about your undergraduate, graduate, and professional school years?

Ambassador Braun: I grew up just as the Civil Rights Movement and women's rights movement began. The good news is that my parents had always encouraged me to be the best that I could be, so they didn't give me any limitations based on race or other circumstances. When Dr. King came to Chicago, I was 15, and I marched with him in spite of my mother's fears. I was very active in the Civil Rights Movement. I was too young to be a spokesperson, but I became involved with groups that were pushing for social change and the antiwar movement—Vietnam was going on at that point. I was a student activist in college.

Then I got to law school and discovered that many of the same impediments that African Americans suffered were also suffered by women because there were only five women in my law school class at the University of Chicago and only five Blacks in my law school class. I found myself once again in a situation in which I was advocating for social change. In fact, the first Black Law Students Association (BLSA) chapter was started at Rutgers, and I was the first one to bring it to Chicago at the University of Chicago law school. And that of course caused no small amount of consternation in the administration, with the professors and the like. I was supposed to be grateful for being there and not agitate for other blacks or women. That's been a characteristic of my career all along. I've tried to do what I can to make things better for people who might otherwise be excluded.

Wynn and Farmer: Can you tell us about any individuals, mentors, or role models who have had a significant influence on your educational and career path?
Ambassador Braun: Yes. In high school it was Mrs. Burrell, my chemistry teacher, who was "old school"—a black woman very committed to education. She was an old-fashioned teacher who cared about her students and was very rigorous in her instruction. She really challenged us to be the best that we could be. She gave you no slack, you had to get the work done, you were disciplined in class, but you knew that the discipline, the rules, and the difficulties that she made you go through were out of caring and not otherwise. So I remain to this day very grateful to her. Mrs. Church was my very first teacher who, again, was "old school." When I got beat up in the schoolyard, she would bring me in and put me on her lap and tell me everything was going to be okay.

This generation of students has a much more difficult environment for learning, and the school system doesn't like teachers to hug students anymore, but in the world that I grew up in teachers hugged you out of love, not any sense of perversity. So I benefited from having committed teachers in my life.

Wynn and Farmer: Exactly when did you know that you were interested in law and politics?
Ambassador Braun: I got into both law and politics because of circumstances and times and the timing. It was something I was drawn into. At

one time I referred to it as a calling. I didn't map out a career path; it drew me along. I went to law school largely because I didn't know what I was going to do after graduating from college. A friend of mine said he was going to take the law school entrance exam, and I said, "Sign me up too!"

I wound up signing up for the LSAT and then getting admitted to the University of Chicago. Then after UC, I became a federal prosecutor. My father had always wanted to be a lawyer, and I think that's one of the things that actually moved me in that direction. He was in law enforcement but had wanted to be a lawyer, and frankly, I had wanted to be an art historian. I was more interested in art history at that point in my life than in becoming an attorney. But he encouraged me to go to law school, and so that's what I did. I thought at that point in my life I was going to be a trial lawyer.

But after I got married and started a family, neighbors encouraged me to get involved in electoral politics. In keeping with my community activism, the antiwar movement, the Civil Rights Movement and the environmental movement (all these things were linked together in my mind and in my life), I became involved in a protest to protect the parks in Chicago. So I was agitating for the environment, and people encouraged me to run for the state legislature. I didn't have any political ambitions at that stage in my life. But I responded to a dare: one man told me in a public meeting that I couldn't do it because the Blacks wouldn't vote for me because I was not part of the Chicago machine, the Whites wouldn't vote for me because I was Black, and nobody with any sense would vote for me because I was a woman. That insult was all I needed to sign up and run for that office for the first time.

Wynn and Farmer: Ambassador, after all that experience you actually ran for the Senate and won.
Ambassador Braun: Yes, but it's very important to know that I was in electoral politics and government for many years before running for the senate. My friend jokes that people think I was born at the Democratic National Convention in 1992. In fact, I started off in the state legislature. I served for ten years in the state legislature as an Illinois state representative. I represented a very diverse constituency, in fact, the same district that Barack Obama later was elected from. I was the first woman, elected from that district, and in that election season a record number of women were elected from across the state of Illinois. I think four women got elected to the state legislature. They called it the "Year of the Woman." Later, I ended

up suing my own Democratic Party over racial discrimination in reapportionment. Everyone told me I was going to get run out of town on a rail, but instead, we won that case, creating the first Hispanic district in the state of Illinois as well as additional black districts for the state.

Then Harold Washington was elected mayor and he named me as his floor leader. So in an ironic turn of events I became the first Black woman to move into a majority leadership position in the state of Illinois. I served as assistant majority leader for five years and was ready to retire, but Mayor Washington prevailed on me to stand for countywide office. I was elected the Cook County recorder of deeds, again the first woman, the first Black, elected countywide. Cook County has about 3 million people in it, so that was no small thing.

When Mayor Washington died suddenly I again resolved to leave electoral politics. But then President Bush nominated Clarence Thomas to the United States Supreme Court. Many of my life's opportunities had been made possible by the work of Thurgood Marshall and the Warren court. The Supreme Court had opened doors for me and others like me, and the whole string of decisions that we now associate with the Civil Rights Movement, everything from *Brown v. Board of Education* to *Hansberry v. Lee* came from the leadership of Thurgood Marshall. We grew up in a neighborhood that had been segregated until the *Hansberry v. Lee* decision got rid of the restricted covenants that were used against Black people. So I firmly believed that the nomination of Clarence Thomas represented an unacceptable move backward for America. The fact that he was Black did not contradict his conservative political and policy views, which were diametrically opposed to those of Justice Marshall. For the President to tell the country that he had found the most qualified black person to take Thurgood Marshall's spot was to me an unacceptable outrage.

What inspired *me* to stand for the Senate and to run against a Democratic senator who voted for Thomas's confirmation was that I believed that Thurgood Marshall deserved a replacement on the court who would be committed to carrying out the legacy that he had left for us.

Wynn and Farmer: What do we have to do in the future to get more Blacks elected to the Senate? What can we do on college campuses to turn that around?

Ambassador Braun: I think it all comes out of a climate of public and popular opinion. And I think that when this society gets to the point that it begins to celebrate and not denigrate African American culture, tradition, and history, we will then see greater integration in the United States Senate, in corporate America, and in all different environments in which people interact and shape the direction of this country. The problem is a cultural one. Race still remains the third rail of American politics. Race still remains a bugabear around which there is still no open, cogent, and sensible conversation.

African Americans have yet to get to the point where our particular culture and traditions and history are celebrated by the larger community. That is the challenge we all have, and when that challenge is met we will see a greater receptivity to African Americans in American politics as senators, governors, and president.

Wynn and Farmer: You served as ambassador to New Zealand and Samoa. Tell us something about what you did as an ambassador.
Ambassador Braun: I still use the title ambassador. It was my good fortune to be what I called an ambassador to paradise. I represented the United States in one of the most beautiful and comfortable places in the entire world. It was my job to inspire the people of New Zealand and Samoa to like the United States and to feel good about everything American, the American people, American culture, and the like and to work through such governmental issues as our countries might have. As a result of that I got to travel all around the South Pacific. New Zealand was a particularly wonderful country for me because it is a country that is in many ways like ours, but yet very much unlike our own. It had a woman in leadership and minority people of color whose culture was embraced and celebrated by the whole community. For me, it was like landing in paradise.

Wynn and Farmer: Do you feel that the role of ambassador is more difficult now that the country is involved in war?
Ambassador Braun: There is no question about that. All over the world, this president [George W. Bush] has frittered away the goodwill that America enjoyed following the terrorist attacks of 9/11/2001. All over the world people were supportive of America, but his arrogant leadership has alienated people who might have otherwise identified with us. I can remember getting phone calls, telegrams, and letters from people in New Zealand, Samoa, countries in Africa, and all over the world saying that their prayers were with us and how badly they felt about what had

happened here in the United States. And in the space of six months the bullying and arrogance of this president turned all that around. The war he started will go down in history as a great tragedy exacerbated by arrogance and ignorance. Everything from "Bring it on" to "mission accomplished"—it was just a nightmare. In fact, that's how a French newspaper recently referred to the Bush regime, that with the change in the Congress this last November, "our six-year nightmare seems now to be ending."

Wynn and Farmer: What do you think our young people today who aspire to become lawyers and politicians can learn from your experiences?
Ambassador Braun: I'm kind of old-fashioned. I think the important thing is to encourage young people to focus in on the fundamentals, the values that brought us this far, to focus in on preparing themselves to be able to stand on their own two feet, to be independent, to be able to function in this modern-day society. I think the biggest challenge we face is the kind of unreality that gets sold to young people so consistently that they wind up with their values in a bizarre place that does not inspire building strong families, building strong communities, working together to create wealth, working together to create opportunity and the ability for people to do for themselves. There's an old message that Elijah Muhammad used—"Do for self." It's an old message, but it truly is a message that is as current as any we can give to young people. Create your own jobs; create your own housing. Train to be the doctors, train to be the lawyers, people that navigate the system for you. Train to work on making your own community safe. It never ceases to amaze me—looking at hip-hop culture—that people haven't figured out that a culture of violence only makes their own lives miserable. If your grandmother cannot walk down the street where you live, what makes you think somebody is going to invest money there to create a job for your nephew?

Wynn and Farmer: What are some of your values that have contributed to your success?
Ambassador Braun: I think from my father I learned to dream no small dreams. Reach for your personal best and try to achieve whatever you think for yourself would be your own personal dream, your own personal motivation. And from my mother I learned to do the best job you can where you are planted. Whatever it is you wind up doing, do the best

you can do at that. If it's being a United States senator or being a street sweeper, do the best job you can do at that. Do something for others. This culture of selfishness, modern society, is destructive in every way.

Wynn and Farmer: Looking at the political picture today and thinking about your background, do you have any ambitions to seek political office in the future?
Ambassador Braun: No, I don't. I'm in the private sector now. I have a company, Good Food Organics, and I'm in the process of building the business. I call it my fourth career: from being a practicing lawyer, to being an elected politician, to being a diplomat. Now I am an entrepreneur, and I'm enjoying this phase of my life.

Wynn and Farmer: Tell us about the line of organic food called Ambassador Organics.
Ambassador Braun: Ambassador Organics! Right now we have a line of coffees, a line of teas, and a line of spices. We intend to expand the line and include other high-quality organic products. We will be able to grow the company as we make our products more widely available. At this moment our products are available at Whole Foods and we're about to get into Dominick's. Our products can be bought online at Peapod, the Internet grocer, and our own Web site, www.ambassadororganics.com.

Wynn and Farmer: What are you doing now in law? You have a private practice, Braun's LLC in Chicago?
Ambassador Braun: All the legal practice I do these days is for Good Food Organics!

Wynn and Farmer: You have had a lot of successes. What do you consider your career-defining moment or of which accomplishment are you most proud?
Ambassador Braun: Winning the primary for the United States Senate was a major, major step because that was the one that I think changed expectations. When we first started out with the campaign for the Senate, the response I got, even from a lot of African Americans, was that I couldn't win—people's vision and aspirations just did not go there. When I won the primary there was almost a sense of the inexplicable, but then I went on and won the general. I had two back-to-back, hard-fought

elections. The problem was that I had beaten an incumbent Democratic senator in the primary, and the political establishment made me pay. I wound up getting it from both my own party as well as from the Republicans. That was the bad news. The good news was that it raised expectations and a record number of Black people, male and female, have stood for the United States Senate since then. You've had people running in the primaries; unfortunately, the only ones to get through to the general election have been Harold Ford, Jr. and Barack Obama; Barack is the only one to actually make it to the Senate. If you calculate the number of minority candidates for the Senate after 1992, I think it's telling. The people who worked to elect me to the Senate in 1992 helped usher in a new era in which Blacks, Hispanics, women, and other nontraditional candidates could believe they had a chance to serve, and everybody else could tap into a reservoir of talent that outmoded expectations had previously made unavailable. They helped to expand the expectations about our democracy. That was one of the reasons, frankly, that I decided to run for the presidential nomination in 2004. I felt that by running it would break the mind-set that said a black female could not be president. And I believe, frankly, that has been accomplished in that not only have people been talking about Condoleeza Rice as a candidate on the Republican side but Barack Obama on the Democratic side. Breaking down barriers, helping people to pursue the maximum extent of their own personal abilities, expanding the talent pool in government, that contribution has been the most important one of my career.

Wynn and Farmer: During your run for president your platform was to rebuild America physically and spiritually. You explained that the physical rebuilding of America was broken into three functions: economic revitalization, education, and health care. Would you comment on the current economic revitalization, education, and health care of America under the current administration?

Ambassador Braun: It's all gotten worse. But I'm optimistic that the country is about to make a change in direction. I think the last set of elections was very promising, and I think the overreaching of the war in Iraq and the people who have died will mean that people will take another look. More people don't have health care now than ever before. So I think that's going to make folks take another look at health care and consider universal coverage. Our education system has not kept pace, and we are even falling behind Third World countries in terms of educating our children. Constructive change is going to require parents to say enough is enough. We need to take another look at how we do education. Our economy is working at the top end with CEOs and top executives making multimillion dollar salaries and yet the working people are barely scraping by—even with an increase in the minimum wage—with barely enough to live on. I just think the pendulum is swinging, and to the extent that we can get people to focus on the fundamentals and real values, the better off we will be and the better able we will be to come to grips with the real challenges facing our country.

Wynn and Farmer: Do you have a title or theme you would like to assign to your chapter?
Ambassador Braun: I like the title "Dream No Small Dreams."

CHAPTER 3

My Journey in American Politics

DONNA L. BRAZILE

Political Analyst, Brazile and
Associates, LLC, Washington, D.C.

Some girls grow up and want to become a princess. Some girls just want to marry a prince. But I was a young girl who wanted to help pick a president. Not just any president, I wanted to help select the president of the United States.

Growing up in the Deep South at the peak of both the Civil Rights and women's movements, I got the itch very early in life to become an activist. My hometown, Kenner, Louisiana, was a stone's throw away from New Orleans, where the African American community—in the aftermath of the assassination of Dr. Martin Luther King, Jr.—began to press open the doors of political empowerment.

From the beginning, I knew what side I was on. The only question I faced was when would I get my start. The night after Dr. Martin Luther King, Jr. was assassinated I was literally baptized into the Civil Rights Movement. My time had come, and I was ready to volunteer to do my part to continue King's legacy.

Leadership is standing up for what you believe in—while being in a position to help make a difference. As a child, I had a strong desire to help others and to make a difference in my family and my community. My parents, Jean and Lionel, encouraged their nine children to speak up and ask questions, especially if it involved trying to do the right thing. All I knew growing up was that I wanted to become active in my community and in the Civil Rights Movement.

When I was ready to become involved, a neighborhood activist helped me get my wings. Rosemary Minor, a local civil rights pioneer, became an early mentor for my generation of grassroots organizers. She was a visionary leader deeply committed to helping others, especially young people.

Raised in Jim Crow's segregated South, Ms. Minor taught us to take our civic duty very seriously by standing up for our community and taking on responsibility to improve our neighborhood. She was my hero.

With the encouragement of women like Ms. Minor, we began to take pride in civic engagement. By the time I turned nine years old, I became actively involved in my first political campaign in support of a local city council candidate who promised that if he won, we would get a playground in my neighborhood. Ms. Minor assigned me to go door to door to remind our neighbors to register and vote.

Imagine that. I relished my responsibility to call on others to take up such an important principle as the right to vote. As I rode my bicycle from street to street, I met many new people and got to know my neighbors. A year later, I received my first patronage job in politics: serving as Ms. Minor's assistant coach for a young girl's softball league in my hometown. What a fabulous reward for political activism!

As a teenager, I continued to develop my political skills and worked on every campaign in and around New Orleans. Starting in high school, I volunteered for the Carter-Mondale presidential campaign in 1976, where I helped to register new voters and organized a rally in the French Quarters with other young adults. When it was time to go to college, I volunteered to help organize students for President Carter's reelection campaign in 1980. This time, we were not as successful, and former California governor Ronald Reagan swept into office in a landslide, defeating Carter in Louisiana and much of the country.

Still, I knew my passion for politics could only grow stronger, so I got involved in civil rights causes to help me learn how to build coalitions. While still a student at Louisiana State University, I helped to organize many Black student organizations and was active in student government. The mayor of Baton Rouge, Pat Screen, appointed me to serve on the local Fair Housing Board. With the help of Sybil Taylor, who later became the first Black woman to head up a statewide AFL-CIO affiliate, I learned how to effectively engage citizens at the grassroots level.

By the time I graduated from college, I was well on my way to a career in public service. But first, I had to find a suitable job in Washington, D.C., where I wanted to continue my political career. Luckily, I was hired by the National Student Educational Fund and began lobbying on Capitol Hill for federal financial assistance for students. This is where I met so many great leaders and had a chance to serve as an intern for my home state's member of Congress.

By the end of 1981, I began to attract national attention as the student coordinator for the Martin Luther King, Jr. Holiday Committee, which successfully petitioned Congress to make the civil rights leader's birthday a national holiday. This was a tremendous grassroots victory as millions of Americans signed petitions demanding that Congress designate January 15 as a national holiday in honor of Martin Luther King, Jr.

Two years after moving to Washington, D.C., I accepted an offer from Coretta Scott King (Martin Luther King, Jr.'s widow) to help organize the 20th anniversary commemoration of the historic 1963 March on Washington. Few people believed that, at age 23, I was qualified to organize this national march. The success of the event surpassed the wildest dreams of its conveners—more than 300,000 people turned out to stand up for jobs, peace, and freedom at the Lincoln Memorial in August 1983. From this moment on, I was encouraged to do more, and when the opportunity presented itself, I did.

Later, in the fall of 1983, the Rev. Jesse Jackson, Sr. decided to run for president of the United States. During this historic presidential campaign, I learned more about national politics and became an expert in communicating with various voters, organizing campaign events, and attracting delegates to his cause. I consider the experience gained in the Jackson campaign to have given me a strong foundation in grassroots organizing. I remain close to the Reverend, who has served as a mentor and cherished friend.

In between electoral campaigns at the national level, I often worked on short-term projects like Hands Across America and major grassroots initiatives to help generate public support for liberal causes. With the election of Reagan, many of us believed civil rights laws were coming increasingly under attack. Thus, I spent many years working alongside members of the Congressional Black Caucus and the Democratic Party to help elect progressive leaders to office to reverse these policies.

By 1988, I had become restless again, and after a brief stint as campaign manager for Mary Landrieu for Louisiana state treasurer, I went back to national politics. For the first time, I had several candidates interested in hiring me for various positions. I decided to work for Missouri representative Dick Gephardt's bid for the Democratic presidential nomination. Dick was a leader in the U.S. House of Representatives and had broad support from various interest groups. Our campaign was built on a new emerging model in electoral politics to engage citizens where they lived—a model that helped us win the Iowa caucuses, but we failed to win the Democratic primary.

Later in 1988, I worked for the Democratic presidential nominee Massachusetts governor Michael Dukakis, where I served as a deputy political director helping to build new alliances between the campaign and the minority community. Early on, Dukakis, who did not have much national experience, was labeled an out-of-touch liberal by his opponent. After an impressive convention, the campaign sputtered and eventually lost its momentum. Then Vice President George H. W. Bush spent the final weeks of the campaign nailing Dukakis as a card-carrying member of the ACLU. The loss was a disappointment, but it also made me keenly aware of how nasty and polarized our country was becoming.

I reentered the political scene after taking a much-needed break to mourn the death of my mother, Jean, and to begin to heal after so many bruising battles. In the interim, I volunteered to work at a local shelter for homeless men and women and took on another major political assignment—a march for Housing Now!

Housing Now! was a broad coalition of civil rights, peace, women, and low-income housing activists who came together to urge an end to homelessness in America. When I heard of the group, I decided to get involved by helping to identify and organize ordinary citizens to lobby Congress to provide more funding for low-income housing. We had great success, but soon I returned to my passion— electoral politics.

I decided to manage the congressional campaign for one of my mentors and friends, civil rights leader Eleanor Holmes Norton. Norton, former chair of the EEOC, was the early favorite to win the race for the District of Columbia's delegate to Congress, but we had a tough campaign. After the election, I became Eleanor's chief of staff on Capitol Hill, managing a small staff of 18 full-time employees. Eleanor was a gifted lawmaker who took on tough issues like trying to get the statehood and voting rights for Washington, D.C., residents and fighting to preserve home rule. Eleanor was and remains my friend and mentor. During my tenure, Eleanor would allow me to take a leave of absence to work on various statewide and local campaigns.

In 1998, I designed and then ran the Democratic Congressional Campaign Committee's (DCCC) Get Out the Vote operations, which helped cement the Democrats' unexpected gains in the House that year. We boosted turnout in key targeted Congressional districts, which enabled Democrats to win up and down the line. The DCCC experience gave me another opportunity to expand my campaign skills and to enter a new political arena.

As a result of our successful 1998 efforts, I received recognition for effectively coordinating and mobilizing Democratic constituencies across the country. I was subsequently called on to support then vice president Al Gore's campaign for the Democratic nomination. Initially, Gore named me political director and then later promoted me to serve as campaign manager. As campaign manager my job expanded from organizing voters to managing hundreds of staff members across the country. It was a great experience, but I did not like the way it ended.

The 2000 presidential election is now a legend in American history. George W. Bush was officially sworn in as president of the United States as the result of a 5 to 4 Supreme Court decision that prevented the state of Florida from conducting a thorough recount. This decision overruled a decision by the Florida Supreme Court authorizing a statewide recount—amid evidence of massive voting irregularities, including unprecedented evidence of voter suppression and discrimination in Florida's minority precincts. Black men were singled out for criminal background checks before being allowed to vote. Black voters were required to show as many as three different proofs of identification at the polls. There were other widespread election irregularities, but in the end, Congress ignored the complaints.

Despite the outcomes in 2000 and 2004, I remain passionate about electoral politics and getting people motivated to have a say in who runs their country. This is especially true for young Americans who turned out in historic numbers in 2004. We must encourage them to continue their efforts and run for office.

As the first Black person to run a major presidential campaign, I have to admit that when I began my journey in national politics, I never imagined I could affect how things are done. By working to achieve my goal, I not only gained a seat at the table but also broke a glass ceiling for women and minorities in American politics.

From growing up in racially segregated Kenner, Louisiana, to running a major presidential campaign, I know that anything is possible if we work hard and learn the skills necessary to become an effective advocate. When it comes to voting in America and giving every citizen a voice in the governance of their country, we can do better. We just have to want it badly enough and organize citizens to get involved in electoral politics.

As African Americans, we have come a long way, but to go forward, not backward, and to ensure that every American has access to the American dream, we must break down the remaining barriers to political participation and usher in a new season of hope and opportunity.

My journey is not complete. Over the next two decades, I would like to see *more* women and minorities run for public office, including the highest office in the land. We can and must increase the number of young Americans running for office and help prepare them to run this country one day.

As an organizer, I remain a fervent supporter of civil rights and voting rights for all Americans. From organizing major national demonstrations to developing strategies to help increase turnout of citizens at the polls to investigating voting irregularities after the 2004 presidential election, I remain devoted to improving democracy here in America.

My advice to young people everywhere is to get involved. Whatever your passion, act on it! If you want to help end hunger, join a cause and get involved. If you want to help Black men and women find jobs, start your own business. Don't sit out the next election. I urge you to register and vote in every election—no matter the race, it's your turn to make a difference and to stir it up.

Dr. King was right. The highest calling today is to serve. Continue to soar and serve. It's your calling too.

CHAPTER 4

Blueprint for Leadership Success

CARL BROOKS

President and CEO,
the Executive Leadership Council
and the Executive Leadership Foundation,
Washington, D.C.

The Executive Leadership Council (ELC) is the nation's premier organization of the most senior African American corporate executives in Fortune 500 companies. Before becoming president in 2001, I'd spent 12 years as a proud ELC member, representing General Public Utilities, at the time, the eighth-largest electric utility in the United States. As vice president of human & technical resources, I was responsible for human resources, labor relations, safety, materials system management, procurement, transportation, real estate, environmental affairs, and information technology. Before that I served as vice president (process owner) of finance and administration and was responsible for finance matters, accounting, budgeting, communications, corporate governance, legal, security, internal affairs, and government/regulatory affairs.

Becoming a member of ELC has allowed me to network with the biggest and baddest African American executives on the planet. But as *Blueprint to Success* (an ELC leadership survey) revealed, business success is neither mysterious nor an unattainable prize offered to only a privileged few. There is a blueprint to success. And that's what I want to share with you.

Professional success revolves around five key elements, the five Ps of success: (1) preparation, (2) performance, (3) positive visibility,

(4) predictability, and (5) perseverance. Many people believe career preparation begins the day you enter college or graduate school. I say it begins the day you're born into a family.

The first P, preparation, I learned from my family and from my teammates. My parents moved from Savannah, Georgia, to Philadelphia, Pennsylvania, in the 1940s and raised two boys and a girl with a love and discipline that taught us family values of respect, unity, and goal setting early in life, the latter of which leads to preparation. As the middle child, I was thrust into the role of being a protector for my siblings, an older sister (Barbara) and a younger brother (Nathaniel). I understood early that I needed the heart of a fighter and social skills to gain recognition, to gain respect, and to overcome South Philly's tough streets. Luckily for me, I was good at both, and I had a strong and supportive family in Philadelphia and Savannah to keep me grounded. They instilled in me strong family values, a disciplined work ethic, pride in being an African American, and a social consciousness that inspired me to make a valuable contribution to society. Achieving excellence in whatever I did was not an option but a mandate. Developing the heart and spirit of an achiever was part of my childhood preparation.

My father had played in baseball's Negro Leagues. So in my teens I gravitated to baseball, refining my athletic skills to a level that attracted the attention of the pros. I also took up boxing and martial arts, becoming a Golden Gloves champion and a fifth-degree black belt in karate. Playing in competitive sports prepared me to compete in business. The mental and physical discipline, teamwork, leadership skills, strategic planning, and execution that I learned in competitive sports have served me throughout my career and life. I would encourage any young person to participate in some sort of competitive activity to develop the confidence and maturity that come from preparing, competing, and performing under pressure.

Yet the preparation provided by family, friends, and teammates is just step one of preparation. The second step is to develop the confidence to self-analyze and honestly evaluate strengths and weaknesses, to ensure your continuous development. The journey of development is not over until it's really over.

You've got to ask yourself, what are my skills and competencies? What are my strengths and weaknesses? What skills and competencies do I need to acquire? Do I have what it takes to excel in this company and to advance to the next level? What motivates me to succeed and why? What do I value and how do I define success? How are my values enriched or diminished by my environment? Until one is able to accept critical analysis, you may recover from shortcomings but fail to learn from them.

Mediocrity is a luxury that we can't afford. The second P, performance, is about avoiding mediocrity. We've got to perform at an exemplary level in our chosen fields. If you are an accountant, you've got to be an excellent accountant. If you are a lawyer, you've got to write great briefs and handle your caseload in an exemplary manner. Additionally, young professionals need to acquire competency in several other areas to perform at the highest executive level. Financial acumen is a must along with finely honed articulation skills. As global competition increases, an understanding of and proficiency in evaluating mergers and acquisitions are becoming essential, along with motivational skills. Also take time to continually educate yourself. Profit from the experiences of others by understanding their performance strategies. In addition to the book you're holding in your hands, two texts that I recommend are *Breaking Through*, by David Thomas, and *Cracking the Corporate Code*, by Dr. Price Cobbs and Judith L. Turnock. These books have helped me to understand the unique challenges and tremendous strengths of being an African American corporate executive.

To succeed in corporate America, or to succeed at anything, you must manage your image. Being prepared and working hard mean little if you labor away in obscurity, comfortable in your own world or corner, unnoticed and unrecognized. That's why the third P of professional success, positive visibility, is an important aspect of managing your career. It is important to remember that executives don't discover you; how you promote yourself determines whether your talent will be discovered or remain unnoticed.

As a young go-getter at General Public Utilities (GPU), I made it a point to understand the competitive dynamics of my industry, the inner workings of GPU's corporate culture, and how I could work within it without compromising my principles or values. Before I became a vice president at age 39, I was constantly affronted by critics who believed African Americans lacked the ability to succeed as corporate executives. After being named Division Chief of the Year for four years, and after I was able to effectively terminate the Forked River Nuclear Plant project, which had to be canceled after the Three Mile Island incident, I captured the attention of the entire senior leadership team at GPU. I knew that every officer in the executive suites knew and remembered my name. I was clearly prepared and had demonstrated excellence in multiple critical situations. I had excelled in my performance and now had the opportunity to build positive visibility for myself and achieve status and influence.

During my rise in the public eye, I also took advantage of the executive development and leadership courses that GPU offered internally and externally. I excelled at the Dartmouth Executive Program (Presidents' School) and was committed to continuous improvement and innovation to meet the changing demands of the company.

Positive visibility in the eyes of your superiors is a critical component to achieving career success. Young executives must command respect but still appear approachable; they must appear self-confident without being arrogant. As the only African American executive at GPU, I had no African American peers or role models who could serve as mentors. That's why the ELC has been such an important network to me and scores of other African American executives. The ELC has provided me with many mentors—and good friends.

This brings me to the fourth P, predictability. Backed by preparation, consistency, top-notch performance, and positive visibility, a young executive should be able to catch the eye of the senior team, absent racism and other factors. However, the most certain way to ensure visibility is through the advocacy and support of a mentor. The mentor you attract may or may not be the person you predict. That's why flexibility is essential to your success. No blueprint is etched in stone. Your plan will require slight revisions to accommodate new situations.

Are you willing to look outside your company, your industry, or even the business world to find a mentor? Peers or colleagues willing to share their special expertise and provide critical feedback may serve as valuable mentors. Or individuals in other industries and business sectors may prove helpful. Don't limit opportunities or minimize your support system by being inflexible about whom you associate with or accept as a mentor.

Growing up, some of my earliest mentors and role models were those who coached or taught at the YMCA and Police Athletic League recreation center and our pastor and deacons at the neighborhood church. They taught me valuable lessons about hard work and personal excellence. They also convinced me that I had the skills and aptitude to become a successful businessman. One of my most important mentors in business and in life is a friend that I still have to this day—former GPU chairman, president, and CEO James R. Leva. Jim is an Italian American whose family emigrated from Italy. We were able to bond through our affinity for the martial arts. We were both black belts. Jim has been an influential voice in my career and a very important person in my life.

Exhibiting persistent, predictable performance is critical to building professional stature. That's why it is imperative that young executives find a company that closely matches their personal values. Although there are no automatic fits, many young people, lured by money and company prestige, fail to assess whether an industry or a company's culture is a good match with personal values. When your values are similar to those of your workplace, chances for success are much greater.

The ability to influence others and affect outcomes is the most rewarding part of being an executive. When you understand what motivates your people and can direct their efforts in ways that allow them to succeed, you are fulfilling your job as a leader who both inspires and meets the bottom line.

The final P is perseverance. Talent should be the only thing that prevents you from moving up the corporate ladder path, but there are still more talented people than there are promotional opportunities. Most promotions don't come after a sensational presentation or some other significant event but, in most cases, after a long period of exemplary performance combined with positive visibility and strong advocacy from a mentor. We've got to stay the course and perform at a high level.

I am concerned that this generation of young African American professionals is not benefiting from the lessons of our past. They are not looking back to learn the history of those who came before us and on whose shoulders we stand. Learning the history of African American corporate executives and civic leaders can be inspiring and a powerful motivator to help young people stay the course. People like Naylor Fitzhugh, Dorothy Orr, or Al Martins, have blazed a trail for all of us. We now can dream of becoming the next Stanley O'Neal, Ken Chenault, Richard Parsons, Clarence Otis, or Ann Fudge in corporate America. These are people who wield tremendous power. They are leaders who shape their companies' future and global economic success.

Another area where perseverance is important is in deciding whether or not to make a career change. After GPU was purchased by First Energy, as a company officer, I expressed my "change of controls" rights, in lieu of seeking a position in Akron, Ohio. Relocation to Ohio would have been a hardship on my family, so I decided to retire and seek out new frontiers, perhaps as a pro golfer. My wife, and my golfing handicap, quickly discouraged that thought.

When I was asked to lead the ELC, I recognized an opportunity to give back to corporate America and to the African American community. I could use my management skills and passion for African American excellence to help advance the ELC's staff; create professional development programs for young professionals, mid-level managers, and senior executives; and advance ELC's advocacy efforts in making the business case for diversity.

Leading the ELC required a change in management style. I was leaving a situation where I managed a workforce of 1,600 people and a budget of more than $2 billion to run a small, inspirational nonprofit with a staff of only 12 employees and a budget of around $2 million.

The ELC enterprise is smaller but my sphere of influence in corporate America and the African American community has been significantly broader and deeper. Since becoming president of the ELC in 2001, we've created a CEO's summit that attracts some 30 to 40 Fortune 500 CEOs each year, our annual recognition dinner has grown from about 800 attendees to more than 2,000 people annually, we've developed an Institute for Leadership Development & Research that has global impact as it works to develop African American executives for breakthrough performance, and the ELC budget has grown to approximately $10 million.

As the chief executive of the nation's most powerful and influential network (350 members) of African American executives, we are having a positive impact on our members' corporate careers and the lives of thousands of young, next-generation professionals. My tenure as ELC president has clearly been the most personally rewarding experience of my entire career.

CHAPTER 5

The Drive to Overcome and Excel

ARTHUR L. BURNETT, SR.

National Executive Director,
National African American
Drug Policy Coalition, Washington, D.C.;
Senior Judge, D.C. Supreme Court,
Washington, D.C.

I was born at home on March 15, 1935, in Spotsylvania County, Virginia, in a house without electricity, to a mother who had gone only to the eighth grade and a father who had gone only to the sixth grade. I was blessed with a mother who started reading to me when I was three or four years old and teaching me to recognize and read kindergarten-type books. When I started Summit Elementary School—a two-room school covering first through sixth grade, I was fortunate to have a committed and dedicated schoolteacher named Elnora Lewis, who encouraged me and started using me to teach the class one grade below the grade I was in. When I was promoted to the fourth grade, she moved from teaching the first through third grades and started teaching the fourth through sixth grades and continued to use me to teach the grade behind the grade I was in. Thus, she was my teacher and inspiration for the first six years in school, and she stressed that I had been blessed with a great talent to learn and memorize, and I concluded that I could not let her down. When I transferred to the seventh grade, I went to John J. Wright High School, a segregated school for colored children, and was blessed with a teacher, Sadie Combs, who continued the nurturing and encouragement and used me as her assistant teacher. Upon entering the eighth grade, the principal of the school, Mr.

A. L. Scott, took me under his supervision, making me his office assistant when I was a junior in high school. By this time I had finished most of my high school requirements and spent considerable time working in the principal's office and traveling representing the school in oratorical and debating competitions. I was also encouraged by the Reverend Russell Robinson, the pastor of my Baptist Church, who had me teach Sunday school and deliver youth sermons.

In my senior year in high school, my agriculture instructor, Mr. E. A. Ragland, spent several hours one evening at my parents' home attempting to persuade them to send me to Tuskegee Institute to become an agricultural expert, as I had excelled as a high school student in the New Farmers of America, raising exceptional hybrid vegetables, chickens, and pigs. I won many blue ribbons in our county fair and even won the Modern Farmers Award from the governor of Virginia. When I responded that I was more interested in working with people and solving human problems, my teachers and the pastor of my church encouraged me to go to college to be a teacher and then on to seminary to become a preacher. In 1951 I was told that there was no future for a Negro lawyer in our society at that time, and that those who became lawyers ended up working in the post office, drove taxicabs, or worked as waiters in hotel. To put it rather bluntly, they emphatically stated that there was no future for a "colored" boy in the law. My father's mother attempted to discourage me from even coming to Washington, D.C., to go to Howard University to become a lawyer because Washington was a "city of sin." I would be "corrupted and lose my way" and become the victim of prostitutes, pimps, and criminals. I insisted that I had a mission in life and that I could reject that way of life and become an outstanding Negro lawyer to bring equality to Negroes and change how we were treated in our criminal justice system. I felt called to be an instrument to do something to eliminate segregation in America and especially how Negroes were treated in the nation's criminal justice system.

When I entered Howard University in September 1952 as a 17-year-old teenager, I had not had algebra and my entrance tests showed that my English skills were still deficient, even though I had graduated as the valedictorian of my high school class. Thus, in my first semester, I only took 11 hours of college-level courses as I had to take an additional six hours of remedial high school courses. I made all As, and at the end of the semester, I went to Dean Miller of the School of Liberal Arts and urged him to give me approval to take the normal load of courses plus 6 additional hours for a total of 23 semester hours of work so that I would be even with my classmates. After a lengthy conversation, he approved my request. I again made all As and finished first in my class with a 4.0 average. Based on that performance, although I was very active in student organizations, I took extra courses each semester and at the end of three years in college, I had earned three and a half years of college requirements for graduation, and only needed 15 more hours of college credits to graduate.

In my second year at Howard University I participated in a television program by Congressman Adam Clayton Powell in which I questioned the segregationist policies of America and the resulting inequality. Then, on May 17, 1954, the United States Supreme Court rendered its decision in *Brown v. Board of Education of Topeka, Kansas* (347 U.S. 483 [1954]). Little did I realize how that decision would affect me personally at that time. But as I returned for my junior year in college, James Nabrit, the vice president of Howard University, who had been lead counsel in *Sharpe v. Bolling* (347 U.S. 497 [1954]), the District of Columbia case that had been consolidated with the *Brown* case, called me to his office and told me that he and Thurgood Marshall had been discussing me, and that although he appreciated that I had come to Howard with the idea of going to its School of Law, they wanted me to make an important sacrifice and consider applying to enter a six-year combination college and law school program at the University of Virginia School of Law in Charlottesville and to apply to the other law schools in the top 10 in the nation that had a six-year combination program. I accepted their request and applied. I was admitted to Columbia, New York University, Syracuse, and Boston based on being first in my class at Howard with a 3.93 grade point average. Virginia did not respond to my application.

Mr. Nabrit advised me that he and Thurgood Marshall were going into federal court in Virginia to compel the University of Virginia to admit me. At that time the Commonwealth of Virginia had embarked on massive resistance to desegregation. Mr. Nabrit advised me that they were talking with representatives in the United States Department of Justice to assign two deputy U.S. marshals to prevent the Ku Klux Klan from harming me or others who were supporting efforts to end Virginia's massive resistance to desegregation. After talking with my parents at the Thanksgiving recess in November 1954 and hearing my mother recite the biblical passage that the Lord is your shepherd and "though you walk through the valley of death, you shall fear no evil," and my father saying that there were no two smarter Negroes than Thurgood Marshall and James Nabrit, I was resigned to die, if necessary, for the cause of ending segregation in America and advancing the cause of civil rights.

Then, in April 1955, James Nabrit called me to his office again. I thought he was going to tell me that they were going into federal court with my case to get an injunction to mandate that the University of Virginia admit me to its law school. Instead, he told me that Thurgood Marshall had decided that the NAACP Legal Defense Fund did not have sufficient funds to go forward with a suit in Virginia on my behalf and at the same time deal with the threat that Arkansas would close the schools for Negro children in that state. As we now know, the situation in Arkansas deteriorated to a point where the Little Rock confrontation took place in the summer of 1957. Mr. Nabrit further explained that the Commonwealth of Virginia had agreed to pay all of my tuition and other direct bills to a law school in New York, and that Thurgood Marshall wanted me, a "little colored boy" from Spotsylvania County, Virginia, to go on to Columbia and prove that I could do as well as any Jewish youngster in New York. Columbia University School of Law was then my first choice, but a few weeks thereafter New York University School of Law offered me a full-tuition faculty scholarship and a teaching assistant position in the master's in law program. In addition, Omega Psi Fraternity gave me a scholarship grant, and my former state senator from Fredericksburg, Virginia—Senator Benny T. Pitts—continued the scholarship he had given me to attend college. In my junior year in college I was also elected to Phi Beta Kappa. In September 1955, I enrolled at New York University School of Law with the Commonwealth of Virginia paying my tuition and direct bills and with three additional scholarships.

Upon entering the Day Division Class in the fall of 1955 I was surprised to learn that I was the only Negro student in my class. My law professors were overegalitarian, and every other time they called on a student for recitation in class, I was that student. But having taken to heart Thurgood Marshall's challenge to me, I was always prepared, and instead of being ostracized I was accepted and encouraged by my classmates. I excelled in my classes, and in a couple of my classes made the highest grade. I became the president of one of the student organizations, the Benjamin F. Butler Law Club. I made law review and was designated an associate research editor. By the end of my second year I was 11th in my class. While in law school, I returned to Howard University in the two summers between my law school years and finished the 15 hours of requirements to obtain a four-year college degree from Howard, graduating from Howard University School of Liberal Arts in October 1957 summa cum laude, with a major in political science and a minor in economics.

I had entered law school, with the aspiration of become a judge advocate officer in the Air Force upon my graduation. The height of my ambition at that time was to become a colonel in the Air Force Judge Advocates Corps by the time I retired. But my Jewish friends persuaded me to apply for the Attorney General's Honors Program at the United States Department of Justice. I did so and was selected. While in law school I submitted an article for publication in the *Law Review* advocating the one man, one vote principle, but it was rejected for involving a "political question" with which the courts would not deal. I was most gratified in 1962 when the United States Supreme Court in *Baker v. Carr* (369 U.S. 186 [1962]) adopted the principles I had advocated.

In June 1958, I graduated as a Founders' Day Award recipient in the top 10 percent of my class, 24th in a class of 263 law students. I entered the United States Department of Justice Honors Program in June 1958 and was assigned to the Frauds Section. On October 20, 1958, I was admitted to the District of Columbia Bar as a licensed attorney. While endeavoring to get a judge advocate general's officer's commission in the Air Force, I was drafted into the United States Army and entered active duty for a two-year period from November 18, 1958, to November 17, 1960. While in the Army, I met my wife, Frisbieann Lloyd, a registered nurse, and we were married on May 14, 1960.

While serving on active duty at Fort Ord, California, I rose to the rank of specialist E-4 as an S-1 personnel clerk. I also performed the duties of an assistant adjutant and other officer-type duties for a significant period when my brigade commander served as the post commander after the death of two higher-ranking officers in an aircraft crash. As his aide I performed a number of administrative duties of lower-ranking officers for him, subject to his oversight. For these extra duties, I was awarded the Army Commendation Medal by Secretary of Army Wilber Brucker. I was also commissioned as a second lieutenant Army reserve officer in the Adjutant General's Corps in September 1960. I was discharged from active duty in November 1960 and returned to the United States Department of Justice as an attorney in the Criminal Division. I remained an Army officer in the United States Army Reserves.

Upon returning to the Criminal Division in 1960, I was assigned to the General Crimes Section and began to specialize in criminal obscenity and government corruption cases. I was assigned to be the liaison representative of the Criminal Division to Attorney General Robert F. Kennedy to keep him advised of all of the major criminal cases being handled by the United States Department of Justice and the United States attorneys throughout the country. In August to September 1961, I was assigned as a special assistant United States attorney in East St. Louis, Illinois, but had to stay in the Ambassador Hotel in St. Louis, Missouri, because the Department of Justice could not find any safe place in East St. Louis for me, my wife, and my daughter to stay and be in view of the civil rights controversies and threats at the time. During that time I also worked on a number of major government corruption cases and in 1962, Robert Kennedy assigned me as the special assistant United States attorney to work with United States Attorney Joseph D. Tydings in Baltimore, Maryland, in the prosecution of Congressman Thomas F. Johnson and former congressman Frank W. Boykin for conspiracy, conflicts of interest, and related offenses. There were two other defendants. This criminal prosecution may well have been the very first such government corruption case in which one of the principal prosecutors was a Negro.

In 1963, I received the Attorney General's Sustained Performance Award for the quality of my work in that case and in the Criminal Division of the U.S. Department of Justice. Before the Fourth Circuit Court of Appeals in 1964 I served as the chief counsel for the government in arguing the case on appeal (*Thomas F. Johnson v. United States,* 337 F. 2d 180, 4th Cir. 1964). I also served as a monitor of the Martin Luther King movement for the attorney general to make sure there was no evidence of infiltration of the movement by the Communist Party. During the March on Washington in August 1963, I was one of the United States Department of Justice attorneys who made sure there would not be any disorders or other major problems during the encampment on the Mall.

Although I worked on some of the most exciting criminal cases in the United States Department of Justice, I yearned to be in the courtroom, and in April 1965, I transferred from the Criminal Division of the Department of Justice to the United States Attorney's Office in the District of Columbia, where I served for almost four years until December 1968. During that time I served as a federal prosecutor of misdemeanor cases in the city's Court of General Session, then in the Appellate Section of the Office, then as the presenter of felony cases before the Federal Grand Jury, and finally as the veteran prosecutor of all major felony cases in the United States Attorney's office. In December 1968, I became the first legal adviser of the Metropolitan Police Department (a position now called general counsel) to advise the chief of police and all police officers on how to comply with the constitutional requirements of the decisions of the United States Supreme Court dealing with arrests, searches and seizures, lineup procedures, and obtaining confessions to crime. I prepared general orders to make sure that the practices of the police comported with constitutional requirements and to protect against civil rights violations and use of excessive force by police officers of the Metropolitan Police Department. Many of these provisions remain in effect today and have been responsible for preventing many of the problems experienced by many other police departments during the past four decades or more. I planned an expansion of the office that was ultimately approved by the United States Congress, but before the law was enacted to authorize additional attorneys, I was appointed on June 26, 1969, as the first African American United States magistrate in the nation, a position now described as United States magistrate judge.

I served as one of the United States magistrates in the United States District Court from June 26, 1969, to December 1975. During that period I served on the Training Committee and on the Legislative Committee of the United States magistrates and developed the principles and standards to make sure that the principles of handling the issuance of arrest and search warrants, bail releases, preliminary hearings, and petty offenses— and later misdemeanor offenses—were all race-neutral and administered by judicial officers across the nation without discrimination or inequality. I also frequently lectured to federal magistrates at the Federal Judicial Center and to state judges at the National Judicial College in Reno, Nevada, on principles of probable cause for arrest, issuance of search warrants on factual allegations, and legal concepts that would apply to all persons and circumstances in the same manner. I also wrote and published law review and journal articles implementing these principles for the guidance of federal magistrates and state judges.

I set up the test case of *Coleman v. Burnett* (477 F.2d 1187 [D.C. Cir. 1973]) in the United States Court of Appeals for the District of Columbia Circuit, which led to Judge Spottswood Robinson's writing an opinion that established the legal principle that defense counsel had the right to subpoena witnesses in a preliminary hearing, if such witnesses would negate probable cause, showing, for example, that no crime was committed, or that the government had arrested and charged the wrong person. The principles of this case were later adopted in the formal rules for the United States magistrate judges system. When the magistrates were assigned the function of conducting pretrial proceedings and conferences in civil cases, I also wrote extensively on the principles to be applied in these proceedings, with equality to all litigants in all federal courts throughout the nation.

In the fall of 1975, I was approached and asked to consider becoming the assistant general counsel of the Legal Advisory Division of the Office of General Counsel, U.S. Civil Service Commission, which functionally made the position the legal adviser for the Civil Service System for the entire Executive Branch of the United States government. With great reluctance, and after considerable reflection and deliberation, and considering that I might have more time to spend with my five children as a result of having a staff of attorneys working for me, I decided to leave the position of United States magistrate and to take the position. Jimmy Carter then became president and decided to make the reform of the Civil Service system a centerpiece of his administration, and I was assigned to work with the White House Counsel's office in the several reorganizations and statutory changes he was seeking.

I worked on several of the reorganization plans and legislative initiatives, serving as one of his principal lawyers in dealing with the United States Congress on all bills dealing with personnel matters from appointment through retirement. I personally wrote the initial drafts of the reorganization plan that split the United States Civil Service Commission into the Office of Personnel Management, the Merit Systems Protection Board, and the Office of Special Counsel and the draft bill that would further define the functions of these three separate entities and the new Federal Labor Relations Authority, which became the Civil Service Reform Act of 1978. For this work, I was the recipient of the United States Civil Service Commission's Distinguished Service Award on December 6, 1978. Subsequently, for my work in implementing the Civil Service Reform Act of 1978 and for lecturing around the country on the new requirements, on January 24, 1980, I received the U.S. Office of Personnel Management Director's Award for Meritorious Service.

On January 29, 1980, I was appointed again to the position of United States magistrate for the District Court for the District of Columbia. I again served on the training and legislation committees and in other activities of the national organization. In 1983 to 1984 I served as the president of the National Council of United States Magistrates, leading the national organization. I am the only African American ever to have held that position. During this time I served as a trial judge in an increasing number of civil cases by consent of the parties, sitting with the same powers of a district court judge. In 1985, I presided over more civil cases trials than any United States District Court judge that year. Probably the most notable case I handled as United States magistrate was the preliminary proceedings, including commitment for mental examination, in the case of John Hinckley, who, at the time, had been accused of shooting president Ronald W. Reagan and was later convicted.

In November 1987, President Ronald W. Reagan appointed me an associate judge of the Superior Court of the District of Columbia, and I served in that capacity until October 10, 1998, when I retired and became a senior judge of the Superior Court of the District of Columbia, a status I am entitled to hold for the rest of my life. Probably the most notable case I handled while on the Superior Court was presiding over the trial of Carl T. Rowan for alleged illegal possession of a weapon and ammunition in connection with his arrest when two youths broke into his backyard and went swimming in his swimming pool. In addition, I became the court's expert judge in handling neglect and abuse, termination of parental rights, and adoption cases in the Family Division, later renamed the Family Court Division of the Superior Court of the District of Columbia in 2001. From October 1996 until August 2004 I handled more adoption cases than any other judge in the history of the Superior Court of the District of Columbia since its creation in 1970. When I retired on October 10, 1998, it was to become judge-in-residence with the Black Community Crusade for Children of the Children's Defense Fund as a volunteer to plan and develop programs to reduce juvenile delinquency and crime in America, to improve the foster care system, and to advance and promote adoptions in the United States. I engaged in this work part-time, while continuing to sit as a senior judge on the Superior Court until August 1, 2004.

In addition to my professional career, I have had a very satisfying and extensive American Bar Association role. I became a member of the

American Bar Association in 1962, and in 1969, after becoming a United States magistrate, I became a member of the Executive Committee of the National Conference of Special Court Judges. In 1974, I became the first African American judge to serve as chairperson of the National Conference of Special Court Judges for the entire United States. One of the most amusing incidents in my career was my wife telling me that when we were at an Annual Convention of the American Bar Association in Montreal, Canada, and I was seated on the dais as one of the leaders of the bar, a couple of older White ladies leaned over to her and asked her, an American Indian, if she knew what foreign country I was from. My wife responded that I was her husband and that I was from the United States.

In the American Bar Association, I have served on the Council of the Administrative Law and Regulatory Practice Section and as secretary of that section, and I have served as chairperson of its Civil Rights and Employment Discrimination Committee. I have also served on the Council of the Criminal Justice Section, and I have served as the chairperson of the Criminal Rules and Evidence Committee, chairperson of the Criminal Justice Magazine Board, and as a member of many other committees of the Criminal Justice Section over the years.

In 1985, I was the recipient of the Franklin N. Flashner Judicial Award as the most outstanding judge in the United States on a trial court of special court jurisdiction as United States magistrate, and in 1999, I was one of four recipients of the Award of Judicial Excellence from the National Conference of State Trial Judges for courts of general jurisdiction in America. On February 12, 2005, I was the recipient of the American Bar Association Spirit of Excellence Award for my role in the Civil Rights Movement.

I have been a member of the Federal Bar Association since the early 1960s, was president of the District of Columbia Chapter of the Federal Bar Association in 1984, and served at the national level of the Federal Bar Association as section coordinator over all section activities from 1986 to 1988. Before then I served from 1984 to 1986 as deputy coordinator over all section activities. In 1994, I received the Federal Bar Association's President's Award. I received the Earl W. Kintner Award, the highest award given by the Federal Bar Association, in September 2002.

In the National Bar Association, I have been a life member since 1970 and have served as chairperson of the Advisory Committee to Promote Increased Minority Judges and Judicial Officer representation on State and Federal Benches, as cochair of its Drug Policy Initiative Project, as cochair of its Health Care Initiative Committee Project, chairperson of its Juvenile Justice Task Force, and member of numerous committees over the years. In 1996, I was the recipient of the National Bar Association's President's Award. In 2004, I was the recipient of that organization's highest award, the C. Francis Stradford Award, named after one of the founders of the National Bar Association.

In 1994 to 1995, I served as president of the Prettyman-Leventhal American Inn of Court, an organization created to promote civility and the best of professional conduct in lawyers in litigating and practicing in the courtroom. This organization was patterned on the Inns of Court of England to promote the best traditions in courtroom decorum and manner by litigating attorneys before the bench.

On August 1, 2004, I took inactive status as a senior judge of the Superior Court of the District of Columbia for a two-year sabbatical to be the national executive director of the National African American Drug Policy Coalition, a group of 23 African American professional organizations that have joined together to promote a public health and medical approach to dealing with illegal drug usage and addiction as a disease in lieu of criminal prosecution and incarceration. The emphasis is on long-term intensive drug treatment to effect a cure to the physical addiction and dependence on drugs, which is followed by a continuum of services to stabilize such persons so that they do not repeat their crimes, thus preventing recidivism and making communities safer for all persons. A second major objective of this coalition is developing and implementing an intensive drug prevention program directed to our youth, starting in the third and fourth grade through high school. This is coupled with a rewards and incentive program designed to change their attitude toward educational excellence and achievement. Counselor-mentors are provided as early as the eighth grade and internships are provided for juniors and seniors in high school in the career fields or professions in which they are interested. Through these means, our mission is to reduce drastically the number of African Americans who become prison and jail inmates to a point where the number incarcerated may be no more than our percentage in the population at large and to more than double the number of African Americans going into the professions and into career fields with productive lives in whatever they may choose to do.

Finally, it is most important to emphasize that professional and legal accomplishments are not the "all" of life. I regard as my greatest legacy my family—my wife and our five children, each of whom hold double degrees. The oldest, a daughter, is a lawyer and a certified public accountant; the second, a son, is a physician, a prostate cancer surgeon, and one of the principal inventors of Viagra; the third, a son, is a public health administrator; the fourth, a daughter, holds a MBA degree in the science of management and is an executive with Ford Motor Company in its headquarters in Dearborn, Michigan; and the fifth, a daughter, is a doctor of veterinary medicine in New York City.

Though my parents were not even high school graduates, they have five grandchildren who are all professionals with double degrees. My family is living proof that education can be the means to fulfilling the impossible dream and can lead to a rich and rewarding life for every individual. Even with the intensity of professional pursuits and bar activities, I found time to be an assistant scoutmaster, to be an umpire in Little League football games, to be involved in parent school associations, and to engage in other activities with our children to set an example for them of the importance of achievement and finding exciting things to do with their lives. I felt that it was important to give them maximum exposure to what they could become and what they could do with their lives. I always thought it necessary to heap praise upon them for their achievements and successes, to motivate them always to reach for their greatest potential in all that they did. At this stage in my life, I can say without reservation that each child has grown up always seeking to excel and to be the very best in his or her respective endeavors. It is for that reason that I serve today as the national executive director of the National African American Drug Policy Coalition to open the doors of opportunities for as many youngsters as I can for the rest of my life.

CHAPTER 6

My Professional Success as a Political Leader

WILLIAM LACY CLAY, JR.

Congressman, D-Missouri,
St. Louis, Missouri

I am a fifth-term member of Congress, where I represent Missouri's First Congressional District, which includes portions of the city of St. Louis and St. Louis County. In the 111th Congress as of this writing (now 112th), the current Congress at the time of this writing, I serve as the chairman of the House Subcommittee on Information Policy, Census, and National Archives, and I am the ranking Democratic member of the newly created Subcommittee on Federalism and the Census under the House Government Reform Committee. I also serve on the powerful Financial Services Committee, which has broad jurisdiction over banking, financial markets, insurance, and consumer credit.

I am a proud member of the Congressional Black Caucus and the Progressive Caucus, and I serve on the boards of my father's William L. Clay Scholarship and Research Fund and the Congressional Black Caucus Foundation, Inc. I reside in St. Louis and I am the proud father of two children—Carol and Will.

As a profession, politics chose me more than I chose politics.

Growing up in St. Louis, it seems I had little choice but to go into government service. You see, I came from a family of politicians, activists, and community leaders, and my father, former Congressman William L.

"Bill" Clay, Sr. was probably the most prominent among them. Known nationally for his historic election in 1968 as the first African American sent to Congress from the state of Missouri, he had sharpened his political teeth as a member of the St. Louis Board of Aldermen and as a civil rights activist fighting for jobs for people of color in a segregated St. Louis. At one point he went to jail for 105 days because he believed his sacrifice would help advance the conditions of minorities in this nation. Later, he would serve 32 years in Congress.

My uncle, Irving Clay, also served with distinction on the St. Louis Board of Aldermen for 12 years, from 1991 to 2003. He too is part of our family's legacy, which is to use politics to do good for people and to help people and not to hurt them. As my uncle says, "It is not about us. It's about helping others."

In addition, my cousin, Earl Wilson, made his mark as president and executive director of the St. Louis Gateway Classic Foundation, which was founded in 1994.

So you see, politics and community leadership are in my blood. It was not something I realized early on, however. My life would take different twists and turns before I realized how blessed I was to have witnessed with my own eyes, experienced in my own life, how politics and good government can make a difference in people's lives. For years, it seemed it was all I could do to avoid my destiny. Eventually, I would enter politics through the back door, so to speak.

Here is how my life led me into politics.

I was born in St. Louis, on July 27, 1956. I was 12 years old when my father was elected to Congress in 1968, and we moved to Washington, D.C., the following year. Growing up in suburban Silver Spring, Maryland, I graduated from Springbrook High School in 1974. At the University of Maryland at College Park, I spurned my studies and found youthful satisfaction in being an average student. With that attitude, it didn't take long for the rigors of college academics to take their toll. Before long, I had little hope of salvaging a college career of any kind. Eventually, I dropped out of full-time college studies and wasn't doing much of anything else with my life. But, thankfully, my dad wasn't going to let me vegetate at home.

"You're not going to sit around the house," he said, and helped me land a job on the Hill, as the assistant doorkeeper for the U.S. House of Representatives. I worked that job for seven years, during which time I went to night school. In 1983, I finally earned a college degree—a bachelor of science degree—in government and politics. Part of what helped get me through college was myself. I did some serious soul searching. I had to decide that I was not going to fail at college and be a doorkeeper for the rest of my life. In addition to government and politics, I earned a paralegal certificate and began preparations to attend law school.

I had just started law school at Howard University School of Law when a pivotal moment in my political life happened. With the unexpected resignation of Rep. Nathaniel "Nat" Rivers from the Missouri House of Representatives, I decided to make a run for his seat. I moved back to St. Louis and won the race in a special election. I would go on to serve eight years as a member of the Missouri House of Representatives. Later, in 1991, I won a special election for a state Senate seat, replacing Sen. John Bass, who served from 1981 to 1991. I would serve in that capacity for nine years, until my election to Congress in 2000.

During my years in the Missouri State Legislature, I continued to educate myself. I studied real estate and for years maintained a real estate license. I also worked as a paralegal. To help me better negotiate legislative solutions, I attended Harvard University's John F. Kennedy School of Government for Senior Executives in State and Local Government and was awarded an honorary doctorate of law from Lincoln University in Jefferson City, Missouri, in 2001.

Among my legislative accomplishments during my 17 years in the Missouri General Assembly, I helped establish the Rosa Parks Highway in St. Louis County and helped pass a law requiring that history teachers include information about the history of the Civil Rights Movement in America in their curriculum. Near the end of my tenure in the Missouri Senate, I successfully passed measures that allowed welfare recipients to earn higher wages without losing benefits when making the transition from welfare to work. I also created Individual Development Accounts (IDAs) for low-income families to save money for education, job training, home ownership, home improvement, or small business capitalization. In addition, I established Missouri's hate crime law covering crimes motivated by race or religion, which eventually was expanded to include crimes against individuals because of their sexual orientation, gender, or disability. Today, hundreds of young people receive job training through Youth Build, a program enacted under my Youth Opportunities and Violence Prevention Act.

Since arriving in Congress, I have been working tirelessly to ensure that this nation's elections are conducted fairly and that every vote is counted accurately. I am an advocate for new electronic voting equipment that must reflect the accuracy of the voter's personal choice. I continue to be a proponent of paper-ballot verification, thereby creating a legitimate audit trail.

During my service in the U.S. House of Representatives, I have advocated helping economically disadvantaged families create wealth through homeownership and have supported legislation that prohibits unfair lending practices to home buyers. Also, I champion the promotion of financial literacy beginning at the kindergarten level all the way through the 12th grade.

If you want to build a career in politics, you must prepare as early as you can. I urge you to read more to gain knowledge about different social matters. Read cutting-edge material on issues. When I was in the state Senate, I came up with some pretty good ideas for better government. My colleagues would ask me where I got those ideas. The truth is I read a lot and learned a lot. When you expand your universe, you're a better leader, a better government servant. Be persistent and don't give up. You have to set your goals and then create and try to achieve your goals. As that saying goes—"Shoot for the moon. If you miss, you will land amongst the stars."

There are many roads to success in politics. As you know, my journey involves being raised in a political family and the benefits it offered. In my father's book *Bill Clay: A Political Voice at the Grass Roots*, he writes about how these political ties helped me win my bid for election to Congress in 2000. Although some presume that I sailed to Congress on his wings, the reality is that I earned my right to be there.

First, my father announced his retirement 18 months ahead of time to give candidates a chance to mount their campaigns and to avoid critics who might say that I was given an advantage with a last-minute retirement declaration by my dad. That did not happen. And I found that many of my father's long-time supporters in organized labor decided to support one of my opponents and not me, or to break with tradition and not endorse a candidate at all. Also, my major opponent raised more money than I did—some $300,000 more. But when the votes were counted, I had won out over that major challenger: 34,393 votes to his 15,612! My father explained why.

In the opinion of many, Lacy had the leadership qualities to be an effective representative. He had a wealth of knowledge and experience that prepared him for the job. He had a degree in political science and government from the University of Maryland and had served seventeen years in the Missouri legislature. But more important than formal education, he had something that only a few aspiring for public office possess: he grew up around government and politics. "He lived in a household where government and public service were frequent dinner table topics. Living and breathing the anxieties of elections, the slings and arrows of personal attacks, the thrill of campaign victories, and the deflation of legislative defeat—what could be better training for confronting the real world of congressional combat? (Clay 2004, 285–286)

My father went on to say:

There was no doubt in Lacy's camp about the outcome of the election. Weeks before election day, they felt confident that their highly organized campaign structure was vastly superior. . . . Lacy Clay, Jr. won because he surrounded himself with the most experienced political operatives in the area. . . . The campaign staff was adept at developing issues and cultivating volunteer support. They were veteran politicians and political activists who assured that the daily operation was promoted effectively and efficiently. (Clay 2004, 299)

Finally, my father wrote, "The election of Lacy Clay, Jr. was justified because he was the most qualified candidate seeking the office. His background, association, and identification with pertinent public issues plus his nearly eighteen years in the state legislature prepared him for a greater career in a higher office" (Clay 2004, 300)

As you can guess, I plan a long career as a United States Congressman. To do that, I must win reelection to Congress every two years. To win reelection I must earn it. I must serve my district and its 626,000 diverse constituents. Yes, as an African American I have a keen interest in the needs of my particular constituent group. However, I serve all constituent groups within my district, and that means even serving the needs of those who have opposed me at the ballot box. Imagine, if you will, you are the leader, the voice in Congress of more than half a million people comprising Christians, Jews, Muslims, Hindus, Buddhists, atheists, and many others, among them Caucasians, African Americans, Hispanics, Asians, and Africans—the rainbow of humanity—and stir in the rich, the poor, the homeless, the conservatives, the liberals, the moderates, the hawks, the doves, the men, the women, and the children. That is my district, and that is whom I represent to the best of my ability. And that is not all. Add to them the thousands of visitors from around the nation and the world who come into the First Congressional District of Missouri each year to enjoy its benefits and tourist attractions and to find temporary work. Then add the number of people touched by the municipal, county, state, and federal laws that govern this region. The range is indeed enormous.

If I am to continue to succeed as a politician, I must choose my battles with discretion. I must stand on principles that benefit the majority of my constituents. And on those issues where I differ with some of my constituents, I must do so with grace and dignity and be able to explain why I stand where I stand and for what reasons. I will never satisfy all of my constituents at the same time on the same issue. That is a human impossibility. We are too diverse as a region. However, I pride myself in representing a district where the majority of residents believe in basically the same basic human values and political goals.

Part of my role as a congressman is to participate in various caucuses, for example, the Congressional Black Caucus and the Progressive Caucus. My membership and participation in these organizations within Congress help me to remain focused on the issues important to constituents, which the caucuses represent. In addition to their legislative leadership, these caucuses also help send a strong message that I care about all my constituents and their concerns. Although you can't be all things to all people, it is important to send a message that you genuinely care and are willing to participate in people's lives.

For all young people, I advise you to think down the road and avoid doing things that might come back to haunt you. For example, no matter what career you choose, always strive to be a good citizen. To me that means participation in the electoral process. Don't diminish your right to vote, and your power, by criminal conviction or through apathy. A heavy price has been paid in blood, sweat, and tears by Americans to win the right for all Americans to vote. Each vote counts. As a voter, you must consider how your participation in the political process affects the greater good. As a politician, you have a greater responsibility to protect our voting rights, our democracy.

Success in politics is dependent upon learning the history of your nation, the history of your community, and the history of politics in your community. It is also crucial to understand the economy. A skilled politician effectively balances budgets, works for electoral reform, and improves the education of the nation's 72 million students (8 million in nursery school, 33 million in elementary school, 16 million in high school, and 15 million in college). A good politician must develop affordable health care for a modern, civilized nation and must meet the challenge of terrorism in ways that do not foster war—or unduly tread on established civil liberties.

Also, on the domestic front, the national debt and Social Security are concerns for all Americans, no matter what their age. And clearly, the list of congressional challenges is seemingly endless in regards to education, housing, the economy, jobs, health care, senior citizens' issues, and the wars in Iraq and Afghanistan. This is why I love being a member of Congress, because of our ability to create laws and change the nation for the better.

With this goal in mind, I have helped earmark federal dollars for environmental protection, economic development, and senior care projects, and I have worked to secure federal grants for art and other nonprofit organizations. The bottom line is that I don't like politics that hurt people, politics that weaken the nation, or politics that keep Americans from reaching their full potential. I believe the most important work of a United States representative is using federal resources to address issues central to all Americans. For me, these issues include reforming the local election process, developing more local affordable housing, and providing adequate health care to every St. Louis citizen.

I believe my success as a politician in Congress depends on my strong leadership at the local and state level. I have a vested interest in seeing the St. Louis region succeed because my family has been a part of this community for generations.

So, ask yourself, do you want to invest all your efforts into serving the community as an elected official? If yes, then I am flattered and honored that you might one day—*many* years from today—take my place in Congress.

Reference

Clay, William, 2004. *Bill Clay: A Political Voice at the Grass Roots*. St. Louis: Missouri History Museum Press.

CHAPTER 7

Manifested Destiny

KELVIN COCHRAN

Fire Chief, Atlanta Fire Department,
Atlanta, Georgia; Second Vice President
of the International Association
of Fire Fighters, Washington, D.C.;
Former Chief,
Shreveport Fire Department,
Shreveport, Louisiana

As the Civil Rights Movement was gaining momentum, I was born at Confederate Memorial Hospital in Shreveport, Louisiana, on January 23, 1960 to George Levert and Jane Elizabeth Houston Cochran. At that time, home for us was 1133 Allen Avenue in Alameda Terrace, the projects in the Allendale neighborhood where many African Americans lived.

A few years passed. My mother had two girls and we moved twice. From the projects, we moved to Rear Snow Street, not far from the Alameda Terrace Projects. In Shreveport, when the word "rear" precedes the name of a street it means the address is actually in the alley behind the main street. On Rear Snow Street, I have very vivid memories of what life was like. The experiences and revelations gained in that alley would set my life on a course toward my destiny. On Rear Snow Street the realities of poverty were so evident to me as small child; I knew there had to be a better way of life. It was on Rear Snow Street where my dream was born to become a firefighter when I grew up.

The Realities of Poverty

Several things were evident and constant in my young spirit that caused me to have such an unusual awareness of how others disdain those who live in poverty. We lived in a shotgun house in the alley. My three brothers and I slept in the same bed, the two older boys at the top and the two younger boys at the bottom. My two sisters slept in the same room in another little bed. We did not get all new clothes at the beginning of the school year like many of the children in our school. If we wore something new, it was mostly because that item was desperately needed and that all other alternatives had been exhausted. It meant the hand-me-downs had served their time and patches were no longer effective. My mother could not afford new clothes and shoes for six kids, especially at the rate the boys were growing.

My family was on the free lunch program at school, and many times our after-school snack was a mayonnaise sandwich and a cold glass of sugar water. On several occasions, when we flipped the light switch upon returning home from school, there were no lights because my mother did not have enough money to pay the electric bill. Sometimes the gas was off and we cooked our food on an electric plate. My mother would occasionally instruct us to keep all the jugs and pots full of water. A few days later we would turn on the water faucets and no water would come out. The water was turned off, because mama did not have enough money to pay the water bill. During this same time of great challenge for my family, my dad left my mother and died when I was six years old.

The Birth of Dreams

So I dreamed of a day when I would be a grown man, would have a family of my own, and would not be poor. I dreamed of having a wife and beautiful children. I dreamed of having a house in a nice neighborhood where my kids had their own beds and their own bedroom. I dreamed of buying them nice clothes for school and of what it would be like for them to come home from school to find a refrigerator stocked with food and cabinets filled with canned goods, boxes of cereal, cookies, chips, and sodas.

One day after church, while lying on the floor watching television, we heard the sound of a fire truck from a distance. It was coming our way. Hearing the sound of a fire truck was not unusual, but this particular day it was louder than we had ever heard it before. We opened the front door and right in front of our house was a huge red fire truck. The lady's house across the street from our house was on fire. As I watched those firemen donning their coats and boots, pulling the hose off the truck, and entering the house, I experienced excitement and passion like never before. I looked up at my mom and said, "I want to be a fireman when I grow up!" I was consumed. It's what I hoped for. It's what I dreamed about.

While living in the alley, we joined the Galilee Baptist Church at the top of the alley on Williamson Street, where Dr. E. E. Jones, Sr. was still the pastor at the time of this writing. I was a student at Central Elementary School. When I shared my dream with my mother, my pastor, and my teachers, strangely enough they all essentially gave me the same counsel, "If you believe in God, get a good education, respect grown people, and treat other people like you want to be treated, all your dreams will come true." I was determined to do those things, which seemed too simple for dreams that seemed so lofty and far off. One of the things I find astounding, even today, is that at the time my dream was born, Blacks in the south were not allowed to be firefighters. The discrimination was overt and institutionalized, but *no one ever told me I had to choose another dream or career.*

Dreams Achieved

In February 1981, I was hired as a firefighter on the Shreveport Fire Department. I heard someone say, "The last day you'll ever work is the day you fall in love with what you're doing for a living." If it's true, I have not worked a single day in almost 25 years. I absolutely love getting out of bed every day knowing I will be engaging in a career I've fallen in love with.

While in basic training my passion for the fire service grew, there was much more to it than I knew or dreamed of. It was all challenging and exciting, but basic training did not prepare me for the challenges awaiting me as one of the first Blacks in the department. The city of Shreveport was under a federal consent decree and was mandated to hire qualified Blacks and women. The dissension from some of my White coworkers was obvious. Many of the younger generation dealt with it very well. Some firefighters were understanding and supportive. The difficulties came when there were company officers and chief officers in authority who did not accept the idea of Blacks in the fire service. Even greater challenges arose when racial slurs and jokes were used to demean or in some cases were used in a distasteful attempt to lighten the atmosphere. I remained focused and vigilant, believing in my dream, knowing I was predestined to be a Shreveport firefighter. In my heart, I knew the values instilled in me growing up as a poor kid in Allendale would cause me to overcome the challenges. I believed that, eventually, hard work would pay off, as I had always been told.

My career path was like a fairy tale. The officers in basic training class inspired me with the desire to teach. After four years of service I was promoted to the position of training officer. Training and teaching firefighters increased my sense of worth and value to the department. After five years as training officer, I was promoted to assistant chief training officer, a position I had been denied four years earlier. Through the years in the Training Division, I continued to pursue higher education and leadership, management, and technical training opportunities. I felt compelled to continue to prepare myself for future possibilities. On August 26, 1999, against great odds and prevailing perceptions and commentaries, I was appointed fire chief of the City of Shreveport Fire Department, becoming the first African American in that role in the history of our city.

My dreams have been greatly exceeded. I married a beautiful lady of my childhood years. We have three beautiful children who have their own beds and their own bedrooms. I can afford to buy them new clothes, not just at the beginning of the school year but throughout the year. We live in a beautiful house in a nice neighborhood. Our refrigerator is always full of food, and the cabinets are full of canned goods and other good stuff, (unless we get too busy to go to the grocery store). Our utilities have never been cut off. We always seem to have more than enough. My dream of becoming a firefighter not only came true but was exceeded. I became the fire chief in the same city my dream was born, and Blacks were not allowed to be firefighters at the time my dream was born. The scripture is true, "God is able to do exceedingly abundantly above all we ask or think according to the power that works in us" (Ephesians 3:20).

So, I continue to dream and follow the advice I received as a child. I still believe in God, I still strive for higher education, I still respect grown people, and I still treat others as I want to be treated. My personal vision statement provides encouragement and determination:

> I will stand tall, and stand for something;
> I will move forward, and move mountains;
> I will make more than a difference;
> I will make History!!!

The best is yet to come.

CHAPTER 8

Comer Cottrell, Jr.:
A Master in the Game
By Ralph Ferguson

COMER COTTRELL, JR.

Founder and Former Chairman,
Pro-Line Corporation, Dallas, Texas

The Comer Cottrell story is about the will of a man charting a path of success against overwhelming odds. This man is my friend, and it is an honor to provide readers with this narrative of him and his character and achievements. As a boy growing up on the shell-dusted streets of Mobile, Alabama, Comer developed a business to sell rabbits to generate income for himself and his brother. This initial step into entrepreneurship lit a flame in Comer's will that would not let success be denied in his life. These thoughts of greater success came to Comer in an environment where Jim Crow laws and discrimination were rampant and where the majority society used force, violence, and cruelty to deny opportunity beyond his community.

Everyone can reflect on the challenges facing a boy with a rabbit franchise in his community who thinks that one day he can become a business magnate. In communities across the South, we recall local entrepreneurs like Charles Andrews, Will Thompson, Addison Ferguson, and Comer's granddaddy—men who wanted to break the mold, who were heroes to us. Their small businesses were centers of excellence that signaled there might be a brighter tomorrow with a will to achieve. The lessons from these men's family and friends, known and unknown, are the foundation for the strides

Comer made in developing his business values over time. As did his predecessors, Comer has worked in many fields and found success in most of his employment opportunities before the right opportunity appeared. An entrepreneur waits for the opportunity that wrenches deep in his guts, signaling that the time to move has come. There is no guarantee of success when an entrepreneur believes the right opportunity has come, but the satisfaction of building an enterprise outweighs the risk.

There is not enough security in a job for an entrepreneur when there is not a connection with an opportunity to participate in wealth building. During his childhood, Comer learned the risk-reward principle of business, which prepared him for the leap into business when a friend suggested that they develop a business. Comer's collection of experiences—college, military, sales, business failure, and employment—synergized with opportunity at a time when the nation was examining its conscience about war and the Jim Crow practices that denied full access to the market economy to the more than 20 million Americans whose ancestors had faced turmoil for more than 300 years as slaves building the nation.

The will to succeed finds opportunity in the most complex environments. Comer did not fail to trust his ability to dream. This is a very important characteristic for anyone who decides that great success is a goal, though not everyone can translate this characteristic into a significant wealth-building opportunity. When time, opportunity, and position come together, an entrepreneur with a willingness to invest the sweat equity can achieve success. Entrepreneurs understand that success has hummingbird characteristics, that is, one must move quickly to each potential opportunity, and success often defies guiding principles that considered indefinable the catalyst that lifts your business to the next level of growth.

The team, investors and partners, believe in the opportunity. Motivation to succeed takes different shapes; though the participants are in pursuit of the same objective, they are motivated by a variety of interests. The prevailing interest among Comer's friends was to build something of their own. At the time there was a great deal of concern about the lack of businesses and products for African Americans. so the national stage was set for an economic shift in the importance of the minority community in the market economy. Comer was in the middle of social chaos, but understood that it created a ripe business environment for a person who was ready to build wealth.

If you study Comer Cottrell, you will see that the way he took advantage of the opportunity presented to him did not differ from the approach of those before him, such as Madame C. J. Walker, who made her fortune in the hair care business. Comer did not identify the market; that was done by a friend of a friend who already had a market niche. The vision of how to increase the market to achieve maximum profit potential was what Comer introduced to the team. Every organization must have a visionary who dreams about reaching the farthest horizon. Partners, however, often leave the business at the point where their tolerance for risk ceases. Comer's experience was no different. The partners that had felt secure in a small business did not go forward with the growth strategy. The partners that wanted to diversify outside the niche market into different industries did not remain in the organization either.

Comer's story provides great insight into the working of a partnership through the evolution of a business. This is very important to appreciate for those who have an interest in business. Few businesses are the product of one individual's sweat. Business is a team sport, and as with any team, over time the faces of the team members will change, and this is in the best interest of the business. Comer is master of changing the faces of his team. His story is a great lesson about how to switch team members while doing the least amount of damage to the business. This does not mean people did not suffer as he built the company. In these transactions Comer showed an innate understanding of the market that his peers did not have. When there is only one company to grow, the investment resources are scarce, and you cannot risk dabbling in uncertain markets to identify an alternative revenue stream. Bankers, who are key to business growth, prefer to see a clearly defined market before they invest revenue in a company's future. To become a magnate in your industry, others must believe that investing money with you will earn them more money. It takes great faith and character to believe you have identified a path to wealth building that warrants investment in your dream. The more you consider Comer's achievement, the more you come to realize that his success is about business savvy and family values.

Without strong family values, Comer might not have been able to manage the entanglements of his personal life and the complex issues associated with a startup business. His parents did not shrink from the question of setting certain standards with their son. Though Comer could be accused of backsliding from time to time, he did not abandon his parents' teaching at any time in his life. When he was growing up, his mother reminded him on more than one occasion to protect his soul. This is an important message that it is not the external appearance that is important; the internal qualities make the person. Comer spent his life looking for people with those great internal characteristics to be a part of his team. Comer has said, however, that though he has had many triumphs, he has failed many times in searching for that elusive quality spoken of by his mother, and he has forfeited millions of dollars as a result of misjudging character. Undaunted, Comer continued to build Pro-Line into his signature business.

The great-grandson of slaves moved into the corporate boardrooms. Comer earned the opportunity to serve on bank boards. From humble beginnings in Los Angeles, Pro-Line became an international business, generating significant sales in Africa and South America. To maximize global efficiency, Comer decided, long before it became popular, to link manufacturing and distribution through computers. This single concept increased profit margins on every product in the Pro-Line inventory. This strategy reduced waste in the supply chain and gave the sales force up-to-date information on deliverable products to close a sale.

Comer knew that success was not simply the loan that supported the growth of his company. Instead, he knew that the success of his company was due to his partnership with his banker. If others want to follow the Comer Cottrell model, they must demonstrate to a bank that their business may capture a large share of the consumer market. Knowing the important role banks play in the growth of a business, Comer sought over the years to serve on many bank boards and to be an advocate for disenfranchised business owners who were trying to build wealth.

There is no easy way to get to the top, and it is harder to remain on top. Entrepreneurs who scale the tower of success often have no clue that the real work begins after you get to the top. Money equals swagger and power but people with more money have greater swagger and power. Comer realizes that the more swagger and power someone has, the more money he or she likely has, which is a clue when negotiating. Comer believes everyone in business plays to win, not compromise. He did not learn this lesson on the streets of Mobile, but the values he learned there eased his transition into the neighborhood of titans.

Comer joined the Republican Party on the advice of an old and dear friend. Comer is a man who believes Truman made the benchmark decision that changed the course of modern American society when he integrated the armed forces with an executive order, so at first he felt like a spy when he joined the Republican Party. Though Comer faced some early challenges with his new party, he concluded that the party's fundamental values differ little from the teaching of his family. In fact, the emphasis on self-help, importance of family, and prayer are lessons valued in every African American household. Comer continued to wonder why more African Americans are not Republicans. Part of the answer comes to Comer at a luncheon meeting where he sees a prominent Republican leader in California dining with a known racist. Though our political values may be consistent with Republicans, Republicans do not value us. In this difficult environment, Comer saw an opportunity to seize another platform where he could support diversity through the effective use of his power to influence both political and business leaders.

The decision not to be a footnote but an active player in the Republican Party led Comer to relocate Pro-Line to Dallas, Texas. The decision to relocate, however, was not solely about politics but was also related to Comer's need for the banking and business mecca to complete the construction of his dream to build a rich and powerful business. Other than for the revenue needed to grow his company, Comer did not need the business leadership of Dallas. Though Dallas is a banking capital, Comer knew other competing cities would make growth funds available to his proven organization. Dallas and Comer make a perfect partnership. Comer used his perfect partnership to challenge the Dallas establishment to open the door wider so that more minorities would have the opportunity to grow their companies. The Dallas establishment continues to listen to Comer because they see him as a peer.

So, how was Comer able to make Pro-Line a success? Pro-Line sales are to a proprietary market, which insulates Comer from business assaults that may undermine his profit margins. Conglomerates in the hair care industry did not discover African Americans as a viable revenue stream until the 1990s. In an effort to manage conglomerates' access to the African American hair care market, Comer and his peers developed the American Health and Beauty Aids Institute. Since before Madame C.J. Walker, African American hair care has been a domain where numerous African American entrepreneurs were able to build wealth. Comer used the autonomy of his industry to push forward social change in the business community. Comer knows that when the billion-dollar beauty conglomerates decide they want their share of the African American hair care market, they have sufficient resources to take it all. The intent of the institute is to manage information to insulate this proprietary market against predatory business practices of cash-rich conglomerates seeking entrée. In the meantime, Comer continues to use his clout and financial resources to support civil rights, education, and serve with agencies interested in the well-being of the African American community.

Money follows service. In engineering the growth of Pro-Line, Comer made service a hallmark of the brand. Success is not only found in establishing a flagship company or creating marketing strategies that enlarge the economic pie and create employment opportunities for a disenfranchised population. Instead, the triumph is that Comer served as a model that America is open for business if you have the will and do not fear failure. The best businesses grow to serve a market need by understanding their customers' interest in the product. Money is not the priority for a business that wants longevity in the market economy; quality and service give a business the power of sustainable growth. This lesson that he learned in childhood gave Comer an edge on his competitors. Comer impressed the market with high standards for his products, and the focus on knowing the market has kept the Pro-Line promise that their products will be high quality, reasonably priced, and made with the best ingredient.

As an entrepreneur, Comer believes in reinvesting in the community. Comer knows that without the proprietary African American consumer market he would not have the fortune that he has amassed. It is an honor for him to use part of his wealth wisely in supporting African American entrepreneurs, academic scholarships, and other community projects that prepare individuals to be positive contributors to society.

For Comer, the greatest gift is to be able to give back to the people that supported his wealth-building dream. Comer used millions of his dollars to purchase a college campus to retain the rich heritage of historical African American institutions. As a businessman, Comer has struggled with the realization that there is not a sufficient quantity of talented and highly educated African Americans to run and develop businesses and to hire others. Throughout his professional life, Comer has found ways to employ family members and give them the chance to grow with the business. However, the fact that someone is a relative does not guarantee him or her a seat at the table; family members have to prove that they have the education and skill to work in the complex corporate environment. From experiences with his family that lifted the standards of sales and production at Pro-Line, Comer knows firsthand the contribution a person with a quality education can make to an organization. This led him to purchase the property of bankrupt Bishop College. He could have used his resources to develop this prime real estate and make a profit significantly greater than the cost. And though the purchase gave Comer a choice wealth-building opportunity, he did not consider the profit incentive. Instead, he convinced another historical institution, Paul Quinn College, to relocate to the property and donated the land to them. Thus, the great-grandson of slaves used his immense power and resources to preserve a legacy instrumental in our transition to become a free people.

Comer is a dean in the American business community. He understands as much about being leader as a follower. To succeed in the world of business, you must appreciate both roles. Future entrepreneurs must pick up on the nuance of these skills. There is no overnight success in the business. In the beginning, you need every reliable person you can find who believes your product is a winner in the market economy.

Pro-Line delivers a product that is as old as the African American community. The company improves the quality, service, and delivery in a consumer market where such values were not emphasized. If an entrepreneur places success in front of earning money, there is a greater likelihood that his or her venture will be sustainable in the market. Comer believes there are tremendous opportunities in the market economy for individuals who understand when to lead and when to follow. The strong lessons of his childhood—that learning on the job may be more important than the earnings from the job—are always fresh in Comer's mind.

Comer does not believe in entitlements as a way of life. The struggle to overcome poverty teaches numerous important lessons. This does not mean that everyone must experience poverty, however. The concern is that entitlements provide a subsistence lifestyle that simply meets basic needs without teaching recipients how to break the cycle of poverty. Children growing up in that environment do not develop the skills to help them escape the cycle of poverty. A great many young men and women are in a wasteland of entitlement programs and are not being motivated to be interested in the competitive economy. They are becoming a permanent underclass in our society. With his resources, Comer has done everything he can to lift many young people from the culture of entitlements. He advocates that politicians and educators need to do more through their institutions to redefine the use of entitlements in providing assistance to families. If we are to succeed in the future, we cannot afford to let even one person slip through the cracks. For the United States to continue as a great nation, Comer believes we must design a strategy to snap the cycle of the entitlement culture in a family; if we fail, we may forfeit some of our best business and science minds. It is the right thing to do and it will give more people the opportunity to enjoy the benefits of our free society. When a family is strapped by the burden of poverty and the weight of debt and despair, this living situation is as oppressive as living in a society without rights and privileges. America is too great a nation for individuals and families to feel there is no hope for escaping their situation.

The Comer Cottrell story is about a man from a traditional African American family who rose to the highest pinnacle of the business world. Comer does not believe he possesses some special gift that made him more successful than others. In my many years of knowing Comer, he has never claimed to have a special genius that pushed him to the top. On the contrary, Comer is a gentle man who is involved with family, friends, and business associates and who understands that success is having high-quality advisers who are often more knowledgeable than he is. Of course, success requires timing, preparation, and hard work. For some, this alignment may not ever occur. It did occur for Comer, and he is eternally grateful that his hard work produced Pro-Line, so that those who follow into the business world know that with a bit of luck and a favorable alignment of timing, preparation, and hard work they can build a company greater than Pro-Line.

When Comer looks back, he considers that his decision to sell Pro-Line may have been too hasty. As a business manager, you always want a second look at a decision even when the decision makes you wealthier than in your wildest dreams. Comer is no different. The choice to sell his company may haunt him. This does not mean the decision to sell may have been bad. To remain in business and fight cash-rich predatory businesses for his propriety market might have destroyed him and the company. From the sale, Comer has used his resources to support the development of numerous businesses that have the potential of grossing more and employing more people than Pro-Line did. Comer believes his work was not complete with Pro-Line because issues beyond business steered him to sell. Comer's attitude about his business is an excellent lesson. There are few people who do not look back over past decisions to consider asking what if they had done something different. Comer is an exceptional businessman who continues to learn through life's lessons.

In conclusion, this is the story of a skinny kid, the great-grandson of slaves, growing up on the streets of Mobile in the Jim Crow South with no future. Comer did not accept the prescribed destiny for African American men during that period of American history. With only the will to achieve, Comer moved from opportunity to opportunity to feed his interest in business. Comer tells everyone who will listen that opportunity is out there for anyone who wants to be a wealth builder. You now have some insight into the challenges that exist in the world of business.

About the Author

Ralph Ferguson is the executive director for Enrollment Management and associate academic dean in the Graduate School at Texas Tech University. He earned his MPA from the University of Southern California and a PhD in personal finance planning from Texas Tech University.

CHAPTER 9

Left of Center: A Slightly Unorthodox Career Path

BILL FLETCHER, JR.

Executive Editor,
Black Communicator.com;
Former President and CEO,
TransAfrica Forum, Washington, D.C.

My career path to being president and CEO of TransAfrica Forum has been far from a direct route. It has been based largely on political choices that I have made over the years beginning with a choice made at the age of 13.

Reading the *Autobiography of Malcolm X*

At the age of 13, I read the *Autobiography of Malcolm X*. I did so voluntarily. I am not sure what inspired me at that particular moment, though I had heard Malcolm's name mentioned, and being, at that time, a reader of *Muhammad Speaks*, a newspaper of the Nation of Islam, I knew how much they hated him. Yet I was intrigued.

Once I started reading the *Autobiography* I could not put it down. I was moved more than I had ever been moved by a book. After completing the book I decided that I had to make a commitment to the struggle for social justice, and specifically, to the struggle for the liberation of African Americans. I was not entirely sure what that meant, but given that this was 1967, and there were struggles under way around civil rights and Black Power and against the Vietnam War, I felt that it was demanded that I take a stand.

This may sound a bit melodramatic, but one must consider the times. Youth, in some cases those who had not reached their teenage years, were being mobilized in various causes. Issues of the day were being discussed in middle schools, high schools, and of course, colleges and universities. Debates transpired on everything from the Arab/Israeli situation to whether African Americans should integrate or separate and to cultural nationalism versus revolutionary nationalism. These did not seem to be abstract debates; instead, they carried with them what we saw to be significant consequences. In that context, I decided that politics, at the level of movements for social change, would be central to my self-definition.

Decisions During College

By the time I entered college (Harvard), I decided that I wanted to be an attorney, specifically focusing on defending political activists. This certainly was a manifestation of the times—political activists were regularly being harassed, jailed, exiled, and killed. Great attorneys like William Kunstler received attention for their courageous work in defense of political activists, such as the Chicago Eight.

As my years proceeded in college (1972–1976), I underwent important changes. First, I started thinking about other aspects of the law, including antitrust work. Second, I became acquainted with the working class and the trade union movement, largely through political activist friends of mine and through the teachings of someone who became a mentor of mine: Professor Ewart Guinier (at that time the chairman of the Afro-American Studies Department of Harvard). What struck me about organized labor and the trade union movement was that many trade union workers were Black; therefore, they were in a position to influence what the trade union movement did, and they could also use the organization resulting from unions to influence the direction of Black America.

My commitment to social justice led me to believe that it was important to involve myself with a section of the population that remains largely dispossessed: the working class. This conclusion raised important challenges, however, as it could mean that I would pursue a certain line of work that was of assistance to workers generally and Black workers in particular (e.g., being a labor or employment lawyer). It could also mean that I situated myself directly in the struggles of Black workers, not as an outsider but as a participant. After graduating from Harvard in 1976, I chose the latter course.

Entering the Workforce

Harvard is an elite institution that has as its actual raison d'être the repro-
duction and training of a new ruling elite, not only for the United States
but also for major portions of this planet. As such, one is encouraged to
think of one's self as among the best of the best. Irrespective of intention,
schools such as Harvard work on one's self-image, ultimately leading
those who complete their undergraduate education there to believe that
they know, if not everything, most things that are important to know.

In deciding to involve myself in the labor movement and in the cause of
the Black worker, I was deciding that my education was actually incom-
plete, that is, there was much more that I needed to learn, and not simply
through graduate school. Thus, I chose to enter the labor movement not as
a staff person for a particular union but as a rank and file member. Specifically, I took a job as a welder in a shipyard outside of Boston.

I could say numerous things about that experience (which lasted for
three and a half years), but the most important is that it taught me how
much I did not know about life and how much one can learn from people
who have never been to college. I had to learn the skill of electric arc
welding. I had to learn what it was like to work outside in weather that
was 15 degrees Fahrenheit in the winter and 95 degrees Fahrenheit (and
humid) in the summer. I had to work under some of the most dangerous
conditions in the United States. I had to turn to individuals for assistance
who did not know me, and may or may not have had any liking for me.

In the midst of all of this, I was attempting to organize the workers.
The shipyard workers were represented by a local of the Industrial Union
of Marine and Shipbuilding Workers of America, a union formed in the
1930s and that had a once proud history. The local was led by a small,
conservative group of White men who had little interest in including the
growing numbers of workers of color and women in the real operations
of the union. In addition, they were, in effect, asleep at the switch, while
the employer was embarking on major changes in its labor/management
relations (changes in the direction of attack mode). In this environment I
started to learn about real organizing, and I was compelled to cast away all
sorts of illusions. The complexity of working-class people, and the issues
they face, became very real to me, and any notion of romanticizing workers went out the window.

I suffered a serious accident at the shipyard, falling 20 feet, but after a
couple of months recovering, I decided it was important for me to return

to work. I remained at the shipyard until I accepted a position as a community organizer.

Community Organizing and Advocacy

Going to work as a paid organizer was a dramatic cultural shift. Now I was an employee of a nonprofit organization formed to demand construction jobs for Boston residents, minorities, and women. This work environment is much more familiar to many of today's younger activists who, upon graduating from college (if they are fortunate enough to attend), decide that their progressive activism can be best served by working as an organizer (or advocate) for a nonprofit organization.

My initial foray into community organizing was, overall, a failure. I never received the sort of training that most people need to be an effective full-time organizer. It was also the case that although many workers were interested in gaining employment in the construction industry, this did not necessarily translate into being willing to organize to fight for such jobs.

What was a success, however, is that I found myself deeply involved in the larger issue of desegregating the Boston construction industry. The history of this industry was a history of the racist exclusion of workers of color. It was also the case that women and Boston city residents found it nearly impossible to gain their fair share of the jobs. Though my experience at the Boston Jobs Coalition—the organization with which I was affiliated—ended after one year, my involvement in the fight for fair employment in the Boston building trades lasted till my family and I left Boston in 1990.

In leaving the Boston Jobs Coalition, I was in a quandary about what to do next. Given my interest in the struggle for equality in the building trades, I offered to volunteer some time to help implement a court decision that formally desegregated a building trades' local of the Ironworkers Union (Local 7). This case was being handled by Greater Boston Legal Services (GBLS). The lead attorney for this case decided that it would be worth bringing me on as a paralegal to assist in the effort. Thus, I went to work at GBLS expecting that I would be there for no more than one to two years. Instead, I stayed for four and a half.

Through my work at GBLS, I ended up not only working on the Ironworkers' case but also went on to involve myself in other employment-related legal matters, including representing individuals at administrative hearings (e.g., unemployment). At about the same time an underlying interest that I had in teaching flowered into an opportunity to become an adjunct faculty member at the University of Massachusetts-Boston (in the program directed toward adults who were returning to get a bachelors' degree). I had designed a class on the history of African American workers, and through the assistance of Local 285 of the Service Employees International Union, I was able to gain access to the college. I went on to teach this class on a regular basis, and in time taught classes in employment discrimination law and unemployment compensation law.

This period of time represented a major fork in the road for me. Because I was very successful as a paralegal, many of my colleagues encouraged me to go on to law school. Although I gave it very serious consideration, I decided against it for reasons that may seem a bit obscure. In my gut I did not want the world to interact with me as a "lawyer." To put it in another way, it was my sense that all too often a professional interacts with the world always wearing the hat of that profession. One is boxed in, in other words. I was not convinced that being a lawyer was to be my defining feature.

Reentering Organized Labor as a Staff Person

The employees at GBLS were represented by two unions, both affiliated with the National Organization of Legal Service Workers (of District 65 of the United Auto Workers). I was elected vice president of the paralegals and administrative staff union and was very active in union affairs.

I was approached by the general organizer for District 65-UAW in the Boston area and asked to take on a position as an organizer for the union. This was not the first time I had been approached by a union, but I decided to accept this offer because (1) I wanted to get more deeply involved in the work of the union movement, and (2) it was clear to me that it was time to move on from GBLS. With regard to reason 2, it is worth saying that my approach toward jobs is to identify what I wish to accomplish, determine how it must be accomplished, and then set about achieving it. Once I believe I have accomplished my goals, it is time for me to identify a new set of objectives for that job *or* it is time to move on. Although I felt that I was accomplishing a good deal at GBLS, particularly with regard to issues related to employment discrimination, I also felt that I needed new challenges.

In the interest of time and space, I will compress my 16 years as a union staff person (serving in District 65–United Auto Workers, the National

Postal Mailhandlers Union, the Service Employees International Union, and the AFL-CIO) into one category and offer some general observations.

My best experience was in the Service Employees International Union, which offered an opportunity to grow and learn. During the time that I served that organization, a team spirit was built up as we grappled with the importance of organizing nonunion workers and building a fighting spirit among our members, often in the face of terrible attacks by employers.

Yet, working in a union is a complicated experience. I have seen far too many individuals enter into the employ of a union believing it to be something close to a panacea. This is disastrous because when reality sinks in, so too may despair and disillusionment. Labor unions are political institutions with members who span the spectrum of political and religious views. They see in the union a vehicle to improve their lives (if they see anything in the union). These members may be racist, sexist, homophobic, or xenophobic, or they may be progressive, if not revolutionary. Working in a labor union means interacting with all sorts and attempting to build unity, while at the same time not appealing to the lowest common denominator.

One of the biggest challenges I faced in my union career was that of being perceived as a threat by many of my White colleagues. The source of the threat could have been anything ranging from my personal politics to the questions I asked, to the fact that Mr. and Mrs. Fletcher did not raise me to be a handkerchief-head. This situation sometimes placed me in a situation where I was not included in the inner circle, where the actual decisions were being made. This is always troubling because it is a reminder that there is no meritocracy in the United States. What one achieves is the result of a combination of one's own talents and abilities, along with one's willingness and skill at organizing one's point of view. This means that in unions, as in other organizations, there is often a glass ceiling that one must confront. This can also force one to move on and seek other employment.

The Current Chapter

I never expected to be offered employment by TransAfrica Forum. When I heard that founding president Randall Robinson was retiring, a number of people encouraged me to apply. I did so, expecting, however, that they would want someone with less radical politics than I serving as the CEO of the organization.

Running a small nonprofit advocacy organization is, as my wife likes to say, *more than a notion.* First, our organization (www.transafricaforum.org) exists to raise awareness in the United States regarding issues facing the nations and peoples of Africa, the Caribbean, and Latin America. As such, our aim is to secure a foreign policy on the part of the United States that advances, rather than retards, the self-determined economic, political, and social development of what has come to be known as the global South. In the current political environment in the United States, this is a difficult task in the face of a set of dominant politics that hail U.S. arrogance and world domination, even at the cost of alienating billions of the world's peoples.

Second, small nonprofits exist only through fund-raising. As became clear when I took over the helm, without constant and vigilant attention to fund-raising, an organization's resources will dry up. This is very different from working in a union, where you have a clear membership base. It also challenges the organization's CEO because the sort of leadership attention that one might wish to give to program development and implementation has to be shared with attention to fund-raising.

Third, and related, in an environment with limited resources, there is never a lack of demand. Nearly every crisis that faces Africa, the Caribbean, and/or Latin America is brought to the steps of TransAfrica Forum with the hope that we will . . . *do something about it . . . ,* even if the *something* is less than clear or focused.

This setting forces one to make some very tough decisions regarding prioritization. Specifically, one learns, as I did years ago, that prioritization is not *mainly* about the order of activities but more about what you in fact choose *not* to do.

No Job or Career Replaces One's Commitment to a Cause

As important as were the various jobs that I took, what has driven me has been my commitment to the cause of social justice. This is very different from those—with all due respect—who have started off with the objective of being a doctor, lawyer, businessperson, or pilot. There have been various jobs that have interested me, but the dominant influences in my life have been how to advance the cause of social justice and how to look out for my family. This has meant choosing *not* to take certain positions (jobs or positions within an organization) because I thought they might be distractions. I do not offer this as some sort of self-tribute but more a statement of fact. I have always wanted my life to have accomplished or attempted to accomplish something more than personal gain. In that light, the choice of a particular job has always been secondary to whether that job helps me move down the right path.

CHAPTER 10

My Journey

RICHARD "RICK" GALLOT

Attorney, State Senator, and
Former State Representative,
Ruston, Louisiana

*Commitment is the one quality above all others that enables a
potential leader to become a successful leader.*

—John C. Maxwell

Commitment has been a major attributable factor to my professional success. While it helps that I had loving parents who instilled strong moral values in me, it has been my commitment to achieving success that has led me down the path that I now travel.

When I look back at my accomplishments, sometimes I am amazed at how exciting this journey has been. That I have been able to achieve a measure of success in my professional endeavors makes my memories of the experiences that I have had along the road traveled even better.

I was born and reared in Grambling, Louisiana, home of Grambling State University, the place where "Everybody is Somebody." Grambling is a city of approximately 5,000 people, 98 percent of whom are black, and it is home to more black PhDs per capita than any other place in the country. Growing up in Grambling provided me with a college-town environment that fostered the expectation of success. My mother, Dr.

Mildred Gauthier Gallot, and my father, Richard Gallot, Sr., are both natives of rural St. Landry Parish in south Louisiana. They both began from very poor and humble beginnings and exemplified what could be achieved through hard work and determination. My mother attended Grambling on an academic scholarship and, upon graduation, began working in the Property Control Department. After earning her master's degree, she began teaching in the History Department. She worked her way up through the departmental ranks, eventually becoming the head of the history department, a post she held until her retirement from Grambling with 44 years of service. My father is a barber by trade and has been a self-employed businessman my entire life. In addition to his barbershop, he has owned and operated gas stations, a café, and a convenience store and has invested in and developed real estate in the Grambling area. My father has always had a very strong interest in politics and has held just about every elected office in the city of Grambling. He has been a city councilman, has been elected to the police jury, has been the mayor of Grambling, and is currently serving as a justice of the peace.

I am the youngest of three children. My eldest sister, Daphne Gallot Knighten, and her husband, Reginald, are both educators in Little Rock, Arkansas, and have three children. My middle sister, Loretta Gallot Lee, and her husband, Terry, live in Bossier City, Louisiana, and have two sons. I have a 13-year-old son, Richard Gallot III, who lives with me in Grambling.

People reading this chapter would undoubtedly say that, based upon my parents' background and the opportunities they were able to afford me, I was destined for success. But I challenge that assertion. No matter what background you come from, you must have the desire to want to be successful, and it has to be your work to secure that success for yourself. Billie Holiday put it best: "Mama may have, Papa may have, but God bless the child that's got his own."

At an early age, I gave much thought to what I wanted to do in life when I grew up. Having worked in all of my parents' businesses, I knew I did not want to run a café or gas station. When I was about 12 years old, I decided that I wanted to be a mortician. Looking back on it, this could be considered somewhat morbid. However, my thinking, for a 12-year-old, was quite methodical. In my area, morticians were well-respected. From all indications, at least in my 12-year-old mind, they made a good living and had money, nice houses, and nice cars—all of the things I wanted. So

I thought I'd be a mortician. When I was about 14, I had the occasion to encounter another professional—an attorney. There were no attorneys in my hometown, and I had never met a black attorney. During a career day at my school, a lawyer was invited to attend. He possessed many of the same characteristics I had observed about the morticians. He was successful, drove a nice car, and had a nice house. Further, he made an honest and good living. That day, I knew I wanted those things and would work to become an attorney, not just because of the material things but also because handling dead bodies would not be involved.

Academics, for the most part, were not difficult for me. I attended the Grambling State University Laboratory schools for my elementary and secondary education. In high school, I was an above-average student, with the exception of math and science. I would have to say that civics was my favorite high school subject. I carry an interest in that subject to this date. After my junior year in high school, I had the opportunity to participate in the High Ability program at Grambling State University, a program where students can earn college credit while still in high school. By the time I started my senior year in high school I had earned nine hours of college credit. My high school career was marked by my strong commitment to high academic achievement. I always had the desire to be ahead of the game.

> *The secret of success in life is for a man to be ready for his time when it comes.*
>
> —Benjamin Disraeli

As a result of my academic preparation, I received a scholarship offer from Dartmouth College in Hanover, New Hampshire. Although the financial support this Ivy League school offered was respectable, it didn't cover all of my expenses. Also, my two sisters were in college. I am sure my parents could probably have covered the expense to send me away to college, but I really didn't want to put them in a position to have to support three children pursing higher education. So, I decided to fulfill my lifelong dream of attending Grambling State University to be a member of the World-Famed Tiger Marching Band. The decision to attend Grambling State University was perhaps one of the best decisions I have made. This one decision prepared me for the future in more ways than I could ever venture to share in this short chapter. I have often said that if you can survive the registration process at Grambling, there is absolutely nothing in this life that you cannot do.

In addition to participating in the band, I fulfilled another dream of becoming a member of Kappa Alpha Psi Fraternity, Inc. Many of the young men from my hometown that I looked up to, and who had proven to be very successful in college life and beyond, were Kappas. During my pledge period, I learned many lessons of trial and triumph. I witnessed and experienced the value of being "my brother's keeper." The lessons learned and the friendships made have been an integral part of the man I am today.

During the spring of my junior year in college, as was the custom during that time, I visited with the dean for an evaluation of the curriculum to determine what courses I needed to take in order to graduate. To my surprise, it was determined that I could graduate during the upcoming summer if I signed up for a trip sponsored by the foreign language department at Grambling, where I would travel to Mexico and participate in several intensive courses. The chance to travel to a foreign country was an opportunity I did not want to pass up. I did participate in the Mexico trip, returned for summer school, and graduated from Grambling State University with a bachelor's degree in history in three years.

At 14 years of age, I identified my chosen profession, and I still had this as a goal on my horizon. However, before deciding which law school I would attend, I had the opportunity to participate in a program designed for minority students interested in attending law school. The program was hosted by a predominantly White university. On the first day of the program, the chancellor addressed the group and, in a matter-of-fact manner, informed us that only one-third of the minority applicants to the university were capable of doing work at the law school level. For many of those sitting around me, there was grave concern. I was one of those students who would not be accepted by that university, but I didn't let that deter me from my goal. I knew who I was and what I was capable of. It would take more than this narrow-minded law school chancellor to derail my goals, dreams, and aspirations.

After much thought and deliberation, I decided to attend Southern University's School of Law. My main area of concern was Southern's historically low rate of students passing the bar exam. I was concerned that if I got a degree from Southern, but couldn't pass the bar, I would have wasted three precious years of my life. My sister Daphne helped put it in perspective for me by saying, "If you don't pass the bar, it's your fault, not Southern's." So it was off to Southern University.

I can recall my first year of law school. There I was, a 21-year-old law student with the hopes and dreams of being the next Matlock or Perry Mason. On my first day of property law class, in walks Professor Harris. With his heavy Cajun accent, he asked, "Why are you here?" He then said, "You don't belong here. You are wasting somebody's money—your mama's, daddy's, Uncle Sam's. Some of you ladies should be at home having babies and raising families, and some of you men need to be out selling cars or farming. You don't belong here!" Of course, I thought he was talking to me, although I knew nothing about selling cars or farming. After I got over the initial shock of my professor telling me that I didn't belong in law school, common sense stepped in and I concluded that he wasn't trying to convince any of us to drop out. Rather, it was a reality check. It was his way of getting our undivided attention and causing us to reaffirm why we were there and causing us to focus on our seriousness of purpose. He was reminding us that if we weren't serious about what we were doing, there were alternatives. Needless to say, Professor Harris wasn't talking to me, and I did earn my juris doctorate degree from Southern.

After graduation, I spent the next six weeks studying 8 to 10 hours per day preparing for the bar exam. During the last two weeks of preparation, I studied between 14 and 16 hours per day. I took the bar exam in late July 1990. It was then time to play the waiting game for the next two months, awaiting my results.

I returned to Grambling while awaiting my bar results. Although I had no concrete plans at this point, I envisioned my stay being temporary. In the meantime, I accepted a position as an adjunct professor in the history and criminal justice departments at my alma mater. My acceptance of this position provided me with the opportunity to give something back to the place that had given so much to my family and me. I enjoyed challenging my students and pushing them to exercise their intellectual muscles. My desire was for students to leave my course feeling that I had cared about their academic achievement, so I stayed after class, extended my office hours, and gave additional help where it was needed. I truly enjoyed teaching, although the pay left a lot to be desired.

On September 21, 1990, I received my results that I had passed the Louisiana Bar Examination. Coincidentally, this was the date that my first nephew (my parents' first grandchild) was born. I was sworn in to practice law in the state of Louisiana on October 5, 1990. I continued to teach for three more semesters. My law practice started to grow, and I started to establish a reputation in my community for doing good. In addition to my ability to practice law in Louisiana, I was further admitted to practice before the Eastern, Middle and Western Districts of Louisiana and the Southern District of Alabama, United States District Courts. I was also admitted to practice before the Fifth and Eleventh Circuit Courts of Appeal and the Supreme Court of the United States.

As I learned about issues that were important to my region of the state, and as my interest in civics had always been so great, after giving it much thought, I tossed my name into the Grambling city council election. At 28 years of age, I was elected to the city council of Grambling, a position I held for four years. During that time, I fought and voted for what I believed was right. Although my position was sometimes not one that was popular, I firmly believed that, in my role on the city council, I took the side for what was right for the community. During the final year of my term, a vacancy occurred in the Ruston City Court when the sitting judge was appointed to the United States District Court. I decided not to seek reelection to the city council in anticipation of running for judge.

The upcoming judicial race would be the first contested election for this position in more than 20 years. It would also be the first time a minority had ever run for judge in the history of Lincoln Parish. When I decided to run, there were a lot of naysayers who didn't think I could do it. What was most surprising to me was the fact that there were elected officials that I had supported in their races who would not openly support me in this race. Other people who supported me expressed concern that running in this election would mean an end to my political career before it actually began. One even went so far as to predict that I would get my teeth kicked in the election. Others believed I would upset the good old boys and that this could not be good for my career. I knew I could do this job, and in my opinion, I thought I could do it better than others who expressed an interest in running. Four entered the race, and I came in second in the primary. In the runoff, I lost by approximately 500 votes. Although I didn't win this election, a number of positives came out of it that I could be proud of. First, I ran a clean race. I didn't engage in any negative campaigning. I stuck to the issues. Second, I received 25 percent of the crossover votes, which definitely showed that progress was being made in our community.

For some people, race was not a factor, but my qualifications were. It was a good election and a great learning experience.

In August 2000, the state representative for the district in which I live, Representative Pinkie Wilkerson, lost her life in an automobile accident. Before this unfortunate tragedy, I had never considered seeking a seat in the Louisiana Legislature. As the news of her untimely death spread, many wondered who would run to fill the seat. Because I had just run in a highly publicized race in the previous year, my name began to surface as a potential candidate. After giving it much thought and prayer, I decided to throw my hat in the ring and run in the special election being held in October 2000.

The lessons learned in the previous year's election made it very easy to hit the ground running. I had more than 2,000 signs left over from the judge's race, so rather than purchasing new signs, I had stickers printed to cover "Judge" with "State Representative." This not only saved thousands of dollars, but it enabled me to get campaign signs out across the district while my opponents were still trying to get their signs designed and printed. There were many other organizational advantages that made it possible for me to run a much better campaign than my opponents. On election night, I led the field of four candidates with 58 percent of the vote, which enabled me to avoid a runoff and win in the primary.

In my second term in the Louisiana House of Representatives, I was reelected in 2003 without opposition. I served as vice chairman of the House and Governmental Affairs Committee and was a member of the Judiciary and Civil Law Committees.

A recent event provided me with the opportunity to get an Ivy League experience, albeit 20 years later than my initial opportunity. In the summer of 2003, I attended the Senior Executives in State and Local Government Program at the John F. Kennedy School of Government at Harvard University. This three-week program was attended by 67 state and local elected and appointed officials from all across the United States, from California to Maine, Alaska, and Hawaii. The program was also attended by officials from Australia and Ireland. During the program, we explored the relationships between citizens and government, studied the ethical and professional responsibilities of those in leadership, and exchanged ideas and discussed policy issues with Harvard faculty and with one another. It was truly an experience of a lifetime and I often refer back to coursework and case studies when analyzing policy and governmental issues.

In 2007, I won my third term in the Louisiana House of Representatives. Ineligible to run for a fourth term, I ran for Louisiana state senator in District 29 in 2011 and was elected.

> When I was young I was sure of everything; in a few years, having
> been mistaken a thousand times, I was not half so sure of most
> things as I was before; at present, I am hardly sure of anything but
> what God has revealed to me.
>
> —John Wesley

As I reflect on my political career, I have always felt guided by a divine sense of purpose. Whether it was coincidence or not, two significant occurrences lead me to believe I am thus far on the right track. Two weeks before the judge's election, I was in church and the message was centered on the idea that sometimes in life we ask for things, and when we don't get them, we think God has turned his back on us or we are somehow not in his favor. However, not everything we ask for is meant for us and God has a plan for us all. I lost the judge's race, but based on the sermon, I believed God had something else in store for me. Two weeks before the legislative race, the sermon centered on the fact that God has a calling and a ministry for us all and that it is important for us to be obedient to the calling and to do the very best we can in all those things God has sent us to do. I won the legislative election and have made it my daily mission to be the best steward that God and my constituents have entrusted me to be. The only way I know to approach this task is with a moral compass to help guide my way. This isn't about church or religion. Rather, it's about an internal, spiritual tool that always leads me to do what is good, to do what is decent, and to do what is proper.

CHAPTER 11

"Virago" from *Lift Every Voice*

LANI GUINIER

Bennett Boskey Professor of Law,
Harvard Law School,
Harvard University,
Cambridge, Massachusetts

Lani Guinier, the first Black American woman to be appointed to a tenured professorship at Harvard Law School, was motivated at a young age by Constance Baker Motley, the first African American woman elected to the New York State Senate and the first African American woman to be named to a federal bench. Following in Baker Motley's footsteps, Guinier joined the NAACP Legal Defense Fund (LDF). In the 1980s, she headed LDF's Voting Rights program, litigating cases throughout the South.

She had been a civil rights attorney for more than 10 years and had served in the Civil Rights Division during the Carter administration as special assistant to then assistant attorney general Drew S. Days when President Clinton nominated Guinier to be the first black woman to head the Civil Rights Division of the Department of Justice in 1993. Immediately after her name was put forward, opponents to her nomination attacked Guinier's maverick views on democracy and voting. Clinton withdrew her nomination before a confirmation hearing. Since then, Guinier has used varied public platforms to speak out on issues of race, gender, and democratic decision making and to call for open public discourse on these issues.

Lani Guinier, *Lift Every Voice*: *Turning a Civil Rights Setback into a New Vision of Social Justice*. Simon & Schuster, 1998. Used by permission.

Before joining the Harvard Law School faculty, Guinier was a tenured professor at the University of Pennsylvania for 10 years. At Harvard, Guinier teaches courses on professional responsibility for public lawyers, law and the political process, and perspectives on race, gender, class, and social change.

Guinier is the author of numerous articles on democratic theory, political representation, educational equity and issues of race and gender. Guinier received her bachelor's degree from Radcliffe College in 1971 and graduated from Yale University Law School in 1974.

Dr. Guinier, during several conversations about her autobiographical chapter, recommended that excerpts from her book *Lift Every Voice: Turning a Civil Rights Setback into a New Vision of Social Justice* be used. In particular, she suggested that we use the excerpt from chapter 2 presented here because it sheds light on her career success.

* * *

VI-RA'GO, vai-re'go or vi-ra'go (xiii) n.

1) bold, impudent, turbulent woman; termagant; vixen

2) [Archaic] a female warrior

        —*A Standard Dictionary of the English Language,*

        Funk & Wagnalls (1908)

My picture, stern-faced and grim, confused even my mother, who called me from Boston to report, "Lani, someone is using your name. I see your picture in the paper but I don't recognize you." I didn't recognize myself.

I was being humiliated by words and condemned to wordless silence simultaneously. This passive spectre was not how my parents, Ewart and Eugenia Guinier, had raised me to be. But while my parents had managed wordlessly to make me understand just who I am, their message involved the use of words: Listen carefully to those who know more, whether simple folk or polished intellects, learn from rather than internalize criticism, develop allies, then speak truth to power. Those were the lessons of my childhood: passivity was not a good strategy for leadership unless it is tied to resistance and grounded in common struggle. Those who triumphed were those engaged in spirited action.

In my father's case, he never spelled out this strategy affirmatively. He used stories instead. My sisters and I would sit for hours while he regaled us with richly remembered vignettes. We begged him over and over again,

"Tell us the story of when you were a little boy." These were our bedtime stories. He never read to us.

His stories, chockfull of details about scarcity and making do without enough money, were uplifting tales of triumph. Almost everyone in them, from his childhood in Linsted, Jamaica, to his coming of age during the depression after leaving Harvard College, was black. They were poor; they were decent; they were survivors.

We knew most of the stories by heart, but hearing his voice recount his own living was magical. My father was grateful for our rapt attention, even though we never hesitated to interrupt him when he strayed off course. He would not, however, be rushed. If his audience got too impatient, he knew how to slow us down. Whenever I or one of my sisters asked something he could not answer, or tried to push him too fast in his recitation, he would immediately chasten us with an old ditty from Jamaica. Especially if we were so rude as to question his most recent version by asking, "Why?" meaning, "Why aren't you telling us what you said last night?" he would quickly recite: "Y is a crooked letter, cut off the tail, leaves V." Gaining steam, with obvious gusto my father would continue the singsong, "V stands for Virago," and with his finger pointing at his interrogator, "just like you!"

As a child, I never heard anyone else use the term "Virago." Nor did I ask my father what it meant. I just knew that a Virago was some kind of rascal or rapscallion. I surmised that a Virago was a loving but nettlesome troublemaker. My father called us Virago—Virago must be wonderful! Yet, for some, I have since learned, Virago is a negative term, closer to churlish shrew than courageous combatant. But for me, a Virago was someone admirable, someone who would not let anyone get away with lazy or loose arguments.

Not all of my father's stories were uplifting.

My father's mother, my Nana, Marie-Louise Beresford Guinier French, had left the West Indies, and her three oldest children, including my father, who was raised by several different relatives, including his great-aunt Sarah. My father's father had been a timekeeper on the Panama Canal. He left his family to study to become a barrister in England; he died in London of pneumonia when my father was six. My father's mother remarried and emigrated to Boston with her second husband, with whom she had five more children. She left my father, his older brother, and a younger sister to live with relatives in Kingston. My father had not seen his mother in many years when, in 1925, alone, he emigrated to Boston to join her. He was fifteen years old.

After an exemplary record at Boston's English High, my father applied to college in 1929. In the early spring, he received a letter from Dartmouth, admitting him with a full scholarship—board, room, and tuition. A little later, he got a letter from Harvard, also admitting him, but without any scholarship at all. He was denied scholarship aid upon admission, he was told, because he had not submitted a photograph with his application. This, he later discovered, was a ruse to discourage his matriculation; Harvard had already admitted a black applicant from Cambridge, inadvertently exceeding its informal quota of one black per class.

Harvard had a policy that all freshmen had to live in the dormitories on campus. This "house system" was designed to deepen the educational experience. The housemasters were generally scholars of some renown; besides teaching, they had the responsibility of setting a tone for the house, encouraging those who did well to do better, and keeping an eye out for students who might have some problems adjusting to the particular Harvard atmosphere. You could only be excused from campus residence by making a written application and giving a good reason, such as poor health.

My father wanted to live on campus. As he told an interviewer later in his life:

> I thought that with the money I had saved from working on the boats, and the prize money I had won at [high school] graduation, and a loan from Harvard, that I could, with careful management, pay the full tuition and room and board for my freshman year, so I did not apply for a waiver of the residence requirement. Besides, I *wanted* to live in the dormitories with all other freshmen. But, in the middle of the summer, I got a letter from Harvard stating that I "had been granted permission to live at home."
>
> By this time I had refused the offer from Dartmouth, and had no way to locate my counselor to seek his advice. In fact, there was no one I could turn to—so I just accepted the situation, and planned to commute from Roxbury as a day student. Had I only known. In a residential college like Harvard, even the white day students were isolated, and the Black freshmen (all two of us) would become invisible.

He made no request to be excused from campus residence. Yet he was not permitted to reside in the Harvard dormitories because they were segregated in the 1920s. Only one or two blacks, including the son of a black U.S. senator, had ever been allowed to live in the campus residences at the time my father applied. According to the Harvard *Alumni Bulletin* of 1923, the official policy was one in which "men of white and colored races shall not be compelled to live and eat together, nor shall any man be excluded by reason of his color." Notwithstanding the official policy, at least six black men were in fact excluded from the dormitories before my father enrolled, including Roscoe Conkling Bruce, Jr., a grandson of Blanche K. Bruce, the U.S. senator from Mississippi in 1875–81. Roscoe Bruce, Sr. (Blanche K. Bruce's only child), had graduated from Harvard, Class of 1902, and twenty years later, in 1923, he wrote to Harvard president A. Lawrence Lowell complaining that his son, Roscoe Bruce, Jr., was not allowed to live in the freshman dorms where residence had recently been made compulsory.

During my father's enrollment in 1929–1931, much of his time on campus was spent alone. Few would speak to him, including upperclass Harvard students he had known previously as classmates in high school:

> During the first week of classes in September, I attended the freshman assembly at which Harvard President A. Lawrence Lowell spoke. There seemed to be a thousand people in the hall. I was the only Black. As we left the meeting I could hear conversations being started all around me,—but no one looked me in the eye; no one spoke to me. As I walked toward a group, they would move away.
>
> I went to the library that was designated for freshmen. The student from English High who, like me, had won the coveted Comstock Prize the previous year was at the desk. I remembered him, and proudly went up and told him that I had followed in his footsteps. He looked somewhere above my head, gave no response, and finally asked, "What books do you want?" He went and got the books, and then turned to the next person.

My father drew a sharp contrast with his other interracial interactions:

> There simply were no rewards [at Harvard] for working hard. No instructor ever called on me to speak in class; no student ever initiated a conversation about the course work, or anything else. Even though Roxbury was no model of integration in those days—or today, for that matter—still my life had included normal interactions with the

white people around me. At English High, although I was certainly in a minority, there was no overt hostility on the part of either the white students or the teachers. To the contrary, I had been rewarded for working hard, and had been chosen for leadership positions.

The first person to welcome him to Harvard upon his arrival, and one of the only people to speak willingly, was a man he met at the Coop, the large bookstore where all the students bought their textbooks:

When I went into the Coop and was looking for the right counter, I caught the eye of another Black man,—we were the only two Black people in a milling sea of white students crowding around the counters. This man, all dressed up and looking like a successful businessman, made his way over to me, and said, "Welcome to Harvard!" It was Ralph Bunche.

Bunche was in his last year at the Graduate School, and was probably at least seven years older than I. He was the first person who spoke to me voluntarily, and gave me some sense of community and connection with Harvard. We talked a little, and he suggested that I try to get a job waiting on tables at one of the private student eating clubs. At Harvard, these clubs take the place of fraternities. They were (and still are today) organized for the elite, and naturally did not admit Blacks as members, only as waiters and kitchen help.

These clubs usually had two older Black men in charge, a chef and chief steward who worked full time. The rest of us were all waiters, and all Black. There wasn't much money attached, although sometimes the white boys would give us a tip, but there were the meals which was almost the same as money, and some sense of companionship. Some of the other Black students, mostly students in one of the graduate schools, would stop around, and we would play cards. I didn't win a lot, but I didn't lose either, and whatever extra money I got was very helpful. But it is ironic, isn't it, that we had to create the only supportive mechanism to help Black students adjust to the university in the kitchens of the white boys' clubs.

These early experiences affected my father's entire life, and, as I was to learn in 1993, my life as well. They became the stock story of my youth; Try hard, aim high, but don't be surprised if the bogey of racism gets there first.

My father did not save his stories for his daughters' bedtime ritual. He shared them publicly. They were his gift to an audience, and he was a generous man. He used his stories to engage his listeners in the intricacies of logical arguments that became absolutely compelling because of his own passionate commitment to them. He was energized by an audience. He never hesitated to speak out in support of his progressive agenda, even at moments when others, with less courage and more wisdom, might have opted for silence.

For example, during the 1949 elections for the Borough of Manhattan presidency, my father was chosen on behalf of the American Labor Party (ALP). The ALP picked him as a likely winner because of his wide constituency in the labor movement and among black civic and fraternal organizations. I believe that my father was chosen to run for Manhattan borough president, the first black candidate ever to compete for that office, for an additional reason. Ewart Guinier was a forceful and spirited public speaker. Soon after his candidacy, my father gave testimony to a U.S. Senate committee, as International Secretary of the United Public Workers CIO in New York City. On several occasions the senators conducting the hearing told him to calm down; he should not be quite so animated when answering questions. After being admonished to lower his voice by Senator Ferguson, my father responded:

> . . . [I]f I may seem to be a bit moved about this, it is because of the hell I have been through because I am a Negro. . . .
>
> In Washington, I could not sleep in the hotel because of the filthy Jim Crow system here. I came here Friday and could not find a place to stay. . . . I cannot even eat in this building in your cafeteria. Why not look into that?
>
> Talk about clear and present danger. Congress is looking all over the world for clear and present danger, and the danger is right under Congress' nose. Is Congress going to want me to help go look over the world when dangers that I suffer burn the guts out of me every day?
>
> I volunteered for the infantry in the last war and went to Alabama and I would like you to know that the first day that I went to Fort McClellan, I had to go to the United States Government post office to buy stamps to write home and I was fearful because I did not know the kind of reception I would get because I was Jim Crowed on my way there.

I had volunteered and I was ready to give my life for my country and yet I do not feel that I had the protection when I was in Alabama.

He then continued:

... I stand against lynching, I am against the poll tax, for the FEPC legislation, I stand against covenants, and for full equality for Negroes in every stand of life, and I want that, and I do not want to wait a thousand years for it.

I think Negroes are full-fledged American citizens and should have all the rights of American citizens and should have it today.

By his example, my father taught me to be dignified in the face of great adversity. He had become a U.S. citizen, fought a war on behalf of his adopted country, and yet never felt fully acknowledged or respected, as even a human being. He suffered so many more profound indignities than I, and yet managed to step above them. He was never bitter. I could not be bitter, either. My father was shunned by his classmates at Harvard. I was shunned by my law school friends in the White House. My father was unprepared for the overt hostility he confronted among his college peers, in part because his prior interracial contact had been relatively comfortable, if not rewarding. I too found myself shocked by the torrent of criticism and hostility that rained down on me in the spring of 1993. Just as my father, during his two years at Harvard College, felt invisible, I too found myself disappearing in Washington, D.C., in the spring of 1993. But having been "invisible" as a college undergraduate, Ewart Guinier never again let himself be silenced.

My mother, Eugenia, helped me in that lesson, too. My mother was not religious, but she conveyed a sense of the Jewish immigrant experience through vivid accounts of growing up in New York. Her parents started with a small delicatessen on the Grand Concourse in the Bronx that they eventually developed into a catering business and restaurant. As a young girl of five, my mother was often put in charge of her brother, two and a half years younger. Her parents worked fifteen- to eighteen-hour days. Her father would come home to fix his two children dinner and then to tell my mother and her younger brother bedtime stories. After tucking them in, he cautioned my mother not to leave the cramped apartment; if she needed something, she should knock on the dumbwaiter and a neighbor would come upstairs. My mother's parents were never home at the same time.

Her family never sat down to dinner as a family unless they were eating at my grandparents' restaurant.

As a young girl, I adored the *All-of-a-Kind Family* books—the children's series about a New York Jewish family by Sidney [sic] Taylor—partly because they mirrored tales my mother told me about her own experiences.

I remember fondly the stories my mother would read to me about Jewish history.

The story of Moses, in particular, always inspired me. I admired the fact that Jews were once slaves, resisted slavery, and became free. The story of Jewish resistance to oppression early on defined my narrative of justice. The terrors of Hitler and Nazi Germany were still quite real to a young girl in the 1950s. My parents had met during World War II, when my father was stationed in Hawaii and my mother was sent there as an American Red Cross volunteer.

My parents never let us forget Hitler's atrocities. My most intense memories of being nine years old came from a lazy summer afternoon when our sixteen-year-old cousin, Sheila, led my six-year-old sister and me into an empty cabin next door to ours, at the bungalow colony where my mother was day camp director. We sat on the floor in a spare room devoid even of furniture.

For several hours my cousin, who had just seen the movie of *The Diary of Anne Frank,* reconstructed, scene by scene, the awful agony of Anne's vigil. Thereafter, haunted by the harrowing images this graphic retelling had planted, I became consumed with the game of "tents." Over and over, under upside-down chairs draped with tablecloths or curtains that were handed down to us from our grandparents' restaurant, we constructed safe houses. We were hiding out from the Nazis. We were in fear of persecution—that was an ongoing dramatic narrative for us.

I could have easily been hiding from the Ku Klux Klan as well, but in our fantasies, we were never pursued by southern racists. No, it was always the Nazis who were on our trail.

My mother's stories taught me to endure slights without becoming enraged. She was often more direct, however, than her stories. When the white kids in Catholic school who lived across the street from us picked on me, my mother did not allow me to dwell on the insults. Instead, she told me, put yourself in their shoes, replay the situation through their eyes. Perhaps they were jealous, not merely prejudiced. They hadn't skipped a grade as I had, so they had to show me up on their terms. "Don't see your-self as a victim," she reminded me. "But maybe you should just not play with them."

When I was in elementary school, I would proudly display my report card to my parents. My father would delight with me in my achievement. He burst with pride, showing off my excellent report card to anyone who happened by. My mother would glance at my good grades and make a brief, casual comment: "That's nice, Lani." She would then turn to me and focus her gaze directly on mine. Certain she had my full attention, she would ask, "But how many friends do you have?" Having changed the subject, she would continue, "Let's talk about your friends."

For my father, it was enough for me to achieve in his image. To my mother, it was more important that I develop healthy relationships with my peers. She schooled me diligently in the lessons that nothing you do by yourself or to benefit only yourself really matters. Any achievements must be measured or balanced by their ability to enhance good deeds. I might be a Virago, but I must be one in pursuit of a larger agenda than my own accomplishments.

We lived in a neighborhood that changed with our arrival—Italians, Jews, Albanians, Armenians, and Portuguese had been living side by side when we moved to Hollis in 1956. Working-class, white ethnics lived in neat, tiny two-family attached houses on both sides of the street. By 1964, there were almost no whites still living on our block except my mother. As the demographics changed, so did our zip code. We were now St. Albans, part of the burgeoning black migration from Harlem and Bed-ford-Stuyvesant to southeast Queens.

We celebrated holidays with families on both sides, but never together. Each side of the family had their own traditions and customs. My moth-er's brother had become a successful entrepreneur, catapulting himself and his family into an exclusive cul-de-sac of upper-middle-class Long Island. He took advantage of his parents' eventual commercial success and became an even more successful real estate developer. Uncle Mur-ray and his family lived in a huge, well-decorated house he built in Great Neck, a predominantly Jewish suburb of New York City. They took winter vacations, played tennis all year round. I remember many wonderful times attending my cousins' bar and bat mitzvahs and family seders, where the sheer quantity of food never ceased to amaze me.

Uncle Murray and his children were always friendly. They welcomed my sisters and me when we came to visit. I don't remember, however, any intimate conversations with my cousins or spending extended periods of time together. We were accepted as family. Our presence made any gathering more colorful, even exotic. But we never pushed our way beyond the outer circle of blood relatives. We were definitely related, but something was held back on both sides.

My cousins on my mother's side visited us two or three times a year. They never said so directly, but within moments of their arrival, the carpeting in our tiny living room suddenly seemed especially frayed; in the few minutes after we greeted them, their presence dwarfed even the physical size of our house, which seemed to shrink, under their scrutiny, from a cottage to a cave. They were always amicable, but I secretly harbored the impression that my cousins felt sorry for us.

My mother's parents, both immigrants from Eastern Europe, were extraordinarily generous with their money. They bought my parents a car; they paid for the braces on my teeth; a savings account they established helped support me in law school. When my parents went to purchase the car, a black Rambler station wagon, with money given to them by my mother's father, they could only go to one dealership—the one my grandfather selected. My braces had to be fitted by an orthodontist they knew. We were grateful, of course, for the additional resources. But I was never quite comfortable enjoying their largesse; it felt too much like charity.

Sometimes their comments betrayed their profound confusion about having a darker-skinned grandchild. Even though he made his considerable living as a shopkeeper, a businessman, a man who worked with money rather than ideas, my maternal grandfather, Grandpa Phil, fancied himself an intellectual. His father had been a rabbi; he was much better educated than my grandmother, who dropped out of elementary school. His Russian heritage was superior in his mind to her Polish roots. Grandpa Phil was well-read, even cosmopolitan. He always challenged me to recite the populations of California and New York, to show what I had learned in school.

When I was little, Grandpa Phil, a funny, outgoing, and very proud man, would sometimes give me baths. He inevitably would end the bath by saying, "Lani, I don't know what it is; I scrub and scrub. You are still dirty. I scrub your elbows and knees, but I never get them clean." He wasn't being malicious. He was making an observation from his limited perspective, but it hurt, nevertheless. I loved him, but his ignorance defined our relationship for me much more than his witty banter about statistics.

My maternal grandmother, Grandma Molly, a quietly assertive, dignified woman would offer me fashion advice. She used to tell me that I should never wear black. "You are too dark, Lani, to wear dark colors," she would admonish me. Black, especially, would only accentuate my darkness.

The daughter of a Jewish mother and a black father, I was only eight or nine at the time. I didn't call myself "black" then. I would say, if asked, "Mother is white and my father is Negro." Or, "I come from a 'mixed' family." My sisters and I were "bridge people," my mother would tell us. We were children who lived in two worlds, but came from no one place. We spanned the experiences of two families of immigrants—Eastern European Jews and West Indian blacks. We were neither black nor white back then: we were interracial.

My parents named me after the woman who had helped them get to know each other in Hawaii. Iwalani Smith Mottl was the eldest daughter of an African American couple, Nolle R. Smith, a rancher's son who migrated to Hawaii from Wyoming in 1915, and Eva B. Jones, a classical music teacher from San Francisco. They raised three daughters and a son steeped in polyglot, multiracial Hawaii. The atmosphere there was so far ahead of its time that Nolle Smith was elected to the Hawaiian legislature in 1929 and eventually became a prominent black statesman and diplomat.

My mom worried that mainland Americans would butcher the name "Iwalani" (pronounced "Eva-Lonnie"), so she named me Carol Lani. But soon well-meaning friends were calling me Carol Loonie or Carolina. Determined to reinforce the romantic and multicultural possibilities she had seen in Hawaii, my mother quickly shortened my name to Lani. Little did she know that Lani, which in Hawaiian means "Heavenly" and signifies great dignity, would later become the object of so much public ridicule.

I may have been taught by my parents that I was interracial, but in junior high school, I became black. The interracial hedge no longer sufficed. The neighborhood of St. Albans that we lived in had long since "tipped," and was then almost entirely black. I took a school bus to a magnet school, Junior High 59, which also attracted a large number of Jewish students from Laurelton and Italian kids from Cambria Heights. The white students were friendly during the school day, but it was the black students who made me feel welcome, especially after classes let out in the afternoon. They considered me one of them. We shared secrets; nothing was held back. I rode the bus home with them to my increasingly segregated St. Albans neighborhood. The other black students and I not only boarded the bus together; they invited me to their parties and their homes.

We all ate lunch together, blacks and whites, Italians and Jews, Japanese and Chinese. But when we left school we walked our separate ways to go to our different buses; that was the end of the socializing. Some of the white kids did call me on the phone and we would talk about schoolwork. But they never invited me to visit them in their homes. That was the way it was. Nothing special was happening to me. It felt natural.

I may have looked strange or foreign. I may have had an unfamiliar name; but what was important was that I did not look white. A clean color line was drawn both because of where I lived and how I looked.

Even earlier, I had noticed the difference between being cherished with tight hugs and loving embraces by my father's family and being loved from a distance by my mother's relatives. I was special when I went to visit my father's family. All of us were. My sisters and I were fawned over and exclaimed upon. My father's mother and his sister and brothers doted upon us. I drew emotionally close to my father's people; their culture became my identity. I wanted to be affirmed, not just acknowledged. I was also by then exhausted by the challenge of belonging nowhere in particular.

When asked, as I frequently am, "Why do you call yourself black?" I say, I am a black woman whose Jewish mother taught me about the Holocaust and about slavery. I am a black woman who grew up "black" because that was how others saw me and because it was black people who embraced my mother when she married my father in 1945. I am a black woman who grew up celebrating both Passover and Easter, and who still occasionally sprinkles Yiddish words in my speech.

I am a black woman whose parents—both parents—introduced me to my heroes, people who resisted injustice, people like Sojourner Truth and Harriet Tubman, Frederick Douglass and W. E. B. DuBois. Both my parents educated me and helped expose me to different cultures and perspectives, but it was my black father's experiences with discrimination that provided the organizing story of my life.

As a child, I lived in a small house on a narrow street in a working-class neighborhood in Queens. I went to integrated public schools on triple session and then became one of only twelve black women in the entering class at Radcliffe College. I grew up with little money, yet I have the benefit of an elite education at both Radcliffe College and Yale Law School.

I have an unusual perspective, I admit. I grew up learning to be both outsider and insider.

* * *

I was twelve years old when I first thought about becoming a civil rights lawyer. It was September 1962. Constance Baker Motley was on the television news, escorting a black man named James Meredith into a building of the University of Mississippi. Meredith was about to become the first black to attend that school. The cameras looked out from the doors of the building as Motley and Meredith walked calmly up the stairs and through a howling white mob in order to register for classes. Or so I remember. I could be wrong, but what I did know was that Constance Baker Motley was a black woman lawyer working for the NAACP Legal Defense Fund.

I don't remember anything that Attorney Motley might have said. I don't know that I even watched her speak. It was her erect and imposing figure that caught my notice. Her proud image spoke to me. Her stately bearing said it all. She was a large-boned woman, but it was less her size than her manner. She did not flinch even as the crowd yelled epithets. She was flanked by U.S. Marshals, as I remember, but she could, for all I cared, have been alone. She was that determined.

I thought: I can do that. I can be a civil rights lawyer.

Ten years later, I was in law school. I rented an apartment on the third floor of a small frame house on Garden Street in New Haven, within walking distance of Yale Law School. It was an apartment passed down through the years from one black woman to another. I never wondered why this particular apartment, except that my friend Nancy had lived there and she got the apartment from another black woman who had lived there before her. It was a modest one-bedroom in which the kitchen was the only room that allowed me to stand tall next to any of the walls. The rest of the rooms were built under one sloping eave or another of the roof.

The landlords were a friendly black couple who arranged the lease to attract students; they did not charge rent during the summer months when they assumed the apartment would be unoccupied. One day the landlady pointed out a big, heavy metal hook on the back door. "That was what

Constance Baker Motley's father used," she explained to me. "Used for what?" I asked. "When Connie or her sister came home after curfew, he would latch the door so they couldn't get in without waking him up."

Every time I saw that latch, it spoke to me. It made me just a little more certain about my destiny. After all, I was living in the third floor of the house where Constance Baker Motley grew up in New Haven as a young girl. On some small scale I was following in Connie Motley's footsteps. She had been a legal pioneer—the only woman lawyer to work for Thurgood Marshall when he was head of the NAACP Legal Defense Fund. I was not a pioneer like Constance Motley. But I was in law school to do what she did: I was going to be a civil rights lawyer.

Becoming a civil rights lawyer would require determination to pursue justice despite the names an angry mob might call you. It would require a passion, not just a mission. For me, that passion came from a belief in the merits of my arguments and in the humanity of my clients. It also stemmed from the abiding conviction that freedom for blacks would bring freedom to whites as well. If we ended the hypocrisy between what America said and what it did for blacks, it would ease the gap between what we said and did for everyone.

That peculiar hypocrisy had plagued me for a long time. I can remember asking Mrs. Buxton, my fourth-grade teacher, how Thomas Jefferson and George Washington could have owned slaves and also could have been true to the Declaration of Independence and the U.S. Constitution. Mrs. Buxton did not take my question very seriously, but when I repeated it that night to my parents, they did. I experienced the disconnection between what the founders said and what they did as an epiphany. My fourth-grade lesson was ultimately a lesson in democracy. I realized that, despite Mrs. Buxton's reticence, real democracy required thinking about questions that did not occur to others. Becoming a civil rights lawyer, in retrospect, was critical to bridging that early gap.

I had another, more personal reason. I became a civil rights lawyer to vindicate my father's life. I had witnessed the way that institutional power, often marshaled on behalf of elites, had been used to isolate and humiliate my own father. I had internalized his stories of discrimination, starting with his banishment because of his color from the freshman dorms at Harvard, and continuing with his humiliation, for the same reason, as an elevator operator for *The New York Times* who could not even show his face on certain floors.

Not all of my information arrived in second-hand bedtime stories. I had also personally witnessed some of the ways my father suffered because of his color. He lived through the mid- to late 1950s as an outcast, punished during the height of McCarthyism because his union had refused, on First Amendment and freedom of association grounds, to expel members who were Communist. As far as I knew, my father was not a Communist, but he taught me to respect the dignity and commitment to workingmen and –women of those who were. In order to support his family, he buried his intellectual gifts and fighting spirit, selling real estate and insurance to upwardly mobile working-class blacks in Queens. Thinking he might have more independence as a lawyer than a union official, he attended NYU Law School at night and easily passed the difficult New York Bar exam even as he worked full time; but the committee of the bar nevertheless denied him a license to practice law because, they said, he had "bad character."

My father was a brilliant man, who might have been a legendary lawyer. He had all of the tools—intelligence, determination, a sparkling wit, a masterful capacity to hold an audience spellbound both as a story-teller and orator, and a passion for justice. He also had one too many deficits. As a Harvard law professor, Derrick Bell, once said about himself, he paid the price for being a black man who was not grateful enough. Like my father, Professor Bell was defiant. He demanded respect. He was given a few opportunities but never accorded real recognition. Like Professor Bell, my father wanted both, not just for himself but for those who would come after.

As my father's daughter, I too was a fighter. I would vindicate my father and all others like him who were not "grateful" enough.

But I was not just a fighter for blacks or other people of color. One of the first cases I ever tried as a young lawyer was a criminal case against several men accused of enslaving migrant workers on a North Carolina farm. As a part of a team of Justice Department lawyers, I helped convict the defendants, including a black man, for holding white and Latino migrant farm workers as "slaves."

After I graduated from law school, I clerked for two years in the mid-1970s for a federal judge in Detroit, Damon J. Keith. Judge Keith later told a reporter he liked the way I analyzed a case and he liked that I often went dancing. He said I seemed like such a well-rounded person, with both mental firepower and common sense, that he hired me on the spot during my job interview. One day—Judge Keith recalled in an interview—he was instructing jurors and told them to retire to the jury room to choose a foreman and a spokesman. Later, there was a note on his desk from his law clerk. I had asked him if he would kindly consider making that "foreperson" and "spokesperson" the next time because maybe that would help the jurors think about selecting a woman.

Judge Keith tried to teach all of his law clerks to respect the rule of law, "but to realize it is a changing thing." That's why he liked my note: it showed "sensitivity" and "awareness of the need for change, even in our most basic speaking." But Judge Keith also likes to tell the story about that note because he appreciated the discreet way I let him know.

In 1981, I found myself walking in Constance Baker Motley's shoes, this time as a civil rights lawyer, not a law student tenant. By then I had worked for four years as special assistant to Drew Days, the first black to head the Civil Rights Division of the Department of Justice. When I was trying to decide, before I knew the outcome of the 1980 presidential elections, whether to join the NAACP Legal Defense Fund staff or stay on as a career lawyer in the Justice Department's Civil Rights Division, Professor Bell had told me: "Lani, you need to get out and travel through the South. You will learn how to be a lawyer if you stay at Justice, but you won't learn how to be a civil rights advocate. Justice Department lawyers know their craft. They are superb technicians. But they are also anonymous bureaucrats who rarely learn from the people with whom they work. Get out there and mix it up. You won't regret it."

I followed Derrick Bell's advice and left Justice to join the Legal Defense Fund in April 1981. I was hired by Jack Greenberg, who was director-counsel of the LDF, to work on the extension of the 1965 Voting Rights Act. The act had been passed by Congress as a temporary measure to address the century-old legacy of black disenfranchisement. It was due to expire in 1982 unless Congress renewed it.

As a result of the act, blacks, for the very first time this century, began to register to vote in large numbers. But throughout the 1970s blacks were still not full participants in the political process. Those blacks who were registered now could vote; yet for the most part they could not elect candidates of their choice. In Selma, Alabama, a majority of the residents were black, but the same white man—who as mayor in 1965 had called Dr. King "Martin Luther Coon"—was still the mayor. In neighboring Mississippi, state NAACP president Aaron Henry declared in 1981 that for blacks it was still easier to buy a gun there than to register to vote.

First-generation problems in just getting blacks registered and voting persisted through the seventies and eighties. But now a second generation of problems came to the fore. Many southern states, in response to increases in black voting, instituted jurisdictionwide elections. In conventional terms, these are called "at-large" or "winner-take-all" voting. Because all voters got to vote on all candidates, a candidate sponsored by the black community could not win unless he or she appealed to at least some members of the white majority. But throughout the Black Belt of Alabama, voting was still very polarized—whites would simply not vote for a black candidate. As a result, in many of the Black Belt counties that had large black populations but not black voting majorities, there were still no black elected officials, even fifteen years after the Voting Rights Act was first passed. These second-generation problems were more subtle and difficult to grasp than direct denial of the franchise. But they were no less a threat to genuine democracy.

As the 1982 extension of the act loomed, Jack Greenberg assigned me to the D.C. office of LDF to work with Elaine Jones, the first black woman graduate of the University of Virginia Law School. Elaine, he knew, was a coalition builder and an experienced lobbyist/litigator. He didn't know much about me. When Greenberg hired me, he emphasized my credentials (Harvard, Yale, a federal clerkship with a distinguished black jurist, Damon Keith), but he was also persuaded by a political manner "as conservative and careful as the business suits" in which I often came to the office. I had worked at LDF as a summer intern for Elaine in 1973 while I was still in law school. He was reassured, Greenberg said, because I was "tall, dignified, and always perfectly tailored, with a soft manner and passionate feelings about race."

I began my full-time career with LDF working out of its Washington office in a space too small to accommodate another lawyer. From the moment I joined LDF as a staff attorney in April 1981, my office was a desk in a corner of the room already occupied by Elaine. Sharing an office with Elaine was no small feat since Elaine's presence fills every inch of every room she's in. Whether she was on the phone or reading her mail, her booming voice animated our small space.

On the other hand, Elaine is a very private person. The fact that she welcomed me into her office and encouraged me to stay reflected our unique working relationship. I felt important, as if Elaine had bestowed on me a special honor. Moreover, whatever its physical disadvantages, sharing an office with Elaine permanently enhanced my powers of concentration. Despite the incredible level of activity, you learn to focus. Even more, the close proximity made it easier for Elaine to school me in the multiple ways to be an effective legislative advocate. Sometimes affectionately called by her friends "the one hundred and first Senator"—a compliment originally bestowed on the legendary Clarence Mitchell, onetime lobbyist for the NAACP—Elaine is a great communicator.

Although LDF policy required all new lawyers to work from New York headquarters, Elaine had convinced Jack to allow me to start in Washington. Elaine desperately needed help in waging the legislative fight to renew the 1965 act. She wanted me to work full time on the voting rights extension.

I was doing the Lord's work, I thought, when I became a voting rights lawyer. On the one hand, it was what my father would call a "fortuitous concatenation of circumstances" that I started working at LDF in 1981, the same year the fight to renew the 1965 act started. I was assigned to work on the renewal because I was at the right place at the right time. Originally, Congress thought the law would solve all the problems blacks faced within five years. Passed in 1965 as an extraordinary but temporary measure, it had been twice extended, and unless Congress took further action, key provisions of the law itself would expire in 1982.

What began somewhat serendipitously became an intellectual, professional, and spiritual cause. It was through my eventual mastery of the Voting Rights Act that I learned to love the law. I found in it a concrete opportunity to begin to bridge the dissonance I had discovered in the fourth grade between American promises and actions. For me, the 1965 Voting Rights Act became a sacred document that took us as a society closer to the fundamental truths of democracy. The Voting Rights Act meant that for the first time in American history, black men and women, Asians and Latinos, Native Americans and Alaskan natives, would all be granted the basic freedom of the vote. If the act were vigorously enforced, I believed that blacks and other people of color might even get to participate in the decisions that affected their lives. But the promise of the Voting Rights Act was not simply a pledge to blacks or other minorities. It was a way to make America live up to its democratic ideals for all Americans. What was happening to blacks was the most visible, but certainly not the exclusive, injustice that needed to be corrected before America could call itself a genuine democracy.

Moreover, I found the story of how the Voting Rights Act came into being as valuable as any lesson of American history, because of what it says about the role played outside the formal electoral process by organized movements for social change. I felt privileged to be part of the 1982 legislative fight to renew the law. I felt myself a witness to history, blessed to be participating in an ennobling synergy of organized outsiders working in tandem with sympathetic insiders. This was America at its finest.

Within a week of my arrival at LDF in April 1981, Elaine introduced me to the twenty-five-person steering committee, operating under the auspices of the Leadership Conference on Civil Rights to coordinate the coalition working on the extension act. One hundred and sixty-five organizations made up the Leadership Conference, ranging from groups representing disabled citizens, women, labor, and education to religious and civil rights groups. The NAACP was central to the lobbying arm of the coalition, as were a number of Jewish organizations, the League of Women Voters, and the AFL-CIO. The Leadership Conference had built a strong relationship with congressional leaders, it had a grass-roots network, and many of its officers had substantial expertise in formulating and implementing legislative strategy.

But the Leadership Conference steering committee, while dominated by Washington insiders, also included representatives of litigating organizations such as the Mexican American Legal Defense Fund, the NAACP Legal Defense Fund, the Lawyers Committee for Civil Rights Under Law, and lawyers working for the Joint Center for Political Studies. Most of the lawyers related more to their clients in the South and the Southwest than they did to the members of Congress with whom they soon found themselves working. Some had relocated temporarily to Washington to work on legislation; others came in frequently to lend support but psychologically their community was outside the Beltway.

Armand Derfner, a frumpled, legally blind (without his glasses) civil rights lawyer from South Carolina, was a crucial member of the steering committee. Armand, then with the Joint Center of Political Studies, and Frank Parker, then with the Lawyers Committee for Civil Rights Under Law in Washington, but before that a civil rights lawyer in Jackson, Mississippi, had been trying voting cases since the 1960s. Both men were seasoned. They were veterans of "the movement." As white Harvard-trained lawyers and outstanding litigators, they nevertheless spent much of their adult lives living and working their principle on the ground. They knew the law inside out. They also knew the needs of black people in Mississippi, South Carolina, and other parts of the South. These were their clients and, even more, their neighbors.

Within a week, I was working full time on the Voting Rights Act extension, participating in all of the steering committee's internal deliberations. The committee met every Friday and sometimes every day in between while the extension was before Congress in 1981 and 1982. Although I attended the first steering committee meeting with Elaine in April, I still operated mostly in her shadow. I had a certain knowledge base, having worked in the Justice Department Civil Rights Division for four years and having helped AAG Drew Days restructure the Voting Rights Section, which exercised most of the responsibility in enforcing a key oversight provision of the act. Most of my recent experience was as a Washington bureaucrat, but in my heart I was an outsider.

In 1972, the summer between my first and second years in law school, I had worked for Julius Chambers. Chambers was senior partner in the first—and at that time the only—integrated law firm in North Carolina. The year before I worked there, the law offices were destroyed by a firebomb; the summer I was there, the firm had taken temporary residence in a local hotel. Though the temporary offices were a constant reminder that the firm had been firebombed by angry whites, it was Julius Chambers that I feared. His expression solemn, he rarely looked at me as he gave me an assignment. His dark brown hands were never still—they were either holding a cigarette or playing with a rubber band. He rarely smiled. He was a compact man, always preoccupied with the pile of papers on his desk.

I remember staying up several nights in the hotel room converted into a law library, pulling heavy volumes of law books off the shelf one by one, trying to respond to Mr. Chambers's request for a memorandum summarizing all employment discrimination cases ever decided. In the age before computers, local civil rights lawyers lacked the resources to network information and were often reinventing the wheel. I did not realize this at the time. I had thought it was probably a "test," a way of putting me, a young and eager law student, through my paces. I was sure someone, somewhere had already compiled all these cases and that an experienced lawyer like Julius Chambers certainly knew them. But I kept my doubts to myself. Despite Chambers's formality and the tediousness of the assignment, I felt lucky to be working there. In my mind, this was on-the-job training more valuable than any law school course. This was training to be a "movement" lawyer.

As I got to know him better, I asked Chambers whether he was ever scared doing the work he did. "I don't know about scared," Julius replied. "We were cautious about what we were doing and about our security. We had a bombing of my house, we had a bombing of my office, we had a bombing of my car. We all knew that these things were possible. But I don't think we were scared." He had been at a mass meeting the night his car was bombed. It was in the late 1960s, and Julius Chambers was addressing a meeting about a lawsuit challenging discrimination in the schools of Craven, Jones, Lenore, and Washington counties. Did he hear the explosion, I asked. "I was speaking at the time when we heard the explosion," Julius answered. He continued, "So we stopped and went outside to see what had happened and then we went back inside to finish up with the program." I was astonished. "You saw that your car had blown up and you went back inside?" I asked. "Yeah," Julius said matter-of-factly, drawing out the word into two syllables. "What could you do? I would not have been able to drive it, so, okay, let's just go on with the program." "Did anybody call the police?" "Yeah, we called the cops when we had finished the mass meeting."

My law student summer internships with Julius Chambers's law firm in North Carolina and the following summer at LDF with Elaine working on cases in Alabama had seared in me a connection to the power of local people changing their own lives. My hero was Julius Chambers—a man who saw his own car blown up outside the North Carolina church where he was speaking, and without skipping a beat continued the mass meeting. I was in Washington now, but like Armand Derfner and Frank Parker, my clients and the people I was fighting for were those who lived well beyond the Beltway.

Formally working as an LDF attorney, I aligned myself with people who also had witnessed firsthand the terrors of an angry white South. I admired the more experienced litigators whose judgment I trusted implicitly. Armand and Frank tutored me throughout the month of May when we worked closely with Democratic congressman Don Edwards of California on the House hearings that were essential to establish a public record as to why we still needed such a law and why, even more, the law itself needed to be strengthened. We burned the midnight oil helping prepare witnesses who traveled to Washington to tell their stories in ways that members of

Congress would find most persuasive. Based on those local stories, we knew that many southern county school boards and local governments would try any strategy available to them to avoid complying with the law. Blacks in the rural South, just like Mexican Americans in South Texas, were still fighting an antebellum mentality. Armand and I also helped former Assistant Attorney General Stan Pottinger (President Gerald Ford's Republican civil rights chief) with his testimony. Stan provided pizza, and from time to time even joined our drafting session in his swank law offices, where we worked until eleven o'clock the night before he was scheduled to appear before the committee.

When the extension was first considered by the House of Representatives in April 1981, Ronald Reagan had just been elected president. But the Reagan Justice Department could not formulate a position on the law, in part because the Assistant Attorney General for Civil Rights slot was still vacant. No one from Justice testified during the twenty days of House hearings that May. As a result, with only isolated dissents from conservative intellectuals, those hearings made a powerful case for why the law was still needed.

Vernon Jordan, then president of the National Urban League, was one of the first witnesses. Seated next to Elaine Jones at the witness table, Jordan appealed directly to Congressman Henry Hyde, Republican of Illinois, who was vigorously orchestrating opposition to the extension. "We are talking in good conscience, I believe, Mr. Hyde, about finding a midground. But I don't believe that for black people, given our history in this country, there is a midground when it comes to voting rights. I don't believe that to do away with this act, to find midground in this act, to find some political solution to this problem, is keeping the faith for those black people and white people who walked that forty-mile distance from Selma to Montgomery."

Jordan decided to remind Representative Hyde how hard blacks had to fight to gain the right just to vote. He read a passage from Pat Watters and Reese Cleghorn's *Climbing Jacob's Ladder,* about the courageous band of black people in Terrell, South Carolina, who sang Baptist hymns to corral their faith and bridle their fears so they would not back down when intimidated by white law enforcement. His voice booming but pitched just right, Jordan described how the old white sheriff of Terrell County and fifteen other white men burst into a voter registration meeting at the Mount Olive Church. The sheriff moved quickly to the front of the church, where the Reverend Charles Sherrod was leading the mass meeting. The sheriff explained how happy Negroes were in Terrell. "We want our colored people to live like they've been living," the sheriff said. "There was never any trouble before all this started."

"As he spoke," Jordan read, "the whites moved through the church, confronting little groups of Negroes. Finally, the whites left. A few nights later, three small Negro churches in Terrell County, one of them Mount Olive Baptist, with Jesus and the American Presidents on its walls, were burned to the ground." Blacks had struggled and had paid the ultimate price to vote. It was too soon to turn back, Jordan concluded.

When Vernon Jordan finished speaking, Colorado state senator Polly Baca Barragan picked up the baton, describing more recent events that affected not just blacks but Mexican Americans. She talked about the May 3, 1980, primary in Frio County, Texas. Juan Pablo Navarro was a poll watcher who observed changes in his own ballot when it was counted after the election. He recognized his ballot because he had written in his own name for one of the offices and because he recognized his handwriting. Yet "his votes for the candidates on his ballot had been changed. He also noticed that many other ballots had been tampered with and, not coincidentally, it was those ballots which affected the race of the Chicano candidate, Mr. Adolpho Alvarez." Nothing, of course, was done about the ballots that had been changed after they had been cast. Nor did white election officials in Texas stop at blatant efforts to deny office to Mexican Americans; they also used more subtle kinds of gerrymandering and at-large elections to keep Mexican Americans from obtaining political power.

Republican Henry Hyde, who originally opposed any extension, had a change of heart immediately after attending a field hearing in Montgomery, Alabama, in mid-May. There Maggie Bozeman, a black schoolteacher, testified that in Aliceville, Alabama, white policeman were stationed inside polling places taking pictures of those who attempted to assist black voters. Mrs. Bozeman also talked about "open house voting." There was no secret ballot—no booths, no curtains; just an open table under the watchful eye of white officials. After hearing testimony about a burdensome reidentification procedure that required all voters to reregister—with registration hours limited to 9:00 A.M. to 4:00 P.M., Hyde said, "I just want to say that I have listened with great interest and concern and I will tell you, registration hours from nine to four are outrageous. It is absolutely designed to keep people who are working and who have difficulty traveling from voting. If that persists and exists, it is more than wrong. The lack of deputy registrars—only twelve Alabama counties have them—demonstrates a clear lack of enthusiasm for getting people registered, obviously."

Congressman Hyde's conversion was critical in convincing the litigators that all we needed to do was to give those simple stories greater visibility. Our most able advocates were local people such as Maggie Bozeman and Juan Pablo Navarro. Their stories were vivid reminders that many Americans still lived in only a partial democracy. Those who suffered the daily indignities of being silenced and excluded needed to tell their stories. It was the plain speech of ordinary people that would help the rest of America bear witness to a different vision.

Hyde's repositioning, however, soon provoked a crisis within the Leadership Conference. While Hyde now conceded the continued need for the act, he was also hard at work to weaken its major provisions. Hyde had been persuaded that the law should stay on the books; his approach was to extend the law in principle but create large loopholes so that each of the southern states could easily escape coverage. Hyde drafted a loosely worked proposal that "recalcitrant jurisdictions could have driven a Mack truck through," as Armand put it.

Some of the Washington-based lobbyists were tempted to endorse Hyde's bailout provisions. After all, Ronald Reagan was president; the Republicans controlled the Senate. What good would it do to stand on principle in the House (where Democrats still controlled majorities) and lose everything in the end?

People like Ralph Neas, the newly installed head of the Leadership Conference; the established civil rights advocate Bill Taylor; and a handful of other lobbyists on the Leadership Conference steering committee saw Hyde's move as an opportunity, not because they trusted Hyde but because they thought they knew him. Michael Pertschuk, in his book *The Giant Killers*, quotes Neas explaining the importance of distinguishing among adversaries.

Now Henry Hyde was someone I watched carefully over a long period of time. Philosophically, he was not uniformly against positions of the Leadership Conference. He had been very effective, for example, in support of the Legal Services Corporation fight, and on certain civil right issues he prided himself on leaving the fold of the conservative

Republican administration; he didn't want to be pigeon-holed solely in the extremist camp. . . . The Hyde [anti-abortion] amendment made him a national figure, and he wanted to compensate for that Far Right image by doing well on the Voting Rights Act. From the beginning, I think he perceived himself as the architect of some type of grand compromise. This was an historic bill. He was playing an historic role.

Lobbyists within the Leadership Conference were also keenly aware that they too were playing "an historic role." They were especially conscious of the changing political climate in Washington following the repudiation of the Carter presidency. In their minds, it was politically expedient to find language that might narrow the gap with Hyde. The principal Democratic Party House Judiciary Committee staffer was Alan Parker. Parker and other committee staff members also argued that we needed to forge a compromise, or else we would doom the entire Voting Rights Act. House Staff thought negotiations with Hyde were essential to establish legitimacy in the Senate. In philosophical sync with the lobbyists, staff on the Hill kept looking for compromise language so that Henry Hyde, a conservative Republican, could be their stalking horse in the Republican-dominated Senate.

Moreover, we all knew that time was of the essence. Congress was getting ready to adjourn for the August recess. If we rejected Hyde's plan, we would really have to scramble to come up with something that the Judiciary Committee could vote on and then take home with them. It was crucial that we a have tangible bill during the August recess so we could energize a grass-roots lobby in the home district offices of individual members.

While there were no plans to stage a confrontation as dramatic as what had taken place in 1965 on the Edmund Pettus Bridge in Selma, we all knew the importance of the bottom-up momentum. Unless members of Congress heard from their own constituents, they were less likely to vote the way we wanted. All civil rights laws were controversial at some level. The Voting Rights Act, as American as apple pie to some, was no exception. Even the more liberal members needed occasional bucking up.

Nevertheless, Armand and Frank opposed the formulation of the compromise. Those who knew the law best were skeptical of the fragile compromise the lobbyists and committee staff tried to hammer out. Why compromise, they argued, when we had the votes to pass the bill in the committee and on the House floor? There would be plenty of time and reason to compromise when the bill reached the Senate. There we would need the strongest possible language as a starting point, knowing that Republican Orrin Hatch of Utah was heading the crucial Senate subcommittee and Republican Strom Thurmond of South Carolina was in charge of the larger Judiciary Committee. With the Justice Department off "studying the legislation," we had the field to ourselves.

It was not just the Reagan Justice Department that was missing in action. The Leadership Conference faced no organized opposition anywhere. Although many of the well-funded conservative think tanks that now line the streets of Washington had opened offices, they were still new to the business of trying to influence public policy in a coordinated and well-heeled way. As Dianne Pinderhughes writes in a paper prepared while a guest scholar at the Brookings Institution, these groups had not yet created "a network of policy institutes, legal bodies and other organizations which actively monitor and aggressively participate in public including civil rights policy formation."

The neoconservatives had only begun to exploit the intellectual backlash to government intervention on behalf of disadvantaged "groups." Soon they would figure out how to tap into the country's weary view that the problem of civil rights had already been fixed by national legislation. But for the moment they were not yet on the ascendancy.

The litigators, with whom I identified, were also furious that the lobbyists—who knew next to nothing about enforcing the law—were controlling the process of negotiations, excluding the litigators who had the substantive knowledge. Frank, Armand, Barbara Phillips (a black woman who had tried voting cases in Mississippi and now worked for the Lawyers Committee) and others, such as Jose Garza and Joaquin Avila from the Mexican American Legal Defense Fund (MALDEF), who were in the business of trying voting cases, immediately went into action to challenge the escape hatch that Republican representative Hyde proposed. The litigators suspected Hyde was simply engineering the escape of the South from supervision through the loosely worded sieve of a bailout provision. Hispanic groups were also wary of any compromise. They doubted the commitment of the Leadership Conference to the bilingual provisions of the act, and feared they would be abandoned in the heat of negotiations. Few of the litigators trusted Republicans. Fewer still trusted Hyde.

By July 1981, Hyde's proposal had prompted an intense and painful breakdown with the Leadership Conference coalition. Principals accused the litigators of trying to torpedo the compromise they were crafting. Tempers were short. I agreed wholeheartedly with Frank, Armand, and the other litigators from the Lawyers Committee for Civil Rights and the Mexican American Legal Defense Fund. I also knew that Elaine, who had begun to defer to me as she worked on other matters, was skeptical about Hyde's larger agenda.

At one point toward the end of July, I was the only one present representing LDF on Capitol Hill. I was inclined to lend LDF's support to the opposition; but with Elaine out of town, I did not know the extent of my delegated authority. Within the hierarchy of the LDF, as well as the Leadership Conference itself, I knew I was low on the totem pole. I had been on the job for less than three months, and with no one else from LDF present, I had to decide what position to take on a proposal that threatened the very integrity of our coalition. I remember trying to hide from Robert Pear, who was covering the extensive fight for *The New York Times*. At one point, a recent black Wellesley graduate, Laura Murphy (whose family published the *Baltimore Afro-American,* the famed black newspaper) and I stayed behind in a stairwell so we would not have to speak to reporters, whose antennae had pick up the scent of a fight but whose coverage would only lock people into hardened positions.

I darted out of the congressional hearing room where Hyde's plan was being debated, found a pay phone, and dialed Jack Greenberg's number at the LDF offices in New York. He listened quietly as I described the competing perspectives. Then he asked me what I thought LDF should do. I told Jack I thought we should oppose the compromise. But I was careful not to mislead him. I was very clear that there might be political costs to be paid within and by the civil rights coalition. From the other end of the phone I heard the words, "Lani, sometimes you just have to do what's right."

Jack Greenberg described this exchange in his book *Crusaders in the Courts*:

As one who made some compromises and had refused to enter many a Quixotic fight, I was hardly an ideologue in backing Lani and Elaine. The law would have been weakened. Our resources might have been drained in needless litigation. Besides, I wasn't sure that if we stuck to our guns we would lose and in fact, we won. LDF's strength lay in large part in the energy and enthusiasm of its lawyers. More than once I said "no," but when I felt I could back the staff I did.

Although some of us stood on principle, it was not our principles alone that won that day. Representative Hyde overreached, refusing to change a key provision in his bailout plan. His stubbornness allowed the lobbyists safe cover for retreat. Once it was clear that the compromise did not command a consensus, the litigators and lobbyists on the steering committee stayed up half the night to forge an alternative. A group of us had already prepared what we thought would be the perfect bailout provision, what we would like in the best of all possible situations. We bunkered down to write a substitute bill using the ideal draft as the starting point, but we did so without the blessing of the House committee staff. They were fuming. By temperament and positioning, they were eager to continue to try dealing behind the scenes with Hyde. The subcommittee staff were so angry with us that they would not help in drafting an alternative. They did, however, let us use their offices while they went home.

As veteran Washington insider Bill Taylor noticed during one of our interminably long meetings on the Hill, each of us played a role much like the "types" or positions taken by countries at the United Nations. Armand Derfner was the Hamlet of our coalition—he could always see both sides. Frank Parker, his views honed on the battlefields of the Mississippi Delta, was the red-bearded principled warrior, adamant and vehement. Ralph Neas, executive director of the Leadership Conference and a former Republican staffer for Senator Ed Brooke, was the pragmatic politician—no one was better at counting votes. I also remember deferring to the nonlawyers on the steering committee when it came to speaking in the court of public opinion. People like Laura Murphy of the American Civil Liberties Union (ACLU) had a facility with plain English and a spirited delivery that always enlivened our joint radio interviews defending the extension.

I don't remember what role Bill Taylor assigned me. I was one of the youngest members of the coalition at thirty-one, and had not participated in the civil rights mass movement of the sixties. I had worked in Washington as a Justice Department insider for four years and knew the players. But by temperament and training, I was more like the litigators. I was never without a briefcase stuffed with all the versions of the compromise, our ideal draft substitute, our talking points, questions and answers, or Xeroxed copies of legal cases interpreting the prior law. My briefcase served as a portable office, overflowing with paper just like the cramped space Elaine and I shared. I focused my attention on documents and finding clear language that we could enforce in court. I was always taking notes, making a record of every meeting I attended. I loved the all-night brainstorming sessions, testing and reshaping our arguments. Sometimes I alienated our allies with my insistence that we get it right.

Ralph Neas, as a principal lobbyist who was not always on LDF's side, saw me as "a very determined person" who could be "fiercely independent, totally committed to whatever [she was] working on, and very aggressive about how [she went] after it." While my tenacity was ever present in Ralph's mind, he later acknowledged that I had other qualities as well, saying that I was "open-minded, a coalition builder, inclusive and effective."

Armand, too, saw me as the bridge person in the struggle between the litigators and the Washington people. In describing my role, Armand told a reporter, "[Lani] had a great deal of knowledge, and her hard work gave her credibility on both sides." Armand remembered my laugh most of all. Armand said. "She can talk to anybody, meaning anybody from presidents to railway conductors, white or black. And she has a terrific laugh; you can hear it from here to kingdom come."

By ten o'clock on the morning after my phone conversation with Jack Greenberg, the Leadership Conference had repudiated Hyde's compromise. A group of us had also produced a new bill. Everyone was in a celebratory mood. All the animosity of the last few days was gone. Nine members of the steering committee had stayed up until 3:00 A.M. and completely rewritten the bill in a way that was, in Michael Pertschuk's words, "so technically sound and carefully drafted" it remained essentially intact in its future passage through House and the Senate. The Leadership Conference working group had also prepared a technical section-by-section analysis of the bill and summaries for the press, something that under normal time pressures would have taken three to four weeks to produce. In the place of the Hyde proposal, Congressmen Hamilton Fish (a liberal Republican) and James Sensenbrenner (a conservative Republican who we were told harbored deep personal antagonism toward Henry Hyde) sponsored a Leadership Conference–backed provision that did not include the dreaded compromise language. Briefed by Bill Taylor just fifteen minutes before the committee meeting, Congressman Fish defended the bill as if he had spent all night writing it. The Judiciary Committee sent it to the floor by an overwhelming vote and it passed the full House 389-24.

That experience crystallized my thinking about social change. I was elated. My judgment and my principles had been affirmed. I had been validated as a civil rights lawyer. I "kvelled," my mother would say, with joys of a hard-won accomplishment. But, even more, I felt connected to a community of people, joined by common ideals and a common project. This was not a one-person or a single strategy enterprise. Nor was it an alliance that walked in the lockstep of a shared single set of experiences. We were a multiracial and multigenerational partnership that came together to attack a perceived injustice. We all worked hard, contributing different insights and perspectives. From this large, unwieldy coalition of "types" and roles, I discovered the importance of creative synergy. The tensions between the litigators and the lobbyists were essential in beating back the Reagan administration's attempt to dilute the House bill in the Senate. The line was held; with the help of compromise language offered by Senator Dole, but crafted essentially by our coalition, the final version of the act was very much like the strong House-passed bill.

The principled stand by the litigators forced the lobbyists to reconsider premature compromise; but the eventual legislation reflected the informed perspectives of a varied and broad-based coalition, one that began as individuals meeting every Friday morning and grew together as a community at heart. We were a community by virtue of our chosen, not biological, identity. We came together as blacks and Jews, litigators and lobbyists, experienced insiders and idealistic newcomers. We shared a common passion for social change, but we did not all share that passion to the same degree or with the same energy. Most of us enjoyed the privileges of an excellent education and good jobs, but we did not always agree either by ideology or temperament. Yet we functioned as a single, loosely coordinated organism, each one pulling his or her weight at different times and in different ways.

We were all experts in our own singular domain, yet our sustained collaboration reminded us that the whole was greater than the sum of its parts. The lawyers knew the law; the lobbyists knew the Hill. But neither the lawyers nor the lobbyists alone could tell the stories of exclusion and degradation experienced daily by blacks in small rural southern communities or Chicanos in the Southwest or recently naturalized Asian-American citizens. None of us could tell the stories of the continued injustice as eloquently as the witnesses who traveled to Washington to testify during the twenty days of House hearings. It was those stories and the participation by those ordinary witnesses that made what we were all doing real and important and fundamentally democratic. It was all made possible as well by the ability of organized labor, the League of Women Voters, and other groups with local constituencies who met during the recesses with their local members of the Congress in their home offices. This was an inside-the-Beltway operation with legs.

We operated by consensus. Ralph was our leader and was authorized to speak for the group, but only after the group itself had signed on at least in principle to the position he was to take. Everyone who sat at our steering committee meetings was encouraged to participate, to speak up, to question the received wisdom. Some observers, like Judiciary Committee staffer Alan Parker, who did not participate in steering committee meetings but witnessed their results, dismissed us as "a civil rights circus." Ralph told Michael Pertschuk that he knew Parker well:

Alan did not appreciate working with what appeared to be an excessively democratic group of people. To him, it looked leaderless, disorganized. To a degree there was some legitimacy to this point of view. It certainly did appear to be an unruly mob at times. This was our formative period; trust and relationships hadn't been established. We hadn't won anything really significant yet. And we were not speaking as one.

In a legislative battle for an inclusive and truly representative democracy, our ragtag group of lobbyists and litigators had practiced exactly what we tried to get Congress to enact. We explored the dynamic tension between different kinds of knowing, among different groups of people, and around different ways of mobilizing power—by those with local knowledge and outsider resources and those with individual access and insider expertise.

Everyone had a chance to speak; everyone's view was respected and considered. While we did not speak as one, we did succeed as a whole. Where others saw chaos, we saw democracy.

It seemed to me that our efforts in 1981 and 1982 had been guided by at least three crucial ideas. One was that direct communication from ordinary people can bring important members of the establishment to the table. Whether it was the determination of many citizens to march in the streets as in the 1960s or the plain-spoken eloquence of the witnesses at the field hearings in 1981, the actions and voices of real folk can inspire powerful people who otherwise do not want to talk or act to come to the table. Mobilizing ordinary people to march or speak gives their leadership the power to back up their demands. Second, a broad-based coalition is necessary. The black civil rights groups couldn't do it alone. Just as in 1965, when white clergy, Jewish leaders, business people all joined the movement as it marched for voting rights, a mammoth collaboration fueled our legislative efforts in 1981. Finally, the movement was not just a plea for special rights; it was a crusade for justice. This was about realizing the promises of democracy, not just gaining voting rights for black folks.

My experience in 1981–82 enabled me to see myself as a civil rights lawyer with a mission and a promise. My mission was to encourage ordinary people to make their own lives better. The promise, I thought at the time, was that by vigorously enforcing the Voting Rights Act, we could do just that. As a member of an itinerant band of lawyers marching throughout the courts of law of the American South, I would help fulfill Martin Luther King's legacy and complete the unfinished business of the civil rights movement. I would be a member of the legal bugle corps, playing the newly extended Voting Rights Acts as my instrument. Having worked to strengthen the act, I now had to implement its terms.

The next step for me was to challenge directly the Reagan administration's civil rights policies, and especially its civil rights chief, Brad Reynolds, who seemed determined to subvert the promise of the Voting Rights Act, at least as I saw it. In an updated version of Nixon's "Southern strategy," the Reagan civil rights enforcers were seeking to abstract racial injustice into a question of formal neutrality, detached from any historical or social context. Thus, Ronald Reagan announced his decision to run for a second term in 1984 in a small town in Mississippi, signaling a willingness to represent the "Old South" and all that it stood for. But they were also energetically repositioning the idea of civil rights itself. Whereas the civil rights movement of the sixties and seventies had engaged in protest and litigation to open up the society to more diverse groups of people, the Reagan idea of civil rights throughout the eighties was to break the backbone of group redress in favor of providing the appearance of individual opportunity.

The problem with the Reagan approach was simple: It ignored the reality in which we found ourselves. It denied the existence of disadvantaged groups who by virtue of historical, social, and economic circumstances were structurally positioned at the bottom, unable to take advantage of formal neutrality. Indeed, it transformed the reality of group oppression into a problem of individual pathology and bad character (and in its more virulent form, bad genes). Moreover, it coopted the rhetoric of formal equality to a principle of inaction. If we simply declared everyone equal, then that assertion spoke for itself. We had absolved society, and particularly its governmental agencies, from acting to remedy or interrupt anything but isolated acts of contemptible racial animus directed at single individuals. By limiting civil rights to discrimination against honorable victims, they individualized a systemic problem and justified doing nothing to help either black Americans or white working-class Americans as a group or a class. In the name of race, they buried increasing inequalities of class or group disadvantage generally.

My job was to take on these ideas in court. In 1983, I was part of an LDF team that fought Louisiana's racially biased redistricting plan, which Reagan civil rights chief Brad Reynolds had reviewed and approved as nondiscriminatory under the Voting Rights Act. The record was replete with racially bigoted statements from one local official who claimed that the plan was engineered by himself and other Louisiana politicians because they wanted desperately to avoid electing any more "nigger bigshots." Yet Reynolds had personally given his blessing to the discriminatory plan, over the unanimous protest of the people who knew the law best, the department's career staff. The Republican governor who engineered the plan admitted that it "looked funny," but testified that it was designed to ensure compliance with his ceiling of 44 percent black voters, a quota he imposed on all Louisiana congressional districts. To Reynolds, such reasoning was evidence of political, not racial, bias.

A three-judge court eventually threw out the Reynolds-approved plan. The following year, I gave a presentation about the case at an LDF luncheon in New York to which all the chiefs of the Civil Rights Division of the Justice Department, past and present, were invited. I had a big map which we had used during the court case to persuade the judges that the plan deliberately served all of the black wards and none of the white wards. On it I traced the Reynolds-approved plan, revealing how similar it was to a picture of Donald Duck superimposed on the city of New Orleans.

When I finished, Mr. Reynolds turned to the audience and tried to strike a note of polite irony laced with discomfort that he had been served up for the other luminaries to feast on: "Thank you for inviting me to lunch. I didn't know I was to be the main course. Lani Guinier is obviously an able advocate, but as you know every story has two sides. However, I have to leave to catch a plane so I don't have time to give my side."

During the early eighties, I also found myself representing clients such as Mrs. Maggie Bozeman, the fifty-five-year-old black schoolteacher from Pickens County, Alabama, who had been prosecuted by the state authorities for assisting elderly blacks to vote by absentee ballot. Maggie Bozeman had taught school in Pickens County since 1947; in 1978 she was charged with voting fraud, with voting more than once, and with forging absentee ballots. She was convicted by an all-white jury in Pickens County in 1979 and sentenced to serve four years in the Alabama penal system. The prosecution was able to prove that some of the ballots cast by black voters, which were supposed to be signed in front of a notary, had in fact been signed out of his presence. Aside from the fact that Mrs. Bozeman knew many of these voters, there was no evidence to connect her to the improper signatures. Moreover, apart from the evidence that the ballots were improperly notarized, there was no evidence that they were fraudulent.

At her trial, the only testimony directly linking Mrs. Bozeman to the election came when a witness said that Mrs. Bozeman was in the same car as her friend, Mrs. Julia Wilder, parked outside the courthouse on election day, and that one of the ladies in the car walked into the courthouse carrying a brown paper bag. The lack of evidence apparently was no barrier to conviction.

"I didn't know I was in trouble," Mrs. Bozeman told the historian and journalist Roger Wilkins, explaining in a 1984 *Esquire* magazine profile what had happened the day she was arrested.

> I was doing exercises with the children in the playground when I saw all these cars come up to the school. They weren't police cars, honey. They were sheriff's cars. I took the children back into the school, but I told them not to worry because the sheriff was supposed to help. I was going to get my tea from my thermos to relax myself.

But the sheriff's cars had not come to help Maggie Bozeman; they had come to collect her. Before she would have her tea the principal summoned her over the intercom system.

> One of the white children in my class began to cry and I told him not to worry, it would be all right. I thought the principal was joking with

me, but he wasn't. When I got to the office, Louie Coleman, the sheriff—he's big and heavy—said, "Maggie, come with me. You have been charged with vote fraud." Then he read me a little card. And so I went back to the classroom and told the children that the sheriff had come for me. I left, and Louie Coleman walked me out like a criminal. But he let me drive my own car down to the courthouse, and all these sheriff's cars followed me right from school. It was like a funeral procession.

When asked what she had done to merit this attention, Mrs. Bozeman explained to Roger Wilkins:

I was trying to educate people; trying to inform them about the political process and how they should be involved. My primary role was to gather information and to put it in the people's heads and to inform them about what the law was.

I got my information from the Alabama Democratic conference that put out a memorandum written by Alabama Assistant Attorney General Walter Turner that gave, according to the law, the steps—one, two, three—on how you could assist people to register to vote. Before that, we didn't have the information to educate the people.

That's what bothers me also, I followed the law and still I got convicted.

Maggie Bozeman's real crime was that she was trying to get some political power for blacks in Pickens County. Forty percent of the population was black and yet the county had never had a black elected to anything. Upon hearing this, Roger Wilkins was incredulous. "Not to anything?" he asked. Mrs. Bozeman answered, "To no thing, honey. To NO thing!"

Blacks had run for office, but they were always unsuccessful because all county offices were elected at-large rather than by district. Thus the black vote, though a large minority, was swallowed up by the larger white majority. These were exactly the kinds of problems Mrs. Bozeman had testified to during the field hearings on the 1981 extension of the Voting Rights Acts. It was in part because of Mrs. Bozeman's forceful testimony that Congressman Hyde changed his mind and decided that a federal presence monitoring local voting practices was still needed.

Because voting was not only at-large but winner-take-all, the winning majority won all the seats. And because *whites as voting majority tended to support the same white candidates* and still refused to vote for any blacks, the black minority was never able to elect anyone: "To no thing, honey. To NO thing!"

Prosecuting Maggie Bozeman of Pickens County seemed part of a pattern by Alabama authorities to keep blacks from gaining office. Bozeman's convictions had a predictably chilling effect. Black absentee voting in Pickens dropped off sharply, as did black voting generally, especially when the Alabama Supreme Court upheld her convictions.

Several days after Maggie Bozeman and her seventy-year-old co-defendant, Julia Wilder, began serving their sentences Jack Greenberg read about their plight in *The New York Times.* He studied a picture of the two women serving time in the Tutwiler state prison on a work release program under the sheriff of Macon County. Jack summoned me to his office and showed me the article. "I want you to do whatever it takes to help these women. If necessary get on the next plane, file a habeas petition, and argue the case in federal court. Just get these convictions overturned." With the help of Siegfried Knopf, a volunteer lawyer who had graduated earlier that year from Columbia; Anthony Amsterdam, a brilliant law professor with photographic memory of legal opinions; and Vanzetta Penn Durant, a bright, energetic, LDF cooperating attorney in Montgomery, Alabama, we did just that.

Buoyed by our victories in the Bozeman case and the Louisiana redistricting, I told Roger Wilkins when he interviewed me in 1984 at my work, "Voting right is an idea whose time has come. Black people have a lot of hope in it. I feel good as a trustee of that hope. It is the community choosing the agenda, not the lawyers running the show." My role as a voting rights attorney, I explained to Wilkins in 1984, is as an "energizer of movement. I want to encourage people to make their lives better—to activate their spirit and concern."

I became a law professor in 1988 when I joined the faculty at the University of Pennsylvania Law School. Now I was a legal scholar and educator. I could help train and inspire the next generation of legal advocates. I also seized the opportunity to interpret and reflect on my own advocacy experiences. I began to see a need to change direction and momentum in the fight for civil rights.

My experiences fighting to amend, extend, and implement the Voting Rights Act became part of a larger battle to bring democracy to life. I saw participatory democracy as a system in which the people, all of the people, get to participate in making the decisions that affect their lives.

I was convinced that genuine democracy was a prerequisite for genuine freedom. After all, democracy, "the rule of the people," in what the historian Arthur Schlesinger, Jr., terms its "unarguable sense," means that all of the people collectively decide the course of their own historical fate.

Participatory democracy was not just a racially inclusive version of government by and for elites. Participatory democracy meant giving ordinary people—those whose power depended on their willingness to struggle in association and relationship with others—the incentive and the opportunity to have a voice in public policy. It was not enough to vote, although universal suffrage was a precondition. People deserved the opportunity to cast a vote for someone who could get elected. But in addition to the vote, they also needed a voice.

A vote and a voice that mattered. This was, in my view, what the early civil rights movement had fought for. Many activists turned to electoral politics to awaken ordinary black folk to their humanity, their heritage, and their potential, as citizens, to participate in democratic self-government. As one activist observed in 1964:

> I think one of the things that made [us] so hopeful, so expectant, was the fact that people had made a discovery that there is a way out of much that is wrong with our lives, there is a way to change it, and that is through the execution of this vote. . . . That's the way we [felt]—really excited about the fact that we were at long last going to be able to participate, to be represented.

Like other proponents of the participatory democracy, civil rights activist Septima Clark (who organized citizenship schools to teach blacks to read so they could pass literacy tests) and Ella Jo Baker (an SCLC youth organizer) had faith in the ability of ordinary people to provide much of the leadership for their own struggle. For this reason, Clark once wrote a letter to Dr. Martin Luther King, Jr., asking him "not to lead all the marches himself" so that other leaders might develop who could lead their own marches. Dr. King read that letter before the SCLC staff, Clark remembered. "It tickled them; they just laughed."

Black elected officials, and white officials who were accountable to all voters, not just the narrow elite, would be the vanguard for a new social justice agenda. Indeed, civil rights activists sought the right to vote in part so they could elect more government officials who would be responsive to the needs and concerns of poor working-class folk generally. But to the people like Septima Clark and Ella Jo Baker, it was about much more than electing people to important jobs. Full political participation was necessary, not just universal suffrage. The aim was not just to teach blacks how to pass literacy tests; nor was the purpose of local organizing just about getting people registered to vote; the goal was to create involved citizens and to discover local community leaders.

I worried that the ideals that originally animated the civil rights movement were getting lost. We were all pushing to enforce the Voting Rights Act, but it was becoming primarily a vehicle to create geographic election districts in which blacks were the majority and thus could elect a candidate of their choice. I became concerned that majority black single-member districts were not necessarily the best tool for broad-based community empowerment. And I became critical of the single-minded devotion to a strategy that puts more black faces in high places rather than mobilizes ordinary people to get more involved.

The issues were changing and we needed to change our thinking to keep up. When I left the LDF in 1988 for Penn, I continued to work with Dayna Cunningham, who clearly understood this new terrain. As Dayna explained in 1993 to *Washington Post* reporter David Von Drehle:

> They're changing the rules so minority representation, can't function. I have a case in Shelby County, Tennessee, where redistricting required two-thirds vote of the commission, but after an election they found they couldn't get two-thirds without winning some black members. So [to avoid having to reach out to black representatives] they changed it to a simple majority.
>
> You see all this, after a while you realize that simply creating a black district is not going to solve the racial problem in our government. We need mechanisms that will make people cooperate, build coalitions.

"I learned that from Lani Guinier," she told him.

I was not satisfied that any one of us had all of the answers. I was not sanguine about simply recommitting the federal government and its resources to enforcing a 1960s vision of formal equality. I believed that new, innovative remedies were needed to address a different, more complex set of problems.

Blacks, as University of Texas professor Gerald Torres taught me, function as a miner's canary—the fragile bird carried into coal mines to detect whether they harbor poisonous gases. The canary's death by suffocation signals the miners that it is time to beat a hasty retreat. By the mid-1980s, the New Democrats, with whom Bill Clinton had early on affiliated, wanted to reclaim a Democratic majority by downplaying "group rights." It was as if the canaries had banded together and made demands based primarily or exclusively on special interest or identity politics. We were all the same, the New Democrats responded to the canaries' plea for relief. But as a law professor in the 1990s, working with progressive scholars like Gerald Torres and my Penn Law School colleague Susan Sturm, I began to see the possibility of a different solution, which did not involve ignoring the canary's warning or the canary's special experience. Indeed, the canary's very visibility helped focus our attention in a way that could then be used to expose more systemic problems. I thought we should take note of the canary's admonition, not to fix the canary alone but indeed to improve the conditions of the mines so that neither canaries nor humans risked asphyxiation.

In particular, I came to see in the voting rights context that the problems blacks had being represented by candidates of their choice was a problem experienced by many whites, too. Our conventional notions of democracy were entirely too passive as far as the role played by voters was concerned. In current election districts, representation was a function of living and breathing in the right district, even if the representative was chosen by others with whom you disagreed. I thought representation should be the result of community mobilizing and voter organization instead. Thus, cumulative voting, one of the alternative election systems I now began to explore, was a way of encouraging voters to mobilize and organize at the grassroots level consistent with the mission of the Voting Rights Act (if it were used to remedy proven violations) to better protect democracy for everyone. It would express a more active view of democracy generally. Groups would define themselves as political actors by their interest and by their ability to mobilize like-minded voters.

Cumulative voting was a way of rethinking the role of voters and their representatives from the bottom up. It was a rather simple yet democratic vision: 51 percent of the people should not necessarily get 100 percent of the power, especially if they use that power to exclude a significant portion of the 49 percent. If 30 percent of the voters back a particular party or candidate for legislative office, I began to ask, why aren't those voters represented at all in the legislative body? Why should they sit empty-handed while 51 percent of the voters gobble 100 percent of the seats?

Moreover, when the losers get nothing even though they represent a significant segment of the electorate, we are not necessarily acting in the best interest of the majority or the minority. When politics is "winner-take-all," the stakes are high. Politicians are encouraged to go negative, to drive up their opponents' negatives and drive away their opponents' supporters. A "winner-takes-all" culture suppresses voter participation. It reduces politics to a game in which voters become spectators rather than active citizens and it limits the ability of those with integrity and good intentions to remain so, if they want to continue to play ball.

By finding more inclusive and participatory electoral systems, I thought we could reinvigorate a new kind of politics in which all voters' votes count and in which all voters vote for someone who can get elected. Where everyone can win something, genuine collaboration is possible. These ideas of power sharing and "taking turns" were behind law review articles I began to write describing alternative election reforms like cumulative voting and other winner-take-only-some election and legislative rule changes.

Abbe Lowell worked with me in the Justice Department during the 1970s in the Carter administration. I understood "great concepts," Lowell said, but I never forgot Maggie Bozeman and the other LDF clients I had worked with. Even after I became a law professor, I still identified with "struggles on a human level." To Abbe Lowell, I became "a scholar with a heart."

But in 1993, neither the experience of my career, the many lessons it yielded, nor my actual views were important. For many people, what I did or what I believed did not establish my identity. "Who are you?" "What are you?" they demanded to know. Many of these people were white; but some were black. They were suspicious of me—was I really one of them? The questions were prompted by curiosity; they were also a plea for reassurance. A black waitress, London Sengale, was quite insistent as she served me lunch in a Hartford restaurant: "What is your ethnic background, going back to your grandparents? I know you're black, but who are you? I know you're black, but what are you?"

That was the sound bite in the spring of 1993. We know you are black, but what are you? And, without waiting for my answer, members of the establishment media supplied one. To my mother's great horror, I was once again "Looney Lani." I was also "Bill Clinton's Quota Queen."

What spoke was not how I looked to those who knew me. What spoke was not what I had done. What spoke was not what my mother had in mind when she named me after her Hawaiian matchmaker friend. What spoke was my "type," a black woman of the lunatic fringe. Too black was too crazy. Too black was the threatening Virago in my father's ditty—I was a troublemaker. I made white people feel uncomfortable. That made me not just black, but "too dark."

Too dark, too black, in other words, meant, in the eyes of my audience, that I was about giving blacks more than whites—I was "for" black people.

Too black meant too much of something unfamiliar and dangerous.

Too black meant someone too scary to let speak.

CHAPTER 12

Achieving Career Success by Being Aware

PAUL B. HIGGINBOTHAM

Judge, Wisconsin Court of Appeals,
District IV, Madison, Wisconsin

I am my parents' child; I am a product of the Civil Rights Movement and of the 1960s and 1970s; I now sit on the Wisconsin Court of Appeals as the first African American to sit on any appellate court in Wisconsin's history. The following is a brief history of my influences and inspirations and the strategies I have employed to achieve professional success.

I am a twin. My twin brother, Stephen, and I were born in Philadelphia, Pennsylvania, in 1954. My father shortly thereafter was ordained into the Episcopal priesthood. He moved the family to Providence, Rhode Island and then in 1957, to Columbus, Ohio, where we lived for the next 10½ years. My father headed up the largest Black Episcopal Church in Columbus; my mother raised the family of six. Growing up in segregated Columbus, where "whites only" signs dotted the landscape, my parents instilled in me the strong moral values that led me to a career in the law based on the principle of equal justice for all. There, I experienced the strife and turmoil related to the Civil Rights Movement. I grew up in a segregated world where death was the price some paid for seeking equal rights.

During the Columbus period (1957–1968), the country experienced tremendous upheaval, both politically and socially. My father was a leader in the Civil Rights Movement in Columbus. He was involved in the counter sit-ins and marched with Dr. Martin Luther King, Jr. in Montgomery, Alabama, and in the March on Washington in 1963. Because of his activities we received numerous bomb and death threats and obscene phone calls. I recall the many civil rights strategy meetings held in our home and at my father's church; I have a clear image of members of our church boarding the buses for the March on Washington.

The seeds of my future were planted during this period of my life. I was inspired by my father's activism and my mother's comforting and generous love. My passion for justice was fueled by these experiences. And, as many Black parents taught their children the value of education in those times, my parents always inspired us to be highly educated. In high school, Steve and I were very active in the Civil Rights Movement, the antiwar effort, and the Episcopal Church. We developed our leadership skills through these experiences, skills both of us employ today. That activism continued to grow after I entered the University of Wisconsin–Madison in January 1973.

After graduating from high school in Nashville, Steve and I considered following in my father's footsteps: I intended to go to Trinity College in Hartford, Connecticut, with an eye toward become an Episcopal priest, and Steve went to school at the University of Maryland–College Park with the intention to enter the Episcopal priesthood. A chance trip to Madison in October 1972 eventually led me to change my mind about entering the priesthood. After attending the University of Wisconsin, I eventually decided on a law career, inspired by my cousin, the late A. Leon Higginbotham, a noted civil rights champion and a judge on the federal Third Circuit Court of Appeals in Philadelphia. I was also inspired by other great Black lawyers of his day. My cousin was a well-known authority on civil rights issues. To this day I still ask myself how Leon would have analyzed and decided a certain case or issue, which helps inform how I approach my own judicial decision making.

Steve, on the other hand, also gave up his dream of the ministry and pursued the path of education, politics, and community service. He received a degree in special education from the University of Wisconsin–Madison and taught in various schools in Wisconsin. Not satisfied with just teaching, Steve received a master's degree in journalism, eventually working as a news director for a local community radio station and as a freelance writer. Steve served three terms on the Dane County Board of Supervisors, which he left to manage the Urban League of Greater Madison.

Similar to me, Steve is strongly committed to improving the life of others in our community. Indeed, when we were 16 years old, we made a solemn pledge to the other to work on behalf of our community for the rest of our lives. So far, we have done just that.

I paid my way through law school and for everything over and above the grants that I received from the Legal Education Opportunities (LEO) program at the University of Wisconsin Law School. The LEO program recruits and retains students of color, students with disabilities, and others who are economically disadvantaged. The program provides an informal academic and social support network for students while they are in law school. I have been working since I was 11 years old and always had to fight for myself—so it was nice to get that support from LEO; it was wonderful not to work through the law school process alone. There was a point, however, when I was ready to ditch it all. I was struggling in law school and my personal life. The support system the LEO program provided was critical to my decision to persevere and finish law school. The LEO program is all about helping students move through law school so they come out knowing "I can do this." It is fair to say that without the LEO program, I probably would not be a lawyer, much less a judge, today.

Following law school I worked for the Legal Aid Society of Milwaukee concentrating on civil litigation. There I was able to practice employment and housing discrimination law. I also became involved with the Metropolitan Milwaukee Fair Housing Council as a tester and eventually as one of its legal counsel. After a relatively short period in Milwaukee I returned to Madison and practiced law in a small law firm, continuing my civil rights litigation work. After another one and a half years of law practice I began working with Dane County Executive Richard J. Phelps as the county's minority affairs coordinator. Four years later Madison Mayor Paul Soglin appointed me as the city's first Municipal Court judge, where I served for nine months and then as acting executive director of the Madison Equal Opportunities Commission. One year later I was elected as the first African American circuit court judge for Dane County. After serving nine years on the trial bench, I ran for the Wisconsin Supreme Court; I lost the election but was then appointed by Governor James E. Doyle to the Wisconsin Court of Appeals. I was the first African American, indeed the first person of color, to serve on any appellate court, including the Supreme Court, in the state of Wisconsin. After this historic appointment, I ran unopposed in the spring 2004 election and was elected to a six-year term.

My personal philosophy of the judicial system is that any appellate court, federal or state, should have balance. The judiciary should represent a cross section of society. The people are best served if members of the judiciary represent the full range of political and social belief and thought and come from different experiences in life. A diverse court promotes a full and well-informed dialogue regarding the issues involved in any given case. The law is best developed by the natural tension that is created from a healthy diversity of thought and experiences at the conference table.

I also follow the philosophy that extremism of any sort has no place in the judiciary; there is no place in the judiciary for any personal or political agendas. The law must be developed with precedent in mind, keeping an eye toward legislative intent in interpreting statutes and constitutional provisions, while maintaining a deliberative approach to law development and interpretation. My diverse professional and life experiences provide me with a strong base from which to review the law and its impact on people. Although my politics are progressive, I approach my decision making as a judicial moderate. And this is as it should be. I firmly believe in equal access to the courts. I believe in the jury system and the right to have matters heard by a representative group of citizens. I also believe that our federal constitution was created with the purpose of protecting individual rights and to diminish the intervention of government in our private lives. In the final analysis, judicial decisions must be based on a careful examination, consideration, and interpretation of the law as written by the pertinent legislative body.

The recipe for my success is an unusual one. It started with being passionate about what I do and where I wanted to go. Many doors opened to me just by following my passion. Of course, a strong work ethic and a broad education allowed me to be poised for the opportunities as they arose. I eventually learned that although what you know is very important, who you know may also be very important. The real question is how to strike the proper balance. I am an innately curious person, so seeking knowledge came naturally. But so did developing that all-important network. Through the years, I have been active in my community, wherever I lived. My activism has not been driven by a desire to pump up my resume, but by a natural drive to improve the quality of life of the people in the community. And, as it turned out, my passion to help people created the network that eventually led to my professional success.

In retrospect, it is amazing that I have been this successful. Much of my success has essentially come to me, rather than coming as the result of my pushing for professional success. I simply followed my passion and was prepared for the next step—whenever that step presented itself. In short, I appeared to always be poised, and to be in the right place at the right time, when the career opportunities became available. When I was in law school, I had no idea that my career would take the path it did. What I did know was that by working hard, developing important professional skills, and developing an extensive and broad network I would eventually be in the position to move career-wise. But, most importantly, I had to know myself—emotionally, mentally, and spiritually.

Spirit is my guiding force. My father periodically refers to me as a "frustrated clergyman." Perhaps he's right. As I stated earlier, I once seriously considered following him into the priesthood. I feel, though, that the work I have done throughout my life has been guided by God. I simply have listened and followed the guidance of Spirit. Being aware of my spiritual center grounds me; the values that spring from that spiritual journey inform my passion for justice and to do good for the community. People see this; they are influenced by it and see the strength of passion and Spirit I bring to my work. It's important to recognize, though, that my spiritual journey is mine alone; I am not on this journey for the purpose of achieving career success or to influence people. By being in my light, I naturally affect others. Jesus Christ taught this; the teachings on Buddhism also teach this.

A strong family unit has also been a significant part of my success. I am married to Cora, who is also an attorney. We have two sons, who are four and two years old, respectively. My life is extremely full between raising two wonderful and gregarious boys and doing the important work of the court of appeals. I have developed a deep respect for the challenges my parents faced and the challenges single parents face in raising a healthy and wholesome family. Cora and I are fortunate to live close to our parents and to my twin brother and his family. I never had the opportunity to live close to my extended family during my childhood. I am thrilled that my boys will have that experience, which will be so important as they grow to understand the importance of family and community.

One other piece of advice: if you want to be effective in your community, find that key decision-making point where you are part of the decisions being made. I call this point the "bottleneck," the place between dreams and demands, and the place where those dreams and demands are brought to life. That place is the anvil upon which real and meaningful action occurs. I learned over the years that demanding or trying to persuade someone, including the government, to do something beneficial for the community, for the country, and for the world did not necessarily translate into beneficial action. Throughout my professional career I have sought out that place where I could be most effective at making decisions that would positively affect a whole host of people. Ultimately, that place for me was the judiciary. For others that may mean running for elected office or serving on the board of directors of influential businesses and nonprofit corporations; and for others that may mean sitting on boards of regent of higher educational institutions or becoming chief executive officers and presidents of large and small businesses. The key is to find in yourself what that place might be and to go for it.

To conclude, my advice to young professionals, particularly young Black professionals is this: be aware of your passions and follow them, develop a good work ethic, establish an extensive network of other professionals and friends, be active in your community by giving back, value your family, work for positive and healthy change, be courageous and patient, persevere, and let your light shine.

CHAPTER 13

Daughter of the Delta

HEATHER MCTEER HUDSON

Mayor, Greenville, Mississippi

"If you keep doin' what you always did, you'll keep gettin' what you always got." This quote by Jackie "Moms" Mabley became the mantra of my first mayoral bid for election. My name is Heather McTeer Hudson, and I serve as mayor of the city of Greenville, Mississippi. At age 27, I became the first African American, first female, and youngest mayor of Greenville, the fifth-largest city of the state of Mississippi and the largest city in the western part of the state. At the time of this publication, I am the nation's youngest African American mayor. My journey to this position was not an easy one, but it continues to be well worth every pebble, rock, and boulder along the way.

I am a true daughter of the Mississippi Delta. I was born on December 28, 1975, and raised in Greenville, Mississippi. Though I am from the Delta, my parents are not. Both my parents are originally from Baltimore, Maryland. While in law school, my father spent his summers in Mississippi working on various voters' rights projects in the Delta.[1] After his graduation, he and my mother moved to Mound Bayou, Mississippi.[2] They originally planned for only a two-year stay in the Mississippi town affectionately known as "chocolate city," but they never left Mississippi. Instead, they moved to Greenville, where my father continued his law practice and my mother worked as a teacher in the public school system. As a result, my younger brother, Marcus, and I are native Mississippians.

Because my father originally traveled to Mississippi to serve the people as a legal advocate for civil and voter's rights, my childhood was inundated with memories of people and places that were involved in the civil rights struggle. Our Sunday afternoon drives were on the roads traveled by those bringing information and civil liberties to the people of the Delta. Living with a mother who was also a teacher meant that those drives were also educational. I knew who Goodman, Chaney, and Schwerner were before I could sing the national anthem,[3] I traveled on part of the Rev. Jesse Jackson's presidential campaign in Mississippi at age nine. Election days were virtual holidays at our house because I got to go with my dad to watch the ballots come in and sit at the television station as they did live reports. To this day, I can still get from Greenville to Memphis without coming "above ground."[4] Both my father and mother have been a tremendous impact on my life—past, present, and future. They were both community advocates in their own ways, and watching their commitment and dedication to people not only inspired me but also taught me that part of my responsibility as a person is to help someone other than myself.

It is unusual to be from the Delta and not have a lot of family in the Delta. Everyone has cousins, aunts, and "big mammas" who live and work in the same community. Greenville is a close-knit community where everyone knows or is related to everyone else. Because my brother and I didn't have family in the Delta, we did what any other southern child would do, we made up family. We had a host of adopted aunts, uncles, play cousins, god-sisters, and god-brothers that made up our daily lives. They loved and treated us as if we were their own flesh and blood. These people not only aided in our childhood rearing but they also helped to mold the culture and heritage in which we were raised. I will be forever grateful for the time, money, and energy they invested in my upbringing.

My brother and I are only 2½ years apart in age, so we spent a lot of playtime together. As children, we lived in a predominantly White neighborhood and were two of only four children on the block. Though it was 1982, there was still a lot of racial reconciliation that needed to take place in Greenville, Mississippi, and the rest of the South. Nevertheless, it made absolutely no difference to us that our neighboring playmates were White: they were our friends. Together, our worlds were filled with the imagination and explorations of any child. No day was complete if it wasn't filled with a little dirt, a few bugs, dogs, a scant escape from death, and two mothers yelling across the fence to come home. We climbed trees and scraped knees, and I still have a scar from a painful brush with a barbed wire fence. The four of us were hometown celebrities when we appeared on the front page of the *Delta Democrat Times* for promoting our lemonade stand on one of the busiest streets in Greenville. If Katie and Daniel's mom was going to the store, we all jumped in the car. If my mother was going to the store, we all jumped into the car. Completely unaware of any unusual and suspecting stares from people curious about the lady with four children (two of whom were obviously not her own), we created play and easily amused ourselves regardless of our environment. That all changed once we hit middle school.

Schools in Greenville are highly segregated. At the time of desegregation, private schools began appearing all over the Delta, and in 2005, the public schools were 95 percent African American and private schools had the same ratio of Whites. Greenville is a town of approximately 42,000 citizens and there are five high schools in the city limits. Only two are public. Usually, White students start out in public school but transition to private schools by the time they enter junior high or middle school. It was no different for us in the 1980s. As we grew older, I entered Solomon Junior High School,[5] and our neighbors attended St. Joseph. Our cozy, comfortable world of childhood dreams and imaginations began to widen and fill with the truth and separation of the real world we lived in. As I think back, it saddens me that as new friends drew us away from one another, we were unable to introduce those same people into the world we created. Nevertheless, today we still get excited when we see each other. I truly believe that our pure childhood coexistence influenced our lives today. Katie teaches in a Mississippi Delta public school, Daniel serves in the military, my brother Marcus is working on a master's degree in forensic science, and I'm the mayor.

People often ask if I wanted to be mayor when I was a child. The answer is always a resounding no. Though many of my afternoons were spent at the library directly across the street from city hall, I had no clue what a mayor was or did. I was, however, very involved in student politics and government. I was student body president, a member of the mock trial team, and a member of the Mississippi State Youth Congress. I also involuntarily volunteered for just about any and every political campaign for which my parents were working. I graduated from T. L. Weston High

School in 1994 and went on to attend my dream college, Spelman.[6] My time at Spelman was filled with life experiences only an HBCU[7] can offer, and I learned lessons too numerous for these pages.

I majored in sociology and further developed my love for people and community. I traveled abroad to Santiago, Dominican Republic, where I studied Spanish and Dominican culture. I also worked a summer in Kenya for the Africa Crossroads Program.[8] In Kenya, I was part of a team of women sent to work and develop women's groups and show them how to build income and businesses based on their local trade. My favorite service project was serving as a Girl Scout Leader in East Point, a predominantly Black suburb of Atlanta, Georgia. I also worked as a legislative aide to Senator Donzella James for two years while I was in college. Senator James taught me a lot about staying close to your base. She would take community events over a reception any day. She authored a number of bills and had a genuine concern for the people she represented.

As an aide, I did everything from write speeches to attend local community information sessions. By watching and learning Senator James's methods of communicating with people, I discovered that one of the most important aspects of working in public office is keeping the people informed. This is not always the easiest task, as one must learn how to communicate to different kinds of people in an equally effective manner. I graduated from Spelman in 1998 and headed to New Orleans for law school.

I attended Tulane University Law School in New Orleans. Any law student can tell you that there's not much you do in law school other than study. So it was for me. I was active in the Black Law Student Association (BLSA) and, through it, worked on two campaigns for former BLSA members in their bid for state legislature. My summer intern experience was for former Mississippi Supreme Court Justice Fred Banks. My final year, I worked in a law clinic and represented indigent women in domestic violence cases. I also married a childhood friend, Abe Hudson, Jr. Abe and I decided that whatever we did in life, we would eventually make our home in Greenville, Mississippi. We had been so blessed by the opportunities afforded to us by our community that we knew we had to put back into that same community. Flight of the best and brightest is common in Mississippi. So many young people achieve their education and then decide to move away to work and raise a family. Our decision was based on our commitment to the people and community that raised us. We knew Mississippi would be home forever.

I served extensively in community development, law, and politics before running for mayor. I worked as an attorney with the law firm of McTeer & Associates. I am also cofounder of Project Give Back, a nonprofit organization that helps seniors in the Greenville Public Schools to complete college preparation materials. I currently serve as the executive director of the McTeer Foundation, a nonprofit organization that serves more than 25 Mississippi school districts and more than 2,000 students. It is our family's foundation and our way of constantly and increasingly giving back to the community that has so warmly welcomed us and enriched our lives.

My decision to run for mayor was actually conceived and birthed in prayer. I am a woman of faith, and I asked God to use me however he saw fit to move Greenville forward. The Bible clearly states that "the last shall be first and the first shall be last." We've been last for quite some time, so I knew he had to have something in mind for us soon. It seemed as though everywhere I went people were discussing how the city was deteriorating and how city government officials seemed unable to do anything about it. I often found myself joining in these coffee shop conversations and listening to the complaints, wishes, and desires of the people. Toward the end of 2002, it really began to bother me that no one seemed interested in actually doing anything other than complaining. A few times, I even mentioned the fact that we need to find "somebody" to help bring Greenville back to life. Little did I know that the "somebody" would be me! During a quiet night ride, the thought of running and my actually winning began to take over my thoughts. For every excuse I gave for not doing it, God gave me two for why I should do it. I knew that people would say I was too young and had no experience. I knew that though the town of Greenville was 65 percent African American, neither a Black person nor a woman had ever won the election before.[9] I knew I was up to a challenge like none other. But I also knew something else. I knew that God would not grant me anything I could not handle. I knew that the people of the community had raised me and put into me everything they wanted to see succeed. I knew that all my years of work with various politicians, community projects, and legal aid had prepared me for running and managing this city I called home. I knew that the people believed in me and saw me as their child. I knew that despite the odds, I would win.

Once I announced that I was running for mayor, life changed. My father would ask me daily, "How's your base?" I quickly learned that he meant, "Have you communicated with the people who are going to elect you today?" Strategy and money are important pieces of any campaign, but communication with people is ultimately the thing that can make or break an election. Though I had been a sociology major in school and had traveled the world studying different cultures and how they interacted with one another, my campaign taught me firsthand about people. A government official serves the people, and all politics is local. People want you to listen to their ideas and hear their complaints. You must have a vision and plan to share because people want to know where you're going if they choose to follow you. People will develop their own opinion of you regardless of everything you do or say. People you think will be with you will completely turn away, but people you've never met will stay all night to help complete strategies and projects. People expect you to do what you say and say what you're doing. People carried me when I was tired, encouraged me when people spoke negatively, and cheered me when things were good. Greenville, Mississippi, has wonderful people, and those people helped me get elected.

Another challenge of the election was overcoming the age and experience issue. There was a lot of hidden racism and sexism behind the concerns about my age. The going saying was always, "But she's so young!" I simply smiled and talked about my prior work and political experiences and how they had prepared me for the task ahead. I then kindly reminded them that the requirements for the job were simply being a resident of the city and a registered voter. Finally, I mentioned that it was truly sad that at age 18, one is old enough and trainable to die for the country in war, and at 21, I could obtain a license to practice law and represent corporations worth millions, but there are still some who think young people are not capable enough to manage a city. I spoke at every event possible, walked door to door, passed out flyers, and visited schools. When we ordered yard signs, they were gone in one day because so many people were eager to put them in their yards. African Americans in the city were really beginning to feel that they could make a difference—and they did.

On Election Day, the enthusiasm throughout the city was like a drumbeat, constantly increasing in tempo and force. Elderly people were going to the polls on walkers and canes. Cashiers were reminding their customers in line that today was Election Day. One lady even said she went though a drive-thru and the attendant asked her if she had voted today!

The election did not go without its glitches, however. A tremendous number of people were not on the books even though they had registered.

Yet and still, people were resilient. They refused to leave without submitting an affidavit ballot. By the time the polls closed, we were ahead by more than 1,000 votes. Our dedication and commitment to the community and the people's commitment to change had paid off.

As mayor, I continue to work for Greenville. Since I've been mayor, the city of Greenville has seen a 30 percent decline in the crime rate, a decrease in the budget deficit, and the institution of quality-of-life programs such as the City to Community council meetings where I hold a regular city council meeting in the local community. Currently, I'm working with our federal officials to include Greenville in more federally funded projects. Part of what I learned by listening to Greenville citizens is that our lack of infrastructure improvements is a major problem. Today, we're working for more street, sewer, and water improvements. Economic development and job opportunities are also at the top of the priority list. We are heavily marketing the community as a Delta Mecca for retail and industrial growth. Greenville is the largest city in the Mississippi Delta, and it has the perfect foundation for a future in tourism and retail industry. I truly believe that, with God, all things are possible to those who believe and I believe the best is yet to come for Greenville.

It has been a blessing to receive numerous awards and honors. I was named one of the 50 most influential African Americans in Mississippi and have been featured in the *Jackson Clarion Ledger*, the *Jackson Advocate*, *Jet* magazine, and the *Mississippi Business Journal*. In 2005, *Essence* magazine named me one of the 35 most inspiring women in the world. I still serve in the community and continue to attend my childhood church, Agape Storage Christian Center, where I serve as teen ministry leader. I am also a member of Alpha Kappa Alpha Sorority, Rotary Club International, the Mississippi Bar Association, the Mississippi Municipal League, the National Conference of Black Mayors, and the U.S. Conference of Mayors.

Through it all, I cannot forget from where I came. I realize that this is just the beginning of my life of service to Mississippi. The citizens I serve are family to me. They've raised me, nurtured me, and admonished me. I am thankful that I am able to return even a small portion of the investment that they have put into me. I can only hope that others in Mississippi see the hidden treasures in our state and return home to help develop the land that gave birth to them. Mississippi is truly God's country, and I'm glad to be part of it.

Notes

1. The "Delta" is the Mississippi Delta region located in the central western part of the state. Though it is the poorest region of the state, it has the most fertile soil and is famous for its southern writers, blues music, and catfish.

2. Founded by ex-slaves in 1887, Mound Bayou, Mississippi, is the oldest Black municipal government founded by Blacks in the South.

3. Reference to the three civil rights workers, Andrew Goodman, James Chaney, and Michael Schwerner, who were killed in 1964 in Mississippi.

4. A common term used by civil rights workers that means to travel certain back roads and avoid the highway so as not to attract attention.

5. Currently Solomon Middle School.

6. Spelman College is a historically black college for women of color. Founded in 1881, Spelman is often ranked in the Top 10 of colleges and universities in the nation and is famous for producing outstanding women who achieve. Spelman College is located in Atlanta, Georgia.

7. Historically Black College and University.

8. Africa Crossroads is a program that allows college and graduate-level students to volunteer and work in various African countries on needed projects.

9. African Americans and women had run for the Greenville mayor's seat in the past; however, none were successful.

CHAPTER 14

Be Secure in Who You Are

By Neari F. Warner

BERNETTE JOSHUA JOHNSON

Associate Justice, Supreme Court
of Louisiana, Baton Rouge, Louisiana

Justice Bernette Joshua Johnson is one of the first African American women to attend Louisiana State University law school, where she received her juris doctorate degree in 1969. She received her honorary doctorate of laws from Spelman College in 2001. Justice Johnson was the first woman elected to Civil District Court. She was elected in 1984, was reelected without opposition in 1990, and elected chief judge in 1994. Justice Johnson has spent much of her legal career working for the poor and disadvantaged. She served as a law intern with the U.S. Department of Justice, Civil Rights Division, Washington, D.C., and as a legal services attorney with the New Orleans Legal Assistance Corporation (NOLAC). During the 1960s, Justice Johnson worked as a community organizer with the NAACP Legal Defense and Educational Fund in New York City. During the 1970s, she helped to organize household workers to receive Social Security benefits and a minimum wage.

Justice Johnson is the recipient of numerous awards including, but not limited to, the Outstanding Women on the Bench from the New Orleans Association of Black Women Attorneys; the first Ernest N. Morial award given by NOLAC; 1994 Woman of the Year from the LaBelle West Chapter, American Business Women Association; the Daniel Byrd award and the A.P. Tureaud Citizenship Award from the Louisiana State conference, NAACP; and the American Bar Association's prestigious Margaret A. Brent Women Lawyers of Achievement Award. Justice Johnson is currently an associate justice of the Louisiana Supreme Court.

Dr. Neari F. Warner interviewed Justice Bernette Johnson on October 18, 2006, for this book.

Dr. Warner: Let us begin with your early background, including information about your parents, siblings, and overall childhood experiences.
Justice Johnson: I was born in Ascension Parish near Donaldsonville [Louisiana] and grew up in a family with three brothers and my parents. My dad was in the Navy. In a parish like Ascension in the 1940s, when you got back from the war, there was no job opportunity in a farming community. That's how I wound up in New Orleans with my family. I attended segregated schools in New Orleans, and I think it is important for young people to understand that although we had segregated schools, we had excellent educators who gave us grounding and the basics. Also, I think what might be missing from young people today is that they don't have the encouragement and the motivation; and perhaps they don't have the teachers who expect them to excel. It seems that we just expect failure in schools. Even in the segregated schools, there was the expectation that we would excel and do well, so we did. I left high school in New Orleans and went to Spelman College in Atlanta, where I became involved in the Civil Rights struggle. Returning to New Orleans and attending LSU Law School, I have been in the New Orleans community ever since, working as a lawyer for Legal Services. Immediately before seeking a judgeship at Civil District Court, I worked in the city attorney's office. I was a trial judge in civil trials for 10 years in Civil District Court. I was elected to the Louisiana Supreme Court in 1994, where I have been 12 years now. Time goes by so swiftly.

Dr. Warner: During those experiences, are there any particular individuals that you would acknowledge as being your mentor or your role models?
Justice Johnson: Absolutely. I guess when we talk about segregated schools, I can still remember being at McCarty Elementary School in the Lower Ninth Ward. That's significant now because this is that area that was destroyed by Hurricane Katrina. McCarty School doesn't exist because it was replaced by Martin Luther King Elementary School. I met

the principal of that school, and he's doing a marvelous job trying to get this school back up and running. Mrs. Zenobia Johnson was the principal of McCarty Elementary. I still recall that when *Brown v. Board of Education* was decided, she called an assembly and made the announcement. Like everybody else, we expected that life was going to change overnight. We didn't realize what *all deliberate speed* meant in terms of school desegregation, and we didn't anticipate the turmoil. The desegregation of schools was a struggle. In fact, that's where I did a lot of my work regarding school desegregation—the NAACP Legal Defense Fund.

Dr. Warner: Yes, I do understand what you are saying about our schools. We did happen to go to the same high school, and we had wonderful experiences.
Justice Johnson: Yes, Cohen High School. Cohen was a school! Walter L. Cohen was a school everyone wanted to attend—the best of schools, I think. Of course, we get into competition because I have a brother who graduated from Clark High School. McDonough 35 has a 70- or 80-year reputation for educating African Americans. Cohen High School was a school where everyone wanted to attend. The principal there was a person who motivated me. I think Mrs. Bradley at Cohen High School and all of the teachers and the principals there—Mr. Sorrell and Mr. Perry— all of those educators were absolutely motivating.

Then when I went to Spelman College, I also had excellent role models. One was Dr. Moreland, one of the instructors who taught political science. There, I had the chance to meet some lawyers in the Atlanta community and to work for the Legal Defense Fund. I also had the opportunity to meet Julius Chambers and Constance Baker Motley—all of those wonderful people. It was just a great experience and that, I think—the NAACP experience—was what motivated me to return to Louisiana and enroll at LSU Law School. LSU had not had a Black student in 10 years. Attorney A. P. Tureaud filed a lawsuit to desegregate the LSU System. His son, by the way, attended undergraduate school at LSU and was one of the first Black students. Dutch Morial and Robert Collins were the first two Black students in 1955. My classmate, Camille Grey, and I got to the law school in 1965. There had not been anybody in that 10-year span, and that was motivation for me.

I met great lawyers. I worked for Dutch Morial as a law clerk after law school. I had a chance to meet Mr. A. P. Tureaud, who is a giant in terms of the civil rights struggle. I have been blessed with lots of role models—lawyers, teachers, and, of course, my parents. I said to some young lawyers recently at a board ceremony that the things learned at home are really the things that ground children—parents who teach them how to resolve disputes and parents who insist that they can't bring anything home that doesn't belong to them. These are the children who understand *do not steal* and *do not kill*. We must have that moral foundation and the moral grounding. I had wonderful parents and a large extended family that have just been encouraging throughout my career.

Dr. Warner: Can you pinpoint what specifically motivated you to pursue the judicial area?

Justice Johnson: Working with lawyers encouraged me to go to law school because growing up I knew teachers, but I didn't know any Black lawyers. Then, I had the opportunity to work for the NAACP Legal Defense Fund. Jack Greenberg and all of those lawyers who were part of that process helped me to see that there are Black lawyers out there and that they are doing some really great things. That, too, motivated me to go to law school. When I graduated from LSU in 1969, I returned to New Orleans. The first Black judge in New Orleans was Israel Augustine at Criminal District Court, and that might have been about 1970. Then, I clerked for Dutch Morial in 1969. I think in 1970 he was appointed a judge at Juvenile Court. Prior to then, he was in the Louisiana Legislature, the first Black in the legislature—then the first Black at Juvenile Court. So it's a progression. I tell young people all the time, "Your aspirations are tied to what you see is possible." If you've never seen a Black lawyer, how do you know you can be one? If you've never seen a Black judge, how do you know you can be one? If you've never seen someone from the NASA space program, how do you aspire to that? I'm always encouraging our African American judges to get out into the community for Law Day and Black History Month and church programs and all of these things because young people have to see us up close and personal because it lifts their level of aspiration.

Dr. Warner: What are the key milestones or the turning points that you feel put you where you are today?

Justice Johnson: I guess you would think about it in terms of forks in the road, a choice of A or B. One significant thing was that during my senior year in high school, I had a choice of Dillard University or Xavier

University because that was all I knew. Then, Spelman College happened to send someone down who showed me a film about Spelman College. It was then that I decided this is what I wanted to do. So, off I went to Atlanta for four years. That was a fork in the road. Finishing Spelman College, I had the opportunity to work, as I said, with school desegregation cases all over the South. The Legal Defense Fund hired me along with two of my Spelman classmates. When my parents came to Atlanta for my graduation, I packed a bag to send home with them, but I said, "Well, I'm not going home. I'm on my way to New York." So, I left Atlanta and went to New York for my orientation for my first summer of work. We sat down with a group of lawyers, and they explained to us what they were doing in terms of cases. We think of *Brown v. Board of Education* as one big monolithic case that desegregated every school district, but that is not the case. The fact is that in every state and in every parish in Louisiana, we had to file lawsuits against that school board to desegregate that particular school system. After that was accomplished, the lawyers were in the community just trying to give people information so they could take advantage of it. Otherwise, it would be a hybrid victory. It would be the case of handling a hundred cases and desegregating a hundred schools but not having anyone to take advantage of them. The Fund hired us, and a stock description of what we did was to disseminate information.

Dr. Warner: Would you expound on some of these experiences?
Justice Johnson: I would leave New York and go to Gadsden, Birmingham, or Montgomery in Alabama. In Louisiana, I have worked in Patterson, Berwick, Morgan City, New Iberia, and Shreveport because every school district had its own set of circumstances. The circumstances differed in every place. In some places like Little Rock, Arkansas, the authorities desegregated high schools in 12th grade; however, in most Louisiana parishes, they desegregated the schools from grade one. I would be in some little community—Berwick, Patterson, or some small community in Alabama—and we had the problem of public accommodation. If we flew into Shreveport, we knew we would stay in a Black hotel in Shreveport. In many of those places, we were lodging with a local NAACP president or an activist because at that time there were no open accommodations in terms of hotels, restaurants, and all of this. We went in and worked with the local community activists in getting information to them about the whole process, much like our secretary of state is doing now in dealing

with displaced voters. We explained the process to them in such terms as "This is how you apply to send your child to one of these newly desegregated schools." There I was, sitting on the front porch trying to convince a parent to send a five- or six-year-old into a situation I knew was hostile. When I thought back to Ruby Bridges and William Frantz School in New Orleans and the mobs almost lining the street and federal marshals having to march her in, I was saying to myself, "You know this is going to be tough for these little kids."

I worked in that for a period of time and then began that whole process of applying to law school. I applied to Boston University and the University of North Carolina. This was another fork in the road. I was relatively familiar with North Carolina because I had done some work in Raleigh and a lot of little towns in North Carolina, South Carolina, and Tennessee. Looking at that whole process, I really wanted to go to school in Boston. Of course, Dr. Martin Luther King, Jr. had studied for his PhD at Boston University, and obviously, this was a school that was accustomed to and comfortable with Black students. This was my fork in the road, and I said, "You know, I really would like to go to Boston University." I had been accepted. Then I said, "No, Bernette, you need to go to LSU because there has not been a Black student at LSU in 10 years. And you can't take the easy way out. You've been sitting on porches telling parents 'Look, I know this is tough; but go ahead and send your child.'" Yes, LSU was tough because my classmates were not all that accepting or receptive. However, in every situation I tell folks, "You know, the glass is either half empty or half full and so take that situation and create something positive with it." With all of the negatives, there are always positives. There are always professors—there are one or two who will help. There are always other students who will assist and give you notes, encourage, and help you. It was not an impossible situation.

Dr. Warner: What about the issue of racism? Tell us how you dealt with the racism you must have encountered, professionally and personally. Justice Johnson: In the LSU situation, it was never violent. It was either one of two things: Either you were ignored or no one was overtly hostile. The staff and the faculty at the law school were all professional in terms of how they handled your paperwork, your loan papers, and all the rest. Whether students were friendly or not is another issue. Some of them were—Margaret Omere comes to mind. This young woman was from Lake Charles and had an Ivy League undergraduate background. She was from the kind of background where her parents had exposed her to various things. So, she made sure—she was a year ahead of me—that I had all the notes everybody else had. Whether I was a member of their fraternity did not matter because I had access to all of that. She made her boyfriend sit in the library and assist me when I needed help with something. That's the kind of access I had. As for the ones who did not want to help, rather than being ugly or verbally hostile, they were just trying their best to ignore me or pretend I was not there. Perhaps, that was how they dealt with the desegregation of their law school.

Of course, I have done work in situations where people have been overtly hostile. I am sure we have all experienced that in terms of overt hostility based on race. I just always try to conduct myself in a professional manner and try as best I can to keep something from becoming physically confrontational while at the same time always letting people know where I stand. It is not my nature to compromise myself or other Black people in any situation. You know that this is my position even though I am just registering my dissent. That is how I have conducted myself professionally, and here at this court. This is how I try to encourage my staff and other young lawyers to approach racism when they encounter it. That is also how I have raised my children. I think that is an important process by which we have to raise our children so that they recognize racism when they see it. I saw just recently the incident in Coushatta in Red River Parish in Louisiana, where the bus driver was seating the Black kids in the back of the bus. If that mother had accepted that, we know we would be back where we were before Mrs. Rosa Parks.

I use such incidents to help our young people understand our past struggles. I tell my son and my daughter-in-law about such things because I have an eight-year-old granddaughter, Mia, who is very bright. She is in school in Atlanta in the DeKalb System. I said to them, "If she doesn't know who Mrs. Rosa Parks is, that's your problem. She has a picture of Mrs. Parks in her bedroom, and it's your job to teach her because she will come along in 50 years, 100 years after Mrs. Parks and will not know what Mrs. Parks did." We have to raise this next generation; they have to raise their children because otherwise we are being propelled backwards. Fifty years from now somebody is going to come along who will try to seat us in the back of the bus; either we will have to accept it or we are going to say, "No, Mrs. Parks did this, and I am going to do it, too. I'm not going to stand for it."

Dr. Warner: What is your prediction for African Americans in the judicial system and what, if anything, can we do to help increase the number of African American judges?

Justice Johnson: I think we have to look at it state by state. I think a lot of it has to do with population. In Minnesota, for instance, there was an African American on the Supreme Court, but we are a small number in terms of population or the number of lawyers there. In the South, I think the majority of African Americans are where we live. Here, I am one of seven. There is one African American on the Mississippi Supreme Court and two on the Georgia Supreme Court. I am not sure that South Carolina has an African American. North Carolina has one, and that is about the way it goes.

In the states where Blacks are, proportionately, not in large numbers, we may not have African Americans on those courts. I think there is some-one African American on the Supreme Court in Maryland. The process, I think, depends on population—our numbers and how we are represented in the general population and among the number of lawyers. I think it depends on whether we have an elective process or an appointive pro-cess. If we have the numbers and we have the districts we can elect Black judges. However, if we are only 10 percent of the population, the only way we can be represented is by the appointment of a Black judge. I think this judge in Minnesota was popular, had gone to college, was an athlete, played basketball or football. He was a rather outstanding person who had come to the attention of a governor who wanted to make an appointment.

Dr. Warner: What kind of advice would you give young people whose aspirations are to be on the high courts?

Justice Johnson: I would say being at this level has to be a long-term aspirational goal. I tell young people all the time that everybody starts at the bottom; everybody starts at the beginning. If you are interested in ending up here, the first thing that you do is study hard in high school, make good grades along with enjoying band and football and every-thing else because you want to enjoy school, too . You don't want to just study. Then, if you can, attend college; and if you can, earn a scholar-ship because that helps your family. There are just lots of opportunities at state and private schools and Ivy League schools. Everybody has a chance for a college education, and so you achieve that goal. Then, if it is possible, you can go to graduate school immediately after college. I did not have a family at that time. I married after law school; therefore, I could somewhat keep my focus on studying. However, some people have family responsibilities and a job requirement to support a family and may have to delay some of these goals for a time. You accomplish that goal all the while you are involved in your community. If you graduate from law school, you build a career there and then look at what opportunities are there to run for judgeships or what opportunities are there for an appointment to a judgeship.

Dr. Warner: Some African Americans consider careers in the legal system as leading to losing their cultural identity. Do you think this is a genuine concern?

Justice Johnson: No, I don't. I don't think I have ever feared losing my identity in any situation. It did not matter where I went to school or where I lived. I recall a time when I was an exchange student in Kansas, where there are few Black folks in Winfield, Kansas. You just have to be secure in who you are. I don't think you need the dashiki all the time to promote or suggest who you are. You are comfortable in yourself. For those folks who want to dress in a certain fashion, that's fine in terms of identity. I don't think you lose your identity; I don't think you lose yourself. I really do not believe that this is a problem. It never has been for me.

Dr. Warner: What is your philosophy of the high court and how do you view yourself as a judge?

Justice Johnson: In terms of what I do, I serve several functions. We, the seven justices on this court, have several functions. We supervise the judiciary. By that, I mean we make rules to determine who will be admitted to practice. We have committees we have established that recommend to us whether a lawyer should be suspended or disbarred. We also have a Judiciary Commission, which, as you know, can recommend to us that we can suspend or remove a judge from office. That is what I mean about supervising the whole system. That is part of it relative to the cases, and we have lawyers who file cases in this court. The cases come up to us on direct appeal—death penalty cases, for instance, and cases from the Public Service Commission and various agencies. We also have what we call writs of circuitry, meaning discretionary writs, about 3,000 of them.

Citizens and lawyers can file those writs here in the court, and we decide whether we want to grant or deny a writ, depending on whether it is a legal issue that we need to decide.

We also decide if there is a conflict in the circuits or if there is some other reason that we need to grant a writ application. We also take up constitutional challenges where a law has been declared unconstitutional by one of the lower courts, and we subsequently decide whether that particular statute violates the constitution. Thus, we do cases, we do writs, we listen to oral arguments, and we write opinions. Overall, however, our major role, I believe, is the supervision of the judiciary—the courts, the lower courts, the judges, and the lawyers in the state.

Dr. Warner: What do you think set you apart from the other judges such that you were able to achieve this appointment?
Justice Johnson: That's an interesting question. It's why me and not maybe 17,000 or 18,000 other lawyers in the state. We say we can't count the number of Black lawyers, maybe a couple thousand, now at least I guess, statewide. So I don't know. Why me of those 18,000 lawyers and a couple thousand Black lawyers? I think the answer may be that, first, I'm here in the New Orleans area. The seat was created so that people from this majority Black area would have an opportunity to elect their choice to the court. That is all a part of our litigation. *Chisom v. Edwards* and *Clarke v. Roemer* were the two lawsuits that we filed in Louisiana that dealt with desegregation of the judiciary. As a result of *Clarke v. Roemer*, we went from 8 or 10 judges to 60, and we created this Black Supreme Court seat as a result of *Chisom v. Edwards*. The fact that I am from the New Orleans area, rather than a judge from Shreveport or Monroe, is one answer. New Orleans is where the majority Black district is.

The other answer, I think, is that I finished law school at LSU in 1969 and that I have been a lawyer for a very long time. Justice Revius Ortique was the first African American on the Court, and we had the mandatory timer that they set. He was here for a number of years. When this vacancy occurred in 1994, upon Justice Ortique's retirement, I had been a lawyer since 1969. I had ten years of experience. When you are looking for someone to run for the seat, the answer is experience. The reason I was able to prevail is years of practice as a lawyer, plus the 10 years as a district trial judge. That was persuasive to the electorate in terms of "let's send Bernette Johnson to the Supreme Court."

Dr. Warner: What are some of your values and personal traits that have sustained you, that have contributed to your success, and that are just noteworthy to know about?

Justice Johnson: I think my religious faith has certainly sustained me. Not everyone has that, but my religious foundation is what keeps me grounded and on track. It helps me to see our world in terms of destiny and purpose. The Creator has me where I have certain skills and certain gifts. There will be and there have been certain doors open to me certainly because of destiny and purpose. I do not see my life as something by chance. I see my life as a purposeful life because of my family background and our emphasis on morality. My paternal grandfather was superintendent of a Sunday school. I grew up in a family where there was a Baptist preacher. That is just our style. Sometimes that kind of style protects you because if you are not raised in a family where everybody is only interested having a good time, it lessens the likelihood for you to be shot or stabbed.

For example, if you attend one of my family functions, all we are going to do is sit around and talk and eat. Nobody is going to be shot at, and the police will never be called because my father, Frank Joshua, didn't like loud people. He just wouldn't tolerate it in his home. The kind of socializing that some families will do—such as you see on television at a wedding reception where somebody is going to start fighting, and the police have to come in to break up the wedding party—is not what we do. We don't do that. That is just not the way we conduct ourselves, and I think it affects a person. I tell my children all the time that rules are there, and that they may seem burdensome at the time, but in the long run they protect you. The fact that you do not let your young teenagers drive protects them from killing themselves. The fact that you do not give alcohol to minors or do not allow alcohol use by minors in your home protects your young people. Your talking to them constantly about unprotected sex protects them from herpes and AIDS, and so all of the rules in the long run protect us.

Dr. Warner: Speaking of family, I understand that you have two children.

Justice Johnson: Yes, both of my children went to school in Atlanta. My daughter, Rachael, got her undergraduate degree at Spelman College and then went on to Smith College to get her master's degree in social work. She recently earned her law degree at Tulane University. My son, David, went to Morehouse College. I think because of what I have seen in the whole system, I think it is good to send young persons to a nurturing environment for that first degree where they are going to run into some supportive staff. When they get that first degree out of the way, I do not have an opinion about where they go next. Do you want to go to the big universities with 40,000 or 50,000 people? That is fine because you are grounded from your undergraduate experiences. I still am extremely close to the women I spent those four years with at Spelman College.

As I said, my daughter graduated with a master's in social work. She worked in adoptions in Atlanta for a while, and then she decided to go to law school. She came home to live with me and went to Tulane for three years. After Hurricane Katrina, everyone's world was just turned upside down. She had an offer to work again with a personal injury firm where she had clerked over the summer. So, she went back to Florida. She took the bar and was admitted to the Louisiana bar. She was sworn into the Florida bar just recently. I am proud of her, and I am proud of my son. He is an accountant. He did computer work and then got the degree in accounting. He is working in Atlanta and is doing well. When I run into someone who has met Rachael or David and who says to me, "You know, this is a great kid," or who compliments me on their work, that makes my day!

Dr. Warner: Surely, I know that this makes you proud. In similar manner, you should know that we are proud of what you do and of the impact that you are making on society. Tell us about your role and your duties and responsibilities.
Justice Johnson: I did trial work for about 10 years. I guess every decision you make impacts someone's life and sometimes you don't even know how. Years later I run into someone who will say, "You were the Justice Johnson who gave me my divorce" or "I was the foreperson on your jury." You can tell that that experience has changed that person's life.

At this level, we are writing opinions, and we are trying to get a majority consensus. Therefore, it is a different process. At the pilot level, when I was a district judge, I made up my mind independently. When I reached a conclusion, I had a judgment presented or drafted by my staff; I signed it, and I was finished with it. The appellate court could overturn it or decide whatever its members thought appropriate. Here we are trying to reach a consensus. Consequently, I need to persuade at least three other judges to go along with whatever I am suggesting. That means that our word alone does not really have to prevail or carry. I have to persuade three others that this is the way we have to do this. Sometimes that means adding some things they want to the process or to the language.

So it's like seven cooks in the kitchen. I cannot cook it the way I want it. It is not just you; everybody has to have a bit of it. That is different with the appellate court. We can see that play out in the U.S. Supreme Court with Justice Sandra Day O'Connor. At times, you are with what they call the liberal group, and at other times you are with the conservative wing. You are just trying to build a consensus to accomplish what you are trying to accomplish. It may not be everything you want, but that is the process. Anything else is more canned as being at a trial where I call it the way I see it, and it is my opinion. Here, if some others are signing on, then I have to let them be involved in the process.

Dr. Warner: You are very involved in a lot of professional and civic activities. Why is this important to you?
Justice Johnson: It is important because people have to see judges; we have to be involved in a community. We cannot isolate ourselves; otherwise, how can we motivate young people or be a benefit to them? That's why I am involved in a lot of law and church activities and with the Links and with the Zeta Phi Beta Sorority. For a time, I was involved in the SCLC [Southern Christian Leadership Conference] for women. That was a great experience for my children because I took them to some of those conventions, and they had a chance to see a lot of those heroes or "she-roes." They saw the struggle.

I think we have to be involved. For that reason, I accept invitations to participate in women's day programs and Black history programs at churches and schools and graduations. I certainly do all of these. It is a way to give back, to connect with our community so that they are current about what we do. I do not want my job to be a mystery to young people, and so we invite them here for Law Day. We invite schools to come to the court to see the building, to see our law library. We invite groups to come in for oral arguments. That is a part of the education process. This is a state building, a public building; and we like to be open and to invite them in.

Dr. Warner: What would you identify to be your career-defining accomplishment of which you are most proud?

Justice Johnson: Perhaps there is one, my work at the Supreme Court. I think that is because it is important. My hope is that there will always be at least one African American here at this court because our population pre-Katrina certainly was more than 30 percent African American. Since I have been here at the court, I have insisted that all of our various committees, the Committee on Bar Admissions, and all of the committees appointed by the court actually represent who we are with respect to race, gender, and diversity of the population of the state. We need people from Shreveport, Monroe, New Iberia, Opelousas, and various other places. With bar admission, certainly it would not speak well of us to have a system where African Americans or women or any other group is excluded. This is the group that administers the testing and makes a decision about who practices law in this state. We have to make sure that all of these committees are representative. In the same vein, I think that we have to be sure that we do not let it turn into a situation where African Americans are not well represented in the judiciary.

Dr. Warner: Since this publication, *Voices of Historical and Contemporary Black American Pioneers,* is designed for young professionals who are just starting their careers or are very early in their careers, what advice would you give those individuals regardless of the profession?
Justice Johnson: I would suggest that they seek out mentors and certainly that they be involved with their peer groups. I would also advise that they seek out mentors—someone from another generation who is in fact involved in that profession that they aspire to serve. If you are a meteorologist, you would talk to someone practicing meteorology at a TV station who can give you good advice. If you are interested in science, you would seek out a science professor or a math professor. If it is computers that interest you, seek out someone who is interested in that. For young people who want to be lawyers, meet some of the local lawyers in your community and engage them in a conversation. Ask them questions about their careers and plans and goals. Most important of all, young people should know that professionals are always willing to give advice and talk about their careers.

Dr. Warner: Justice Johnson, Your Honor, thank you for your time and for your willingness to share and to participate in this project. It has been a pleasure working with you.

About the Author

Neari F. Warner, retired professor and former acting president of Grambling State University in Louisiana, currently serves as visiting professor in the Executive PhD Program at Jackson State University in Mississippi. She earned her PhD at Louisiana State University, Baton Rouge.

CHAPTER 15

A Tradition of Accomplishments

EMIL JONES, JR.

Former Illinois State Senate President,
14th District Senate Office, Chicago, Illinois

I've said many times that the Illinois General Assembly is probably one of the best universities. When I was a freshman in the Illinois House in 1973, a veteran legislator told me to sit with people from different regions of the state—that would enable me to have a better understanding of all of the issues confronting Illinoisans. That was an excellent piece of advice—one that I still use today—and one that I believe better enables me to work with all of the members as president of the Illinois Senate.

All 33 members of the Illinois Senate Majority Caucus are distinct individuals who represent districts just as diverse as the people who live in them. I have had the honor of serving as the head of the Democratic Caucus in the Illinois Senate since 1993, first as Senate Democratic leader and since 2003 as the Senate president. As Senate president I represent each and every voice of the Democratic Caucus at the negotiating table with the governor and the other caucus leaders.

Since I have been a member of the Illinois General Assembly, I have made education, economic development projects in underserved areas, and working families my priorities. As the newly elected Senate president in

Note: Before Emil Jones, Jr.'s retirement in 2009, he submitted this chapter for publication while serving as Illinois State Senate president.

the 93rd General Assembly, I set an ambitious agenda targeted to those priorities, and I used the skills that I had learned throughout my career in the Illinois General Assembly to reach those goals.

One of the most difficult tasks before us was to reform the criminal justice system in Illinois. I was the first statewide official to call for a moratorium on the death penalty in Illinois. I followed that call with the appointment of my own task force consisting of lawmakers, attorneys, judges, and law enforcement officials to study the criminal justice system in Illinois. Our findings were issued in 2000, but Republicans, who controlled the Illinois Senate at the time, turned a deaf ear to the proposed reforms. Shortly after our reforms were proposed, then-governor George Ryan announced his own independent panel, which issued a report in 2001 that mirrored many of our recommendations for reform. These, too, were ignored by the Republican-controlled Senate, although hearings were held on the issue.

I made reform to the criminal justice system my top priority after being sworn in as Senate president. The reforms became a reality in 2003, when the legislation passed with overwhelming bipartisan support, and Illinois became the first state in the nation to require the videotaping of interrogations in capital murder cases—a keystone of the reform package.

Illinois also joined other states in its concern about diversity with the passage of a law that requires law enforcement agencies throughout Illinois to record the race of the person in a vehicle stopped for a traffic violation.

Additional reforms that were included in the package are a requirement that police must preserve evidence, disclose evidence of innocence from death penalty cases, and provide all reports and evidence to prosecutors; evidence of a defendant's innocence must be disclosed to the defendant's attorney; executions of the mentally retarded are prohibited; the prosecution must disclose information about an informant, including criminal history, any deals made with the state, and any other information affecting the reliability of an informant or his or her testimony in a case where an informant who is in custody testifies that a confession was made by the defendant. The defendant also has access to DNA information and analysis, including DNA-matching databases.

The battle for justice was not over with the passage of these reforms by the Illinois General Assembly. Another battle was to be fought in the media over the provision that would require a police officer who committed perjury during a capital murder case to lose his or her job. The police unions fought to take the provision out of the bill. Most law enforcement individuals are honorable, but the system must be cleansed of the few who would undermine the integrity of law enforcement by committing perjury. The provision stayed in the bill.

The other priorities on my agenda included establishing a prescription drug discount program for senior and disabled citizens who are without insurance for prescription drugs, requiring equal pay for equal work, increasing the minimum wage, increasing funding for education, and conducting a study of racial profiling.

The Senior Citizen Prescription Drug Discount was passed and signed into law after years of not even being called for a vote when Republicans controlled the Senate Chamber. The legislation establishes a program that allows seniors to pool together so prescription drug prices are reduced by up to 40 percent and those on limited incomes aren't forced to choose between heat and medication.

Legislation also passed the Illinois Senate to ensure equal pay for equal work—another piece of legislation that did not see the light of day during the previous decade. Statistics show that women in service positions currently earn 71 cents on the dollar for what men earn for the same job. In management positions, the disparity is larger—68 cents on the dollar. The average working family loses $5,000 annually when the same work is not rewarded with the same pay. With an eye on doing more for working families, I also fought to increase the minimum wage in Illinois from $5.15 to $6.50 per hour.

Working families also benefited from legislation to expand the Earned Income Tax Credit that, in 2000, finally put Illinois on the same footing with federal tax law in not taxing its poorest citizens. When the bill passed in 2000, Republicans put an expiration date on the law. In 2003, we made the legislation permanent and refundable, which provides a hand up, not a handout.

Education funding reform has been discussed in Illinois since the 1970s when I was a member of the Illinois House. Although we have yet to eliminate Illinois's outdated and unfair system of primarily funding schools with property tax dollars, we have been able to increase the state's commitment in per student funding. Illinois's current system is inherently unfair in that some schools are able to fund a student's education at $18,000 annually, while others fund at only $4,964.

Although we have increased funding for schools, true reform is needed. Briefly, here is what we have accomplished in two short years, despite extremely difficult budget constraints. In 2003, a $250 per student increase was passed despite the nearly $5 billion budget deficit Illinois was experiencing. In 2004, despite pressure from some in the General Assembly to pass a zero-growth budget, I fought for and won a $389 million increase for Illinois schoolchildren.

My commitment to education continues. As I gave my initial remarks to the 94th General Assembly, I told my colleagues in the Senate that I would seek common ground on the education-funding reform issue and work with them in a bipartisan fashion to reach that goal. Recently, I created the Select Committee on Education, which is charged with that monumental task.

Although 2003 was a critical year of accomplishment, and many people point to it as groundbreaking since it was my first year as Senate president, I can point to many critical accomplishments during the 1990s when I served as Democratic leader.

Although some try to downplay the role of Democratic leader, many were surprised at what I was able to negotiate during that time. The two following instances underscore what determination and knowing the concerns of the other negotiators at the table can achieve.

In 1997, the governor called a special session of the Illinois General Assembly to work on the education funding crisis. This special session followed a spring session that was marred by Republican infighting over the Republican governor's education proposal to raise the income tax in exchange for a reduction in local property taxes. When it appeared as though nothing would be accomplished on reforming the funding formula, I took to the negotiating table a compromise that would increase general state aid for poor school districts to $4,225. Further, my proposal made education funding an entitlement, similar to Social Security on the national level. That meant education funding was dedicated up front in the budget for three years.

Putting this proposal on the table accomplished what the governor wanted—an increase for schools—and what the Republicans wanted—no increase in state income taxes.

In 1998, the Republican leadership was calling for major tax breaks for business; however, the average Illinois citizen had not received a tax break since the state income tax was passed in 1969. I was the first of the legislative leaders to call for doubling the personal exemption on the state income tax. Both measures passed with overwhelming support.

Though many would like to label me as a Chicago Democrat, my record speaks to the efforts that I have worked to achieve for our state. Education funding reform; health care initiatives; construction and maintenance dollars for schools, roads, and other infrastructure improvements; tax breaks for working families; equal pay; and an increase in the minimum wage.

This year I have also targeted efforts to provide more funding for underprivileged women who are victims of breast cancer. Senate Bill 1 would create the "Ticket for the Cure." The net proceeds from the sale of this ticket would go primarily to services for women who are undergoing treatment and recovery from this disease. In some instances, low-income women do not seek treatment because they cannot afford transportation to the clinic or hospital, or they do not have child care. Other hurdles they face are affording the medication. Some must choose between paying the heating bill or paying for their medication. Estimates show that the "Ticket for the Cure" could raise as much as $5 million a year for breast cancer. Illinois would be the first state in the nation to create a lottery for breast cancer. Canada currently has a lottery for cancer.

My advice to young men and women entering the workforce is to always be open to new experiences. As I indicated earlier in this chapter, the best advice I received as a freshman legislator was to get to know legislators from other areas of the state: southern, rural, and suburban. After serving for more than 30 years as a state legislator and establishing those relationships, I believe it has helped me be a Senate president who truly represents all of Illinois. That ability to serve all of the people is what I consider to be my greatest accomplishment.

CHAPTER 16

A Lawyer's Life in Brief

KIM M. KEENAN

Principal, Keenan Firm, Washington, D.C.;
General Counsel of the National
Association for the Advancement
of Colored People (NAACP),
Washington, D.C.; Past President,
National Bar Association

If there is no struggle, there is no progress. Those who profess to favor freedom and yet deprecate agitation are men who want crops without plowing up the ground; they want rain without thunder and lightning. . . .

This struggle may be both moral and physical, but it must be a struggle. Power concedes nothing without a demand. It never did and it never will. . . . Men [and women] may not get all they pay for in this world but they must certainly pay for all they get.

—Frederick Douglass

The quote at the start of this chapter is one of my favorite quotes. My mother used to always say, "Power concedes nothing without a demand." She was referring to remarks made by the late former congresswoman Shirley Chisholm, who made this into her personal mantra. This quote has weathered the test of time because it touches at the heart of what it is to be Black, and in my case, female in America.

I am the eldest daughter of an autoworker and a social worker. Little did I know that my parents' work ethic would serve as the foundation for my legal career. I watched them both work very hard. Through Buffalo, New York's blizzards, layoffs, cutbacks, and plain old setbacks, my parents were unwavering in their desire to provide their children with the best education possible to prepare them for their future.

My first true brush with injustice came in third grade. I attended a Catholic grammar school, and for each of the three years that I had attended, I received First Honors at the end of the school year. First Honors was given to the child with the highest grades. At the end of the third year, the teachers told my mother that I could no longer receive First Honors, even if I deserved it, because it was disheartening to my classmates, who were predominantly White. I was only one of a few Black children in my class, and it never dawned on me that my performance could leave such a permanent impact on my classmates. But this experience did leave a permanent impact on me. I had never seen my mother so focused. She explained the situation to me and pointed out the injustice of their position. Of course the teachers did not intend for me to leave the school, but in fact, my mother felt that they left her no choice. She would never tell me to settle for second best, even if my teacher was a nun. I had been trained from birth to do my best and to compete against everyone without regard to color, gender, or anything else.

My mother was the first real advocate in my life. Like my father, she was fearless when it came to her children. She told the school officials that she would remove me from the school rather than allow me to accept second honors. She promptly enrolled me into an experimental school, which just happened to have a swimming pool, and swimming was my favorite activity. Suddenly, injustice was only a memory.

Against my Baptist upbringing, I went from a White, private, Catholic school to Build Academy, a new school with a decidedly Black focus. Imagine a school with the first Black principal, numerous Black teachers, and a decidedly Afro-American flair. (I have the afro-puff pictures to prove it.) We studied Black history, we used *Ebony* magazine to explore creative writing, and we celebrated with Black Santas and Black Easter Bunnies. For Christmas, we received Temptations albums. My favorite recollection was studying Bach, Brahms, and Stevie Wonder in music class, with James Brown and the Jackson 5 serving as our incentives to listen and appreciate all music. At Build Academy, I learned to be proud of my history, proud of my people, and proud of myself. Unfortunately, the Build Academy experience ended at sixth grade, but the roots of my love for all culture, and especially my culture, were planted by these pioneers who taught me that brilliance comes in all colors.

By the time I reached high school, I had been to every type of school. I spent my eighth grade at a College Learning Lab, another term for a school where teachers learn to teach. The really great thing about this school was that the class was 50 percent Black and 50 percent White. For Buffalo, New York, in the 1970s, this was nothing short of revolutionary. From this experience, I learned some core values. First, always strive to be the best, and when you achieve it, people, whether they like it or not, will ultimately have to respect talent. It may not get the same recognition, but ultimately, right is right, good is good, and the best is just better. Second, people you like will come in all colors. The corollary is that people you dislike will also come in all colors. Third, align yourself with people who are focused on improving themselves. Learn some trait from them that will make you better. This last tenet is straight from my mother. Her motto was "try to spend your time with people who can teach you something." This does not mean become them. It simply means take the best of any situation and leave the rest. This motto serves me well to this day.

In high school, I discovered my talent for diplomacy and politics. My maternal grandmother was from Mobile, Alabama. If images of great home-cooked meals and southern hospitality dance in your minds, then you understand my history. It turns out that my grandmother was the most gracious person I had ever met. Although this may not seem like a core skill for a lawyer, you should note that one of the greatest lawyers of our time, namely the late Johnnie Cochran, was known not just for his skill but his grace. Using these skills, I campaigned for everything from student government representative to student body president. Politics is really about relationships and coalition building. If you can find common ground, your message will resonate to the masses.

I chose the School of Foreign Service at Georgetown because of the rigorous course of study, the beautiful campus, and best of all, the opportunity to live in our nation's capital. To be honest, I was 17, and going away to college was my true priority. Only in hindsight am I able to admit that a challenging education was the best thing that could have happened to me. At Georgetown, I majored in international economics: finance and commerce. The study of economics is the process of analyzing data and drawing conclusions that can be used to change fiscal reality. Although the subject matter is the world economy, as a practical matter, you learn how to think about using data to make changes or draw conclusions. Ultimately, this is the core skill all lawyers use every day. I try to blend my analysis with common sense so that I can keep it real.

Although I applied to law school my last year of college, I deferred my admission in order to work for a year to earn enough money to pay for at least some of law school. Also, I wanted to obtain residency in Virginia so I could pay lower tuition at the University of Virginia Law School. Obviously, studying economics had left a mark on my psyche. I am grateful for the work experience I obtained during that year because it taught me that working is a marathon. Some days you accomplish something important and some days you have to navigate the politics of your employment. Indeed, sometimes the politics of working with others transcends the nature and quality of the work that is actually completed. Moreover, you have to have the stamina to work hard every day, day in and day out. Believe it or not, this was also very valuable to my legal training because sometimes you are working hard and you cannot tell whether your work is heading in the right direction or whether it is proceeding in any direction, but ultimately, you must have the fortitude to see it through to the end.

My first year of law school was very hard, not difficult or merely challenging, just hard. Mr. Jefferson's university, at first blush, was not a welcoming place. I felt isolated at times and out of touch with the process. There were even times when I felt that lawyers looked at the world in a way that was totally in conflict with my personal reality as a Black woman in America. Second year was actually more difficult because, in addition to covering more ground in less time, I had the added pressure of job hunting, which often required out-of-town travel. Third year, quiet as it is kept, is more about getting ready for your future as a lawyer than actually studying the law. You still need to work hard, but it is not the primary focus. In hindsight, I am lucky to have studied at the University of Virginia Law School, and I suspect that they feel the same way about me. We left mutually indelible marks on each other.

Ultimately, I learned that the legal training is just the beginning; it is up to me to bring all that I am to the process to make a difference. Around the time I figured that out, law school proved to be my greatest triumph to date. By the end of my law school experience, I had been elected to student government and received one of the highest grades in trial advocacy. Hard work does pay off, not always when you think it should, but I would not trust anything else in a clutch situation. The key lessons I took away from my law school experience:

1. Never, ever, give up.
2. Rely on your inner strength to keep you on track.
3. You can learn from anyone.
4. A true friend will also give you tough love.

While in law school I was fortunate to meet other Black attorneys who provided me with insights and advice. To this day, I am grateful to them for sharing with me their triumphs, their tribulations, and, ultimately, their wisdom. One thing I know for sure is that everyone needs help, and when you get help, value it! Treat people who are willing to offer constructive insight like gold and you will always have them. These people do not help you because they owe you. Maybe they owe Charles Hamilton Houston (the legal mastermind who engineered the end of desegregation in America) or Charlotte E. Ray (the first Black woman to be admitted to a bar association), but they do not owe you. So do not take them for granted nor abuse this privilege. Try to call these mentors just to see if there is something you can do for them or to let them know how their good advice has worked out for you.

It is amazing how the qualities you learn at home can take you a long way. One piece of advice I received was to try to obtain a judicial clerkship. Serving as a judge was always on my career radar, so I jumped at the opportunity to apply for such positions. After forwarding my transcripts, writing samples and references, I was given the opportunity to clerk for the Honorable John Garrett Penn on the United States District Court for the District of Columbia.

To say that this was the best job I have ever had is really not an overstatement. Judicial law clerks provide research, drafting, and other office services to a judge. In short, you are there to provide whatever assistance the judge requires to accomplish the task of interpreting the law as it applies to the cases at hand. In return for this service, you have the opportunity to learn the inner workings of the practice of law from "your judge." In the federal trial court, judges can have two or more law clerks; one clerk is more senior, but essentially both clerks perform the same tasks. This position typically lasts one to two years. My clerkship was two years, and I honestly believe that the first year of the clerkship is to teach you the job, and the second year is so you can actually be helpful to the judge! In any event, my experience taught me that despite the appearance of ease, judging is difficult, time-consuming, and rigorous. On the other hand, watching the judge make a difference, while interpreting the law correctly, was very rewarding. Reluctantly, after my clerkship, I was compelled to actually find a new legal job.

Somewhere in all this, I took the bar exam. This shows you how selective the memory can be when it comes to painful details. Imagine completing your greatest educational triumph, law school, only to find that you cannot practice law unless you pass a two-day closed-book exam. You know it is coming, but reality is always more sobering than anything the imagination can produce. Once again you remember that you can never let anything turn you back and that if others can do it, so can you.

After my clerkship, I began work at a very large law firm in Washington, D.C. The firm was very diverse, and it had the only Black managing partner in the city, and possibly the nation. It was an exciting time to be a lawyer in Washington. I was assigned to work in the special litigation section of the firm. So what is special litigation? Essentially these are high-profile cases. Whether it was a unique issue, a complex civil case, or the defense of a noted white-collar criminal, these were all examples of special litigation at my firm. I was only three years out of law school at one of the largest firms in the country, so my primary role was to research and draft motions, memoranda, and other documents to keep the case on track. This experience was really about training. No matter what course you choose for a career, the goal is to receive the best training you can. Training is the difference between amateurs and professionals. No matter what happens, at the end of the day, your training goes home with you.

We, the new associates, were very lucky because we had a legal giant in charge of our professional development, Inez Smith Reid. Her career spanned every possible type of position, including serving as the chief legal counsel for the District of Columbia. You could not outwork her at any age and she demanded the highest quality in work product. She selected me and a colleague to work on a pro bono employment discrimination case involving laborers in Front Royal, Virginia. The experience was humbling, frightening, and exciting all at the same time. These were men who had been denied admission to the laborers' union. Because this was an unskilled laborer's union, it is unlikely that they were denied for any reason other than skin color. We took depositions and traveled around the Commonwealth of Virginia recording the stories of the men who were indelibly altered by the inability to obtain work. In the process, we learned how to take depositions and advocate for our clients. In sum, we became lawyers in the true sense of the word.

Meanwhile, back at the firm, we still had to keep up our quest for the maximum number of billable hours. We had to have many, many billable clients to underwrite our pro bono service. Without the paying clients, our pro bono work would have come to a screeching halt. As expected, these billable clients were demanding, and rightly so. Consequently, we were always jockeying to get good assignments working for the senior partners, preferably the rainmakers. Sometimes gender and color were barriers that could be overcome with hard work; unfortunately, this was not always the case. No matter what the situation, though, the goal, my personal mantra, was to get the best experience possible to enable me to strategically advance. I quickly recognized that in order to attain partnership status, I would have to leave and either work as an assistant United States attorney or practice in a firm that provided more opportunities to appear in court. Luckily, one of my mentors intervened. Mabel Haden is the president emeritus of the National Association of Black Women Attorneys (NABWA). We met in law school when I entered and won NABWA's scholarship competition. Her example as an attorney has meant more to my legal career than any other single moment or event. When you see that something can be done, you should be able to replicate it with your own style. Attorney Haden recommended that I apply to work at my current firm. Not only did she support me in this endeavor, but I believe that her reference probably trumped any credentials that I could possibly have produced. I still remember my interview with Jack Olender, who is the founding partner at Jack H. Olender & Associates. He read every deposition that I provided and all of my writing samples. This precision and attention to detail would become one of the key skills I learned from working with him. When he asked how hard I was prepared to work, I could actually recite the number of hours I worked per month, both billable and nonbillable. Needless to say, I wound up with a position that still challenges me today, 14 years after that initial interview.

Over the past 14 years, I have represented catastrophically injured persons in medical negligence cases. I have represented mostly women and children, as they are most likely to suffer the ill effects of such treatment. In cases ranging from blindness, to failure to diagnose cancer, to death,

I have had the rare privilege to share the lives of courageous individuals who carry on in the face of devastating circumstances. Over the years, I have taken thousands of depositions, settled numerous cases, fought vigorously at lengthy trials, and argued before the Court of Appeals (successfully). To this day, I am still humbled by my clients. I have learned something from each of them and I am grateful for the experience.

Along the way, I have tried very hard to participate in community and professional activities. I have served on the board of directors of numerous nonprofits aimed at expanding opportunities, promoting equality, and serving those in need. These experiences allowed me to use my legal skills more creatively and have served to improve my advocacy skills in different arenas such as negotiation, mediation, and public speaking. In my past position as president of the National Bar Association (a position to which attorneys are elected), I have worked with lawyers across the nation to, among other things, improve and protect voting rights, advocate for true diversity in the profession, and weigh in on judicial nominations. In partnership with professional and other community-based organizations, the National Bar Association has been able to effect a far-reaching agenda on numerous other issues. We do this because we owe it to those who made it possible for us to be here. It is not optional nor is it delegable. We have a job to finish. My pride in the men and women of the National Bar Association comes from their commitment to serve on the front lines of the battle for equality, justice, and the American way.

The life of a lawyer is challenging and as unique as the individual. I have never regretted my decision to become an attorney, but there is always a price. The dedication to my craft, the sacrifice of time, hour after hour pouring over research books, studying motions, depositions, oppositions, etc., brought me to the pinnacle of my success. But it was not easy by any stretch of the imagination. I encountered racism, sexism, and other isms too numerous to mention. Life hasn't always been fair, but my life as a lawyer has given me and my clients a fair shot at justice. I would not trade any of it because, at the end of the day, it is the practice of law, not the perfection of law. As long as we are a nation of free individuals, we will always be challenged to live up to our creed of freedom and justice for all. I am proud to be a torchbearer for justice.

CHAPTER 17

Damon J. Keith: A Guiding Light for Equal Justice Under Law

DAMON J. KEITH

Judge, U.S. Court of Appeals
for the Sixth Circuit, Detroit, Michigan

I was born in Detroit, Michigan on the Fourth of July, Independence Day. I was the youngest of six children born to my parents, Perry and Annie Louis Keith. Growing up in a large family was truly wonderful. I was blessed with a loving and caring mother and an industrious father. There was a great deal of emphasis on education in my family, and my dad was determined that I would be the first of his children to attend college—he insisted on that. I grew up in the Detroit Public School system, and in high school I was an honor student and earned three varsity track letters. But throughout my entire public school education, I was never taught by an African American teacher. I never dreamed of becoming a lawyer or a judge, as I didn't know any, and in fact, we had virtually no professional role models to emulate.

That changed when I attended West Virginia State, an all-Black college. West Virginia State was an eye-opener for me. For the first time I saw Black professors, a Black college president, and most importantly, I saw and listened to the great Black leaders of the day who visited the college to speak to the students. Among those who came were G. Carter Woodson, Mordicai Johnson, Benjamin Mays, Adam Clayton Powell, Channing Tobias, Mary McLeod Bethune, and many others. It was as if

I had awakened from a deep sleep, as if someone had lifted cataracts off my eyes.

I graduated from college in 1943 and, with degree in hand, was drafted into the segregated U.S. Army. I served in the army for three years in what was then described as an "all-colored" unit. Despite my college education, similar to many World War II African American soldiers, I was inducted as a private, the military's lowest rank, and was assigned to the quartermaster corps, where our job was to drive trucks and take care of the other soldiers' supplies. I remember my military experiences as being absolutely demeaning. Every single officer in our "all-colored" unit was white—the captains, the lieutenants—we had no Black officers.

When I left the army in 1946, I decided to go to law school at Howard University in Washington, D.C., seeking the same uplifting and inspirational experience I had found as an undergraduate at West Virginia State. And it was. At Howard I learned about the U.S. Constitution, its promise of "equal justice under law," and the importance of that promise to Black people. We were taught by such professors as Charles Hamilton Houston; Thurgood Marshall; William H. Hastie, Jr., who later became America's first Black federal judge; James M. Nabrit, Jr.; Spottswood W. Robinson III; and William R. Ming, who became America's first Black professor at a White law school. As students, we were very much involved in the preparation of important civil rights cases that these outstanding lawyers were championing in the courts. We helped with the research and listened to the oral arguments, and occasionally we made suggestions as they polished their theories and presentations. We would go to the U.S. Supreme Court and hear our professors argue their cases before the Justices. We were blessed to have had these unique and everlasting experiences.

My classmates elected me the chief justice of the Court of Peers, the student government body, an honor that meant a great deal to me. I also recall that many of my Black classmates at Howard who were from the Deep South were paid to attend Howard by their home states, which maintained White-only law schools. Washington, D.C., in the 1940s was also segregated, and I remember that the only place we could eat a meal in downtown D.C. was the Union Station. Experiencing segregation firsthand was good for me, in a sense. To this day, I have never forgotten how deeply and severely racism affects its victims.

After graduating from Howard, I returned to Detroit to launch a new law firm with my good friends, Nate Conyers and Herman Anderson, from Wayne State University; Joseph N. Brown, from the University of Detroit; and Myron H. Wahls, from the Northwestern University Law School. The firm would eventually become Keith, Conyers, Anderson, Brown and Wahls. They were all brilliant lawyers and, as you know, each has achieved great success either in practice, in business, or on the bench. I have always been proud of them and for what we accomplished when it was exceedingly difficult for Black lawyers to build successful firms. All the members of our firm were active in the National Lawyers Guild (NLG) and the NAACP. I especially remember the NLG project that sent lawyers down South to help with civil rights, voting rights, and other human rights issues. We were heavily involved. We also represented the major Black companies in Detroit and baseball star Willie Horton. I was also Horton's legal guardian, and I negotiated what was then an enormous signing bonus for Horton with the Detroit Tigers—$50,000. Horton is now a special assistant to the president for the Tigers, and his statue is in Comerica Park with all of the other great former Tiger players.

But among the many problems Black lawyers experienced in the 1950s, none, in my judgment, were more damaging than the absence of Black judges. Many of the White judges simply were not nice to Black lawyers—they did not treat us with dignity and respect as they did other lawyers. Some were actually outright mean, if not nasty, and belittling in their dealings with Black attorneys. In addition, clients saw or knew how poorly Black lawyers were treated in court. Many of the Black citizens in Detroit came from the South and they knew firsthand about racism in the legal system and how it could determine the outcome of their case. Judges, as much as any aspect of the legal system, caused many Black clients to shun Black lawyers. These experiences as a young lawyer made me ever mindful of the power and influence judges wield.

In 1967, President Lyndon B. Johnson appointed me to the United States District Court for the Eastern District of Michigan, where I was chief judge from 1975 to 1977. In 1977, I was elevated to the United States Court of Appeals for the Sixth Circuit by President Jimmy Carter. As a member of the federal judiciary, I constantly treat the lawyers who appear before me with the dignity and respect they deserve as officers of the court—something Black lawyers often did not get when I practiced. In my 29 years on the bench, I have never held nor threatened to hold a lawyer or anyone else in contempt of court.

Throughout my career on the federal bench, I have tried every day to fight to ensure equal justice under law for all who come within the walls of our judicial system. My career has been guided by the belief that each citizen of the United States deserves the undeniable promise of equal rights for all that is found in our Bill of Rights and our Declaration of Independence, and I have sought to interpret the Constitution in a way that is faithful to that belief. But there have been many times when I have found myself in the minority. And many times, it has been important for me to stand up and speak out against injustice, relying on the value and importance of dissent in our democratic society.

During these times, I have recalled the words of the late Dr. Martin Luther King, Jr., who said "This is no time for apathy or complacency. This is a time for vigorous and positive action." Dr. King explained that "On some positions, Cowardice asks the question, 'is it safe?' Expediency asks the question, 'is it politic?' And Vanity comes along and asks the question, 'is it popular?'; but conscience must ask the question, 'is it right?'" (King 1968) I believe in the importance of asking "is it right?"—even if doing what is right requires the courage to dissent from the majority.

Each day we are reminded that we do not live in a colorblind society. We see discriminatory tactics such as racial profiling continuing to plague African Americans and other minorities. Now, additional laws have been enacted that inevitably affect the civil liberties of some groups more than others in the name of national security. All of this demonstrates that it is impossible to live neutrally in a society that has a history of treating its citizens unequally. If we turn a blind eye to inequality and injustice in our country, we jeopardize the integrity of democracy itself. And it is the responsibility of each and every one of us to take a stand for what we believe in, to do not what is safe, not what is popular, and not what is politic, but to involve your colleagues and do what is right.

Today we are also living in an environment where there are not a lot of checks and balances on our government. Our Founding Fathers created a government with three branches—the executive, the legislative, and the judicial—that were meant to check each other when one of them gets out of line and veers too far toward injustice. In times like these, when there may not be a lot of dissent from within our government, it is even more important for each of us to use our own voice to take a stand for what is right.

And one who dissents should not be called or labeled unpatriotic for simply standing up for what he or she believes is right. When I was a district court judge in the 1960s, I presided over a criminal trial for members of the White Panther Party who were accused of bombing CIA offices in Ann Arbor, Michigan. In the course of the trial in the case, *United States v. Sinclair* (1974), it came out that the federal government had tapped the defendants' phone lines without obtaining a prior warrant. Attorney General John Mitchell, on behalf of President Richard Nixon, claimed that the president had an inherent authority to issue wiretaps without a warrant in instances of national security. This was a violation of the fundamental right guaranteed to all Americans in the Fourth Amendment of the U.S. Constitution: to be free from warrantless searches and seizures. I wrote in that case that:

> In our democracy all men are to receive equal and exact justice regardless of their political beliefs or persuasions. The executive branch of our government cannot be given the power to investigate and prosecute criminal violations simply because an accused defendant espouses views which are inconsistent with our present form of government. Such power held by one individual was never contemplated by the framers of our constitution and cannot be tolerated today.

The government was ordered to turn over its tapes to the defendants. After my decision was upheld by the Sixth Circuit Court of Appeals, the government issued a writ of mandamus to require me to release the wiretap tapes. I had to hire my own attorney to represent me before the United States Supreme Court, and that is why it is now called the *Keith Case*. The Supreme Court unanimously affirmed my decision, and the government later dropped all charges against the defendants.

The defense attorney in that case, William Kunstler, later wrote in his book *My Life as a Radical Lawyer* (1994) that he was "certain that the timing of the activities that brought about the Watergate scandal was directly linked to the wiretapping decision in the Keith case" because shortly after the decision was announced, the Republican Party attempted to remove the wiretap devices they had installed at the Democratic National Committee headquarters. Joseph Goulden, in his book *The Benchwarmers* (1974), wrote that my opinion in this case was a "prime example of an independent federal judge" who "had the courage to say 'no'" in the face of "a presidency which likened itself to a 'sovereign.'" "The strength of the judiciary," Goulden wrote, "is rooted in just such independence as that displayed by Keith."

There were other attempts to undermine the constitution, including one a few years ago when the Sixth Circuit Court of Appeals heard the important case *Detroit Free Press v. Ashcroft* (2001). In that case, the United States Department of Justice was attempting to block the right of the media to attend public deportation hearings. Our court was able to uphold the First Amendment right of the press to cover the hearings. As the author of the opinion in that case, I emphasized the importance of protecting the freedom of the press and wrote: "Democracy dies behind closed doors. The First Amendment, through a free press, protects the people's right to know that their government acts fairly, lawfully, and accurately."

Detroit Free Press v. Ashcroft was a case where our court made a good decision. But there have been many times when I have disagreed with the majority of judges on our panel and have made it a point to voice my disagreement with the panel in a separate dissenting opinion.

In 1986, our court heard *Rabidue v. Osceola Refining Co.*, a case in which the majority held that vulgar language in the workplace was not sexual harassment. The young woman in that case had to endure many derogatory and demeaning comments about women from a supervisor, and was forced to deal with photographs of nude women that her male coworkers posted in common areas at the workplace. But the majority felt that a reasonable person would not be offended by this decidedly anti-female environment.

I strongly disagreed, and said so in a dissenting opinion that explained the various reasons why the majority's conclusion was wrongly reasoned: "As I believe no woman should be subjected to an environment where her dignity and sensibilities are visually, verbally, or physically assaulted as a matter of prevailing male prerogative, I dissent."

The dissenting opinion advocated for a "reasonable woman standard," because there is a wide divergence between most men's and women's views of appropriate conduct in the workplace. That theory was later accepted by the United States Supreme Court, and today the reasonable woman standard is used to evaluate all sexual harassment claims raised by women.

A few years later, in 2000, a majority on our court issued an opinion in a criminal case that condoned ex parte communications between a trial court judge and the government's attorneys. The Sixth Amendment of the U.S. Constitution creates a right for everyone who comes before a court of a law to have effective assistance of counsel, and it prohibits conversations between one attorney in a case and the presiding judges if the other attorneys are not present. In this case, *United States v. Carmichael*, attorneys for the government met with the district court judge in chambers to discuss various aspects of the defendant's case. The majority admitted that these conversations tainted the judge's appearance of impartiality but said they were permissible because there was no evidence that the conversations affected the verdict in the case.

In my dissent, I said that the majority opinion showed a "distressing and total disregard for the meaning of the sixth amendment." Our criminal justice system is premised upon certain fundamental rights, and the majority opinion vitiated each of those basic guarantees. I wrote in dissent that "[a]s judges of this court we have sworn to serve as protectors" of those guarantees, and in my view, the majority desecrated that sacred oath.

In crafting my dissents, I aim not to merely state that the majority is wrong but also try to involve others in my understanding of what is right. Regrettably, I find myself dissenting more today than in the past, but I continue to be encouraged. As the late Justice Thurgood Marshall once stated: "The legal systems can force open doors and sometimes even knock down the walls. But it cannot build bridges. That job belongs to you and me. Take a chance, won't you. Knock down the fences that divide. Tear apart the walls that imprison. Reach out" (Marshall 1993).

I've enjoyed my years as a judge. One of my greatest honors came in 1985, when Chief Justice Warren E. Burger asked me to serve as chair of the Sixth Circuit Committee on the Bicentennial of the Constitution. Two years later, Chief Justice William Rehnquist appointed me to serve as the national chair of the Judicial Conference Committee on the Bicentennial of the Constitution. In 1990, President George Bush appointed me to the Commission on the Bicentennial of the Constitution. The Bicentennial Committee has placed more than 300 Bill of Rights plaques in the FBI headquarters, the Thurgood Marshall Judicial Center, and courthouses and law schools through the United States.

In October 1991, the committee held a three-day conference in celebration of the Constitution that included the gathering of more than 350 federal judges, the largest gathering of the federal judiciary in American history. I was scheduled to speak at the gathering, and as I was standing outside my hotel in Williamsburg, Virginia, waiting for a taxicab to take me to the conference, a White man drove into the hotel's driveway, stepped out of his car, handed me his keys, and walked off, saying, "Boy, would you please park this car." My good friend and fellow committee member, Judge Frank Altimari from the Second Circuit Court of Appeals, wanted to confront the man, tell him who I was, and deride him for his transparent display of prejudice. But I stopped Frank and told him not to bother. I told him that I experienced such situations—to a greater or lesser degree—every day of my life, and that if I attempted to set every such perpetrator straight, my days would consist of little else.

Not a day goes by that I am not reminded that I am an African American. I will continue to work and devote my energies to a time when people will not be judged by the color of their skin, their religion, their sexual orientation, or their gender but by their intelligence, their character, and their devotion to helping people. These have been exciting times. I have always known how rampant discrimination is, and I always keep a sharp focus on the U.S. Constitution and its importance for social change. I have tried my best to enforce the goals of equal justice under law that are so deeply imbedded in the Bill of Rights, the Declaration of Independence, and our beloved Constitution.

I am thankful to God that I am on the second-highest court in the country and have had the opportunity to practice a personal philosophy that is so deeply engraved in me—that whoever you are, you should work to make things better and to make a difference. I hope that when others think of me, they will see a person who believes in the Constitution, has sought to ensure equal justice under law, and has tried to use the law to make things better and to make a difference.

References

Goulden, J. C. 1974. *The Benchwarmers: The Private World of the Powerful Federal Judges*. Weybright and Talley.

Kunstler, W., and S. Isenberg. 1994. *My Life as a Radical Lawyer*. Carol Publishing Corporation.

Marshall, Thurgood. 1993. "Acceptance Speech, Liberty Medal." Independence Hall, National Constitution Center, Philadelphia, PA. July 4.

CHAPTER 18

Riding a Fire Engine
on a Rollercoaster to Success

OTIS J. LATIN, SR.

Director, Homeland Security
and Emergency Management,
Austin, Texas; Former Fire Chief,
Fort Lauderdale Fire Department,
Fort Lauderdale, Florida

In 1963, I started my freshman year at Bethune High School in Shreveport, Louisiana. I dreamed of graduating, attending college, and majoring in electrical engineering. I graduated in the top five percent of my class but did not get a scholarship large enough for me to attend college and pursue my dream of becoming an electrical engineer. No one in my immediate family had attended college, let alone graduated from college or high school, so I had no such role models. Money for college was not an option from anyone in my family. A full scholarship was my only hope and prayer to become the first member of my immediate family to graduate from college and become a role model for younger relatives. However, that was not the path my life would take.

I was raised by my grandmother (Big Mama) because my mother and one of my aunts had to work two jobs to pay bills and provide for me and three of my cousins. We were like brothers and sisters; two of my cousins were older than I, and one was younger. We did not have a lot of money but we never went hungry or lacked for anything. We were raised with plenty of love, discipline, and a love for God. My grandmother was instrumental in my success in school and life in general. She always encouraged me and my cousins to be the best that we could be and emphasized the importance of getting an education. Big Mama, my mother, and my aunt were strong Black women who demonstrated to me a tireless work ethic, resilience in the face of despair, and a never-give-up attitude. Big Mama was the matriarch of our family and someone I looked up to as a role model, even though she did not graduate from high school. She knew the value of an education and that value was instilled in me at an early age. Big Mama told me time and time again that if you prepare yourself with as much education as you can get, there will be no limit to what you can accomplish. One of her favorite sayings was, "cream will always rise to the top." Another one of her sayings was, "no one owes you anything, and you must work hard for everything you want." I have carried these bits of wisdom with me throughout my life. They have served me well. When I want to feel sorry for myself because of something that goes wrong in my life, I just think of Big Mama.

My upbringing and belief in God have been instrumental in my life. I was taught that you must not run from your responsibilities and that when you make a mistake you must own up to it, ask for forgiveness, and make the best out of the situation. During high school I met and fell in love with my wife, Gloria. She was beautiful, intelligent, and a popular young lady, the love of my life, and she still is today. We wanted to go to college and get married after we graduated. However, she got pregnant in our senior year and our plans changed. I went to my mother and grandmother and told them what had happened; they asked me what I was going to do. I told them that I loved her and wanted to ask her to marry me. At that time I was 17 years old and needed my mother's permission to get married. My mother and grandmother supported me in my decision, and my mother bought a wedding ring for me to give to Gloria when I proposed to marry her. We were married on June 10, 1967, after we graduated from high school. We did not have a place to stay, and I did not have a job. However, my mother was living in Houston, Texas, and we moved in with her until I could get a job and find a place to live.

I was 17 years old so my first job was at Romano Cafeteria as a dishwasher. I stayed there approximately two years and worked my way up to line food server and finally to fry cook before I left to accept a position in January 1969 as a fire cadet in the Houston Fire Department. I knew I had to find a job with career opportunities where I could support my family and further my education. Gloria and I stayed with my mother for nine months. Otis, Jr. was born on November 15, 1967, and we purchased our first home in March 1968. When I got the cafeteria job, we started saving immediately for a down payment on our own home. We bought our first home one month before I got a job in the fire department. I don't want you to be misled and think the events that took place to this point in my life were easy and a bed of roses; by no means was that the case. Gloria and I had a lot of hard times. We were high school sweethearts who overcame the odds of a teenage marriage. Our marriage is still growing strong after 38 years together, and we are more in love today than ever before by the grace of God.

My career in the fire service started because I needed a better job with benefits to pay my bills and feed my wife and son. I have been around the fire service all of my adult life. I started my firefighting career as a fire cadet in January 1969. My second son, Otha, was born in February 1969 and attended my graduation ceremony. Big Mama came from Shreveport to witness this special occasion. I was so proud because the three women I love—Big Mama, my mother, and my wife—were all there to support me as they had always done. This was the first step on my rollercoaster ride to success in the fire service.

With two sons and a wife to support, I knew I had to earn more money. I enrolled as a part-time student at San Jacinto College while also working full time for the fire department and part time at the Sears and Roebuck warehouse delivering furniture and appliances. I worked hard and studied diligently in school and on the job. I knew what I had to do and prepared myself to make my first promotion as chauffeur. On January 27, 1972, my third son was born before my promotion to chauffeur in October 1972. God showed favor on me while I worked two jobs, attended college, and spent quality time with my family. I realize and recognize that without God I would not have been able to progress through the ranks of the Houston Fire Department from firefighter to chauffeur, junior captain, senior captain, district chief, and my final promoted position of assistant fire chief in July 1989. In a demonstratation of God's blessings, I obtained the rank of district chief at the age of 30, becoming the youngest person promoted to that rank within a 10-year period. I also became the first African American and the youngest person to obtain the rank of assistant fire chief in the Houston Fire Department.

A new beginning was open to me in 1993 because of my faithfulness and my belief that I can do all things through Christ who strengthens me. The mayor of the nation's capital was looking for a new fire chief, and I got a phone call from the mayor's office asking me to send in a résumé. The rest is history. Mayor Sharon Pratt Kelly, after a national search, hired me as fire chief of the District of Columbia Fire and Emergency Medical Services Department on November 1, 1993. I was the first fire chief appointed from outside the department in its 125-year history. The department consisted of 1,765 employees and 32 fire stations. I was charged with the preparation and administration of a $103 million budget and remained in that position until July 25, 1997. I served two mayors during my tenure.

After nearly four years as fire chief of Washington, D.C., city manager George Hansbury, after a national search, hired me as fire chief/director of the city of Fort Lauderdale Fire-Rescue and Building Department. With this appointment, I became the first African American fire chief in the history of the city of Fort Lauderdale. The department was one of a few in Florida that directed and supervised fire protection, emergency medical services, and the building services department. In 1999, the building services department was assigned to another city department, and in 2003, the Ocean Rescue division was added to the fire-rescue department. I prepare and manage the department's $52 million budget and manage its 12 fire stations and beach lifeguard operations.

As I stated in the beginning of this essay, my dream was to be an electrical engineer, but the God I serve directed my life in the way that he wanted it to go. Yes, I did finish college and received my education; therefore, my dream came true. I completed fire protection technology courses at San Jacinto College and Texas A&M University from 1970 to 1981. In 1984, I received an AAS Degree in Fire Protection Technology, with highest honors, from Houston Community College. I completed studies at the University of Houston and earned a bachelor of science degree in technology, with a minor in psychology (honors) in 1991. I also completed a four-year Executive Fire Officers (EFO) Program at the National Fire Academy in Emmitsburg, Maryland (1991–1996). I completed studies at the John F. Kennedy School of Government Program for Senior Executives in State and Local Government at Harvard University in 1995. In May 2000, I received my master of business administration degree (MBA) from Florida Atlantic University. During 2003, I received the professional designation of chief fire officer (CFO) from the Commission on Chief Fire Officer Designation.

I have always been involved in professional and community-based organizations. I was the first vice president of the Houston Professional

Firefighters Association Local 341. I am a member of the National Fire Protection Association, the International Association of Fire Chiefs, the Metropolitan Fire Chiefs Association, the Florida Fire Chiefs Association, the Fire Chiefs Association of Broward County, and the International Association of Black Professional Firefighters. I also hold memberships in the National Forum for Black Public Administrators and the NAACP, and I serve on the Imperial Point Hospital Community Relations Council, the Board of Directors of Family Central, Inc., the Board of Directors of Kids in Distress, the Executive Board of the Metropolitan Fire Chiefs Association, and the Trustee Board of New Mount Olive Baptist Church of Fort Lauderdale.

I have been married for more than 38 years to my high school sweetheart, the former Gloria Douglas. I am very proud that my wife and I have been able to set positive examples of being a loving husband and wife, faithful Christians, and hard workers. I am a role model to my sons and other family members, just as Big Mama said I would be. She did not live to see it, but my three sons, Otis, Jr., Otha, and Olan, are all Rice University graduates. We have four grandchildren (one girl and three boys) and two daughters-in-law. I attribute all of my success to being raised with lots of love and discipline and faith in God, and I always remember what Big Mama taught me: "cream will always rise to the top" and "nobody owes you anything; you must work for what you get." My road to success has been a rollercoaster ride but a rewarding experience.

Reference

King, Martin Luther, Jr. (February 6, 1968). "A Proper Sense of Priorities." New York: Clergy and Layman Concerned About Vietnam. http://www.aavw.org.

CHAPTER 19

Education Is a Great Equalizer

RITA JO LEWIS

Special Representative
for Global Intergovernmental Affairs,
U.S. Department of State;
Former Attorney, Edwards Angell Palmer
and Dodge, LLP; Former Attorney,
Vanderbilt Partners, Washington, D.C.

Last fall, I started my own business strategy and consulting firm, and I also serve as a senior adviser to the Democratic Leadership Council. I am a lawyer, lobbyist, and former senior association executive of the U.S. Chamber of Commerce, where I served as a vice president and counselor to the president and chief executive officer. I was the first African American woman to serve as a senior officer at the chamber in its 90-year history.

Before joining the U.S. Chamber of Commerce, I worked in politics, law, and government relations. I received a law degree from Emory University School of Law, a master's degree in public policy and criminal justice from American University, and a bachelor's degree in political science from the University of Georgia.

I grew up in Statesboro, a small college town in Georgia. It was one of the major cities outside of Savannah and less than a three-hour drive from Atlanta. My parents, who are entrepreneurs and community leaders, told me repeatedly that hard work and obtaining a college education would be the great equalizer for my siblings and me. I grew up in a community where my parents were engaged in the fight for school integration in the

Note: Before Rita Jo Lewis was appointed to Special Representative for Global Intergovernmental Affairs, she submitted this chapter for publication.

1960s. Despite the fact that I came of age during a time of tumultuous social and political change in America, my parents did not see obstacles that I could not overcome if I obtained the skills and training and continued the work ethic they had instilled in each of us.

My mother was the president of the local NAACP and the state treasurer of the Georgia NAACP chapter. My father is considered, to this day, one of the go-to political advisers for aspiring elected officials in Georgia. My mother, the daughter of a United Methodist minister, instilled in us a belief system and values that started in the home, but also in the religious community, with which my parents were actively involved.

As a daughter of the South, my parents sought to make the principles of *Brown v. Board of Education* a reality for me. They filed lawsuits that ensured that my family and all African Americans in our community would be granted equal rights and opportunities under the law. In addition, my parents were actively involved in the fights for equal voting rights and the integration of public accommodations. Their involvement showed me how active community engagement could bring about change for the larger community in which one lives. Although my parents had six children to raise, fighting for social change and helping to make our community better for all was something that was discussed in our family on a daily basis. One would think that going to law school would be a no-brainer after witnessing my parents fight and win legal battles against incredible odds in the sixties.

When I graduated as an honor student from Marvin Pittman High School, my parents allowed me to decide whether to attend college. At first I did not want to go to college and enrolled in design school instead. That decision was short-lived: I actually enrolled and left the school on the same day.

When I returned home, my parents and teachers were excited that I was going to enroll at the University of Georgia, which had only about 500 African American students among its 20,000 students from in and around Georgia and the United States. Well, they got their wish, and I got a college degree. I was the second person in my family to graduate from college. My parents provided each of us with the opportunity to receive a higher education and, as a result, my siblings and I have advanced degrees, technical training, and thus, successful careers. Once again, my parents were right—nothing happens for you without first obtaining that piece of paper. We talk about that to this day.

After graduating from college, I realized that my career was stalled unless I was willing to put in the time to pursue a graduate degree. I realized, several jobs later, that my upward mobility would be accelerated if I pursued a professional degree. I had delusions of grandeur about working for the leader of the free world.

Before pursuing that dream, I competed in a national competition for graduate students and was selected as one of the first leadership class in the Presidential Management Fellowship Program created by President Jimmy Carter. I was appointed to serve as a congressional liaison to the Drug Enforcement Administration, which is a part of the Department of Justice. After completing that assignment, I was hired as a project manager at the National League of Cities, the largest association of state and local elected officials. This is where I first obtained my first real understanding, skills, and experience in high-stakes, high-profile, public policy debates. I always loved politics and campaigns and wanted to be a part of governing.

As this field relates to the law, I had no choice but to go to law school. I had worked very closely for such notables as Nelson Mandela; President William Jefferson Clinton; First Lady Hillary Rodham Clinton; Democratic Party Chairman Ron Brown; Vice President Walter Mondale; Mayors Harold Washington, Sharon Pratt Kelly, and Maynard Jackson; and Mayoral Candidate and former Cabinet Secretary Patricia Roberts Harris—all lawyers. Each one had encouraged me to get a law degree—echoing the same words as my parents: "If you got it no one can take it from you." The legal training would serve me well throughout my professional career development.

Before my political success, I had a string of defeats. It was not until Vice President Mondale was defeated in his bid for president that I truly understood the meaning of the Girl Scout motto of "Always be prepared." When I decided to go back home to obtain a law degree, it was very difficult to leave a place that I called home, Washington, D.C. However, after working for several historic figures, witnessing and talking about world events, traveling with the Democratic Party presidential nominee, and growing up in a family that valued public service, I was more determined than I had been to obtain legal training. Each one of these people inspired me and encouraged me in my interest in the law.

The adjustment from working to going to law school full time, as you can imagine, was quite a switch. At that time, only a few of us who were in our mid-thirties were attending law school full time. I had no outside income and had to rely on a combination of scholarships, student loans, and my small savings.

However, I did enjoy my law school experience. The outstanding leaders that I had worked for in the past and my law professors gave me a sense of the higher calling of the legal profession. The leaders and my professors instilled in me a responsibility to help the disadvantaged and the poor, to do more for others in my daily practice, and to make sure the rule of law was advanced in every aspect of my professional life with honesty and integrity.

Law school made me really proud of the profession and gave me a heightened sense of responsibility to the public and private sector services. During my three years, I was given the opportunity to clerk for a Fulton County Superior Court judge and to have a summer clerkship with a major New York law firm in Washington, D.C. Upon graduation, I accepted a position in a powerful D.C. law firm and was fortunate to receive excellent legal training.

Additionally, my professional mentors are still advising me to this day. No one walks this path alone. If you do, it is too lonely an experience. I encourage young professionals to seek out advice from people up and down the food chain. A law partner may make a good mentor, but never forget that it can be the support staff members who can make your life much easier and give you the ability to stay on the path to partnership or success. With that said, my mother's motto is always in the back of my head: "someone is always watching you, so always stay alert." Remember, you have the training, you passed the bar, so keep in mind that when they let you out to see the light of day, make sure you network with a purpose. The contacts and relationships you develop will always come back full circle, so never burn your bridges.

Because I have always loved politics, my career has always intersected with presidential campaigns. After serving in local government, I returned to politics, fortunately in the winning campaign of President Bill Clinton. At the White House, I had the responsibility of advising the president on politics and going through the stinging defeat of our party's losing both the House and the Senate under my president's watch. Also, I served as the lead domestic political staff adviser for the United States Olympic Committee, the Paralympics Games, and the World Cup Games held in the United States. Additionally, I served as the senior domestic political adviser for the first Summit of the Americas, which was the first summit held with the leaders of the Western Hemisphere.

I left the White House because it became clear to me that it was an opportunity to serve, but it was not a job. The opportunity to become a partner in a major law firm and to build a legal practice was very appealing. I love being a lawyer. I love being involved in the leading public policy debates of our time, such as the fight for NAFTA (the North American Free Trade Agreement), health care, welfare reform, class action, education reform, small business issues, and diversity initiatives. So my route to being involved with a national business organization like the U.S. Chamber of Commerce was a natural progression for my pro-business interest of seeking common ground on the leading issues of the day.

Were there problems along the way? You betcha. I have been asked on numerous occasions whether pursuing an advanced degree is really worth the time, money, and effort. My answer is always a resounding yes! Educational training is an investment in you. So I encourage young professionals to seek advice and guidance from those who have and have not traveled that path. Education is a key to success, and although an advanced degree can be costly, it is an investment that lasts forever.

As an African American woman, one can imagine that there have been subtle and overt challenges throughout my professional career. I believe the value system I learned growing up in the South has given me the fortitude to press on, however. Also, my support system of family, friends, and colleagues has allowed me to overcome any challenges I have encountered. I live my life as if I am in a marathon race, not a sprint.

My networking and professional experiences have led me to obtain senior roles in the political, legal, and government arenas. For more than two decades, I have had the opportunity to work in some of the nation's powerful political circles: as a special assistant and political director to President Bill Clinton, a senior association executive in the world's largest business federation, the first African American woman partner in one of the nation's largest international law firms, a veteran of five presidential campaigns, one of the first African Americans to travel daily with a presidential candidate, and the lead trip director for Nelson Mandela's first U.S. tour when he was released from prison. I must tell you that each opportunity was enormously challenging and exhilarating.

So, it is now time for me to return to the other side of the table and take my own advice as I learn how to become a successful business entrepreneur. It will not come easy, but what does? The education, skills, training, experience, and relationships and contacts I have garnered over the past 20 years only make me say it is worth it. Thanks Mom and Dad for making me see that the sky is the limit and telling me to always be willing to try something new, to admit when I am wrong, and that education is truly the first step.

CHAPTER 20

Understanding the Code of Legal (Business) Profession

KENNETH A. MURPHY

Attorney, Litigation Partner,
Drinker Biddle and Reath LLP,
Philadelphia, Pennsylvania

As a young child, I was told by the wisest person I have ever known—my grandmother—that I would grow up to be a doctor or a lawyer. At the age of three, I understood that doctors gave pills and needles to the sick. I, however, had no idea what a lawyer did. One thing I did know was that it had to be something good, if grandmom said I might do it one day. By the time I was in the fourth grade, at the age of 10, I had a finer grasp of what lawyers do in both the civil and criminal arenas, and was dead set on becoming one. It was at about this time that I began showing what one of my teachers termed "potential for academic excellence." I would go on to complete junior high school in the Philadelphia Public School system. My father—a master meat cutter (not to be confused with a butcher) by trade—constantly advocated the importance of a quality education and saw to it that I matriculated at one of the region's finest (and most expensive) private schools, the William Penn Charter School. Founded in 1689 by William Penn, the school's name reflects the fact that Penn requested, and was granted, a charter to launch another of his various experiments in the New World.

It was at this private institution that I obtained my first peek at what access, opportunity, and privilege can provide. For centuries, sons of some of the most influential families in the region have been educated at Penn Charter, one of seven schools that make up the Inter-Academic League. It was at Penn Charter that I first came to understand that every organization, profession, and social class has its own language or code, with which any outsider must become facile if she or he is to have any chance of participating at anything beyond a mere subsistence level. For those seeking to gain admission to the group, it then becomes necessary to learn the code (another language), and truly become bilingual.

As a first-generation college-educated Black male, I initially found the corporate law firm culture to be as foreign as the Latin language, which I first encountered as a junior high school student. As I did with Latin, I studied the applicable rules of grammar and conversation in the law firm culture, practiced my conversation mentally before engaging anyone in discussion, and studied long and hard to show myself proficient on every test administered.

I soon discovered that the code of the legal profession/business has at its core two financial truisms. First, the practice of law is more business than profession. Second, business generation is a function of relationships. I also quickly discerned that the first crucial relationship any associate must establish is a mentor/mentee relationship with some partner or senior associate who is universally regarded as a thought leader and/or prodigious revenue generator in the relevant organization. The mentor ensures that the associate will receive challenging assignments that will test his or her mettle and intellect and distinguish him or her from the general population. The mentor also teaches the associate the finer points of relationship building and client account cultivation, and usually facilitates a few client-generation opportunities along the way.

The relationship building and nurturing offered by mentors is integral to an associate's ability to speak and understand the code of the major law firm culture. This is especially true if the associate has no familial or other ties to the culture. Early in my career, I was blessed to find a mentor who helped demystify the political landscape of the law firm environment, and who offered me the sort of straight talk I needed to remain focused on my career development while I navigated the shoals and land mines that some others opted not to identify for me. Before he truly grabbed the rudder to my career, however, I would weather a stormy maiden voyage less than three months out of law school.

Two months into my professional career, I was confronted with one of the stark realities of the legal business environment: Institutions remain; individuals come and go. This is a fact that young lawyers must appreciate early on to ensure that blind fidelity to the institution (read: paycheck) does not cloud their judgment when issues of career development and personal values hang in the balance. I chose my first firm after some thought and deliberation. During the wining, dining, and courting process, I was assured that I would have the opportunity to handle both transactional and litigation matters. The firm had an excellent reputation, boasted an impressive list of blue-chip corporate clients, and was politically well connected. Having clerked at a Philadelphia firm as a summer associate after my second year of law school, I knew that Philadelphia attorneys were either transactional lawyers or litigators, not both. Consequently, I found the prospect of switch-hitting exciting, and my enthusiasm was further stoked by the fact that I would be this Wilmington, Delaware, firm's first Black associate. After two months into my tenure, the Litigation Department chairman issued a memorandum announcing, among other things, various reassignments among the associate ranks. The memo stated that I would work exclusively on litigation matters, and that my specific focus would be insurance defense. Insurance defense work was not what lured me to the firm. Further, the thought that I would now cut my litigation teeth in this practice area left me intellectually depressed. Most important, however, was the fact that this was not part of the agreement, the deal, the bargained-for exchange that I had reached with the institution—or so I thought. When I expressed my surprise at the announcement and reminded the department chairman of the firm's initial representations and promises, I was advised, "No one ever told you that the firm would stop evolving once you arrived!"

I was stunned but soon came to grips with the reality of the situation: The institution had spoken and did not care to hear about my disappointment. As fate would have it, the Philadelphia firm where I had clerked the preceding summer, and whose offer of employment I had declined, again extended itself to me. This time I accepted, and I left my first firm after only four months of service.

After 18 months at this second firm, time spent researching various legal issues, drafting motions and memoranda, and reviewing countless boxes of documents in obscure locations around the country, I accepted an offer of employment from a former partner of the firm who had left to start his own firm before I began as a full-time associate. I first met Greg Miller during my stint as a summer associate. Early on, he offered himself as a mentor and identified himself as a friend. He was the only Black attorney—let alone partner—in the firm, which then boasted 80 attorneys. My mentor was a former federal prosecutor who had begun his career with the Navy's Judge Advocate Corps; his mentor and former boss was the first deputy to the United States attorney general. Greg's professionalism punctuated everything he did. He left no stone unturned in analyzing an issue and left nothing to chance during preparation for trial or deposition. Most important, he had the uncanny ability to galvanize teams of people to work with him, without making them feel that they were working for him. During my summer clerk experience, I had watched Greg as he led a litigation team on one of the firm's largest matters. As a summer associate, I was assigned to the team to research rudimentary legal and evidentiary issues. So, when Greg extended the offer of employment, the decision was not difficult. I joined him and his two partners in 1991; became a partner in 1998; and, in 2004, withdrew from the firm to become a partner at my present firm, Saul Ewing, LLP. My years at Miller's firm afforded me many exposures and opportunities, and confirmed for me the importance of understanding the code of the legal business environment. The legal profession is a business environment. Law firms must make a profit. Their stock in trade is time, and they sell the time of their employees—the associates. Without associates, firms cannot make money. It matters not how much the most senior partner can bill for her time, because she can bill but 19 hours per day, assuming 5 hours for sleep. Consequently, if you have any aspirations of becoming a partner in a law firm (regardless of size), appreciate that to be successful you will have to leverage the time and talents of others; you will have to motivate and galvanize people to perform tasks that they really do not want to perform; and you will have to hone your technical and interpersonal skills to facilitate your cultivation of client relationships that yield business for your firm.

I once heard George C. Fraser, author of *Success Runs in Our Race: The Complete Guide to Effective Networking in the African American Community* (2004), make two statements that speak directly to the code of the legal business. First, "Business generation is a function of relationships." Second, "Business decisions are made, based on emotion, and later justified with objective facts." The bottom line here is that people will decide to hire you because they know you and like you. Assuming a given level of expertise and competence, objective considerations of training, pedigree, and intelligence are matters for discussion only if someone later inquires of your client why she or he chose to hire you.

My advice to young attorneys is to find a mentor early on and endeavor to hone your technical skill set. It is equally important to cast your net wide as you begin to network with other professionals and fellow attorneys. Never compromise on your principles or refuse to advocate on your own behalf. In this regard, I am reminded of an excerpt from Marianne Williamson's *A Return to Love*:

> Our deepest fear is not that we are inadequate. Our deepest fear is that we are powerful beyond measure. It is our light, not our darkness, that most frightens us. We ask ourselves, who am I to be brilliant, gorgeous, talented, and fabulous? Actually, who are you not to be? You are a child of God. Your playing small doesn't serve the world. There's nothing enlightened about shrinking so that other people won't feel insecure around you.

References

Fraser, G. C. 2004. *Success Runs in Our Race: The Complete Guide to Effective Networking in the African American Community*. New York: HarperCollins Publishers.

Williamson, M. 1996. *A Return to Love: Reflections on the Principles of "A Course in Miracles."* New York: HarperCollins Publishers.

CHAPTER 21

Fight for the Things You Believe In

By Neari F. Warner

CLARENCE RAY NAGIN, JR.

President and Chief Executive Officer, CRN Initiatives, LLC, New Orleans, Louisiana; Former Mayor of New Orleans, Louisiana

Dr. Warner: Mr. Mayor, would you start by giving some background information?

Mayor Nagin: I am a native New Orleanian and, like many youth of my time, I was born in Charity Hospital. I grew up in the Seventh Ward of the city and later moved to Algiers, what we called "across the river." My family was like most Black families during those days. My father worked several jobs, sometimes three at a time, to give us, my sisters and me, a good, decent upbringing. My mother worked also.

I attended O. Perry Walker High School on the west bank of the city. At Walker, I played basketball and baseball. In baseball, I was a pitcher, and that earned me a scholarship to Tuskegee Institute (now Tuskegee University) in Alabama. That was a thrill for me because Tuskegee was such an outstanding and well-respected college in the Black community.

Dr. Neari F. Warner interviewed Ray Nagin for this book in October 2006. Ray Nagin's tenure as mayor of New Orleans ended in 2010. He recently wrote his memoirs, *Katrina's Secrets: Storms after the Storm* (2011).

I probably would not have been able to attend that school if it were not for that scholarship. I don't believe my parents could have afforded the tuition and the money necessary for me to be away from home going to school. I am sure that they would have tried to send me, but I know that it would have been a struggle and a hardship on the family. So, when I got to Tuskegee, I tried hard to be a good athlete and a good student so that I would not lose the scholarship. I majored in accounting and, of course, I did graduate. I received my degree in 1978.

After college, I took my first job in Detroit, working for General Motors. I also worked in Los Angeles and in Dallas. Then, like a true New Orleanian, I wanted to return home, and I did. I got a job with Cox Cable as a controller. About four years after that, I became vice president and general manager at Cox. After working in that position for a while, I decided that I wanted to enhance my skills, so I sought another degree. I enrolled in the executive MBA program at Tulane University. I did this because I wanted the skills and advantages that such a program could give me. I wanted to use those skills for improving Cox. I completed the program, and it has been very beneficial for me and my family. Yes, I am a family man. I am married to Seletha Smith Nagin, and we have three children: two sons, Jeremy and Jarin, and a daughter, Tianna.

Dr. Warner: How did you become interested in politics? Was there any particular person or event that propelled you into the political arena?

Mayor Nagin: Actually, I never, ever thought about politics as a career. I never wanted to be a politician. I enjoyed what I was doing at Cox, and some of the things I did as part of my job at Cox put me in the public more than I realized. I would say that one of them was a television call-in show I had for the Cox customers. I had that show only because I wanted our New Orleans franchise of Cox to continue to grow, to get better and to be profitable. I knew that the key to this was the customer and customer service. I wanted to do everything in my power to keep our customers satisfied. In doing this call-in show, I got a lot of exposure. Then, at the time when the mayor's race was coming up, people kept suggesting that I needed to run for mayor, that I needed to put my hat in that race. When it became time for qualifying for the various city positions, I began to think a little about running because the people who were putting their names in the hat did not seem, to me, to have what was needed to run the city. You see, I felt that the city needed someone, not only to run the city but to fix the city.

Dr. Warner: What do you mean by this?
Mayor Nagin: Fixing the city means making it right; making it a place known for more than just partying and corruption. I thought that the usual politicians could not be the ones to run or fix our city. Almost everyone who had expressed an interest in the mayor's race was a career politician. So, after getting so much encouragement from people at all levels (as we say, from all walks of life) and then, after testing the waters with an opinion poll, I got the impression that the people of New Orleans were ready for a new kind of mayor. It was late in the process, but I threw my hat in the race. No one expected me to win, but I was feeling good about it all the time. Now, as they say, the rest is history. After a runoff, I was elected!

Dr. Warner: Mr. Mayor, would you describe some of your accomplishments?
Mayor Nagin: Well, I went into office vowing to fix New Orleans. By that, as I said earlier, I wanted to change the image of our city, especially that image of corruption for which New Orleans was known. And, I think I did that. We brought in business-minded people to work in this administration, and we focused our efforts on cleaning up corruption and cleaning up City Hall. As a businessman myself, I focused my efforts on growing businesses for the city and creating jobs for the city's people. I wanted New Orleans to become known as more than a party city. I think we were achieving some levels of success, but our success was interrupted by Hurricane Katrina.

Dr. Warner: Yes, and the entire nation knows about that interruption; so, would you provide a commentary on Hurricane Katrina?
Mayor Nagin: First, people need to remember that prior to Hurricane Katrina, actually about a year before, the city was threatened with Hurricane Ivan. I called for voluntary evacuation of the city. Over half a million people evacuated, and the hurricane did not hit the city. That ended up being a disaster in itself. It was a bad scene because many of our residents were stuck on the highways and the interstate for hours and hours. Then, almost a year later, the weather service began reporting that Hurricane Katrina was headed to the city. After talking with the weather

forecasters, city council, and the governor, I ordered an evacuation of the city. Of course, many of the people were reluctant about leaving because of what happened during the last evacuation. They were thinking that it was another false alarm. This time, I ordered a mandatory evacuation. I told the residents that this was the real thing.

Many people were able to get out, but many were still in the city when the levees breached. We had people trapped in their houses, on their rooftops, and anywhere they could find shelter. Meanwhile, I was trying to get help from anywhere and from everywhere. I was angry, and I was frustrated, and I said some things that were not so nice. You know, it is easy to sit and criticize, point fingers, and assign blame when you are not the one in charge to make the decision. That is what was happening all around. There was no help coming, but everyone had an opinion or a solution. The media and the reporters were there, but all they wanted to do was to have interviews and press conferences. They were not there to give us the help we needed.

Anyway, we used all the resources that we had and we managed to rescue many people who were stranded. We used the Superdome and the Convention Center to house and shelter them. There were tens of thousands of people in each of those places. We were constantly trying to work while others were offsite criticizing and complaining. Things did not get much better until the National Guard came. The guard was commanded by this John Wayne–type dude. He was Lieutenant General Honoré. The general took charge and began to make things happen. He started giving orders and people started moving and shaking. That General Honoré was tough, and I am thankful for everything he did.

Dr. Warner: Mr. Mayor, would you agree that you are now one of the most recognizable political figures in modern times?
Mayor Nagin: That is probably true, but not always for the right, positive reasons. It is true only because of Hurricane Katrina. I have been on talk shows, have been written about in newspapers throughout the country, have been interviewed by the most well-known political commentators, and have been the target of jokes by the late-night comedians. Of course, I cannot do anything but accept it. I had to think of it as bringing exposure to the city. But many of the things I said were taken out of context. Some of the things I said in haste, and other comments were meant only to keep our city in the spotlight. Sometimes I get so emotional about things in the city that I give answers and make comments that don't come out just right.

That's just how passionate I am about things that relate to New Orleans. Everything that I said and did during Katrina was to either get some help for the city or to encourage people to come back to New Orleans.

Dr. Warner: Mr. Mayor, would you provide some insight into things you are doing or plan to do to restore the population of the city?
Mayor Nagin: I plan to do everything I can do to encourage people to come back to the city. I put together the Bring New Orleans Back Commission. This commission is made up of a group of outstanding leaders—the movers and shakers in the city. The commission was charged with coming up with a master plan to rebuild the city. The commission is made up of several committees, like economic development, health and social services, culture and tourism, public transit, and other infrastructure areas. And, of course, there is that all-important education committee on which you have been working. All of the committees have been working really hard, and I expect that there will be a composite report soon. Meanwhile, I am going to keep doing what I need to do to restore our city, to bring it back, and to make it better than ever.

Dr. Warner: As we conclude, Mr. Mayor, are there any words of wisdom that you would like to give to the young people for whom this book is designed?
Mayor Nagin: I don't have a lot of advice except to say that as young people enter their professions, I simply advise them to always give it their best and always fight for the things they believe in.

Dr. Warner: Mr. Mayor, thank you for your time and for your willingness to share and to participate in this project. As always, it is a pleasure working with you.

About the Author
Neari F. Warner, retired professor and former acting president of Grambling State University in Louisiana, currently serves as visiting professor in the Executive PhD program at Jackson State University in Mississippi. She earned her PhD at Louisiana State University, Baton Rouge.

CHAPTER 22

The Winding Journey of an Encyclopedia Mind

MAJOR R. OWENS

Former U.S. Congressman,
D-New York, New York

In January 1983, in the great chamber of the United States House of Representatives, I, Major Robert Odell Owens, was sworn in as a member of Congress. In December 2006, after 24 years of service in this honorable position, I will resign. My only continuing regret is the fact that neither my father nor my mother lived long enough to sit in my current office to enjoy my magnificent view of the dome of the United States Capitol. I, Major, the son of Edna and Ezekiel, have had the privilege and the pleasure of serving as one of the 535 most powerful legislators in the world. Morehouse men never boast; however, we do fervently enjoy highlighting the truth.

For a youngster who never wanted to be president or governor or mayor, my career trail is littered with contradictions. From 1975 to 1983, I served in the New York State Senate. From 1967 to 1973, I served as the New York City commissioner of the Community Development Agency. Before this six-year appointment, I served from 1966 to 1967 as the executive director of the Brownsville Community Council, a local community action agency, and from 1958 to 1966, I served in various librarian

Note: Before Major R. Owens retired from the U.S. Congress in 2007, he submitted this chapter for publication.

positions at the Brooklyn Public Library. Along the way I also served as a teacher, adjunct college professor, project director, and community organization consultant.

Needless to say, I regard my years of service in Congress as a career pinnacle or mountaintop. But next year, as I resign at the age of 70, I will be taking one more career leap for an unreachable star. I will return to my first and greatest love of creative writing. A forthcoming novel entitled *The Taliban in Harlem* and a nonfiction memoir entitled *The Peacock Elite* (2011) are on their way to be followed by a book of *Selected Egghead Rap Poems*.

Although my career path has been an unusual one, I do believe there have been some constant, stabilizing factors influencing my direction. Every beginning professional should pause and take an inventory of the assets that are seldom printed on resumes. Appreciate the sense of self-worth and self-esteem that comes from nurturing parents and families. Humility is a virtue but acquiescence to lesser beings is dangerous. Without an excess of noise be prepared to wage war against the bullies and the hustlers who wear shirts and ties every day. One should never ignore the value of street instincts and common sense. When I was a child we sometimes experienced a little hunger for food, but I was fortunate enough to live in a home rich with lessons that schools never teach.

Moving to a more explicit listing of career success attributes, let me begin with the need to have an encyclopedic mind-set and to be determined to absorb all relevant information and knowledge available. This is the vital component at the core of my capacity to achieve. It is a character trait that is highly desirable in today's professional environment, which grows steadily more complex as fields of expertise are constantly merging in various combinations and permutations.

Somewhere between junior high school and high school I decided that I wanted to be a writer. Despite a lack of encouraging counsel I surmised that a writer of short stories, novels, plays, etc. had to know a little about everything. Of course, there are other professionals who need to have this same generalist orientation: journalists, librarians, politicians, public administrators. It is my good fortune that I have worked in all of these areas.

The process of always serving as a generalist seems to be a smooth one only when one is looking backward over the decades. I was the son of a factory worker who never earned more than the minimum wage and was often laid off with no salary at all, and I shared abject poverty with seven brothers and sisters. Under these conditions I wrote off the possibility of going to college, but my drive to learn everything possible still persisted. English, history, and languages were easy classes. The challenge was in mathematics, which led me to become the whiz kid of algebra, second to none in the school. My Black teachers established my destiny as a doctor or a lawyer or an engineer.

Like a bolt of magic lightning, opportunity struck at the end of my sophomore year in high school. One of my most inspiring teachers urged me to travel across town to take a test in an experimental higher education program financed by the Ford Foundation. Not only were bright tenth graders who passed the test allowed to go straight to college without graduating but the program offered to pay all college expenses. It was the first great reward for my encyclopedic approach to the world. As a result of my positive addiction to learning, I passed that test, which opened up a whole new universe for the factory laborer's bright son.

When I entering Morehouse College in 1952, like many of my classmates, I was temporarily certain of my career goal. Dutifully I had promised my mother and father that I would use my talent in math and science to become an engineer. My parents' reasoning was that although doctors made higher salaries, the training would take too long. My father was deeply in debt and weary of poverty; he wanted me to graduate, get a good job, and help to support the family.

Although mathematics was my primary focus, in keeping with my early outlook, I found every course fascinating. The discipline required for math studies I applied in all of the required liberal arts courses. I always assumed that the contents of my courses would be useful for some future purpose and appreciated instructors who insisted on maximum thoroughness. Today, in the twilight of my career, I detest college graduates who are hired to work in my office but lack the discipline to correctly record an incoming telephone number. I fire such muddle-minded creatures fast. The computerization and digitalization of office operations has raised the premium on professionals who are thoroughly accurate and self-correcting. The ability to listen, analyze, summarize, problem solve, and create are skills that are absolutely necessary. A mind immersed in factual and intellectual substance must accompany these skills.

Competition among peers and high standards at Morehouse College (where I attended 1952–1956) provided the environment necessary to practice and build the skills mentioned earlier. The training and development that lead to career success involve additional factors, and many are too complex to be fully explained in a short biographical statement. It is important to note, however, that my passion for digesting experiences went far beyond book and instructional materials. Individual personalities greatly affected my development and subsequent ability to cope with the rigors of a strenuous professional society. Faculty members, administrators, and college presidents, such as the legendary Dr. Benjamin Mays, were important mentors, sources of inspiration, and good conventional role models. The Morehouse requirement that every student attend chapel every day was a duty despised by most students, but in retrospect, that daily interaction with the broader world and real problems was as vital as any other component of my education. I always entered chapel with a mind ready to receive new wisdom.

In my junior year at Morehouse, conflicts began to bombard my resolve to become an engineer. Among the inspiring teachers and mentors was a creative writing teacher who rekindled my dormant desire to write. The more I wrote, the more boring the math and physics needed for engineering became. My encyclopedic mind found a home in a grand compromise that allowed me to pursue a career in writing but at the same time earn a reasonable living. Added to my major in mathematics and minor in education was a second minor in library science.

In 1957, with a master's degree in library science from Atlanta University, I had the option of working anywhere in the nation. New York is where the great writers sprout, however, so with great enthusiasm I became a librarian in New York while I launched into creating my great American novel. *Roots and Wings*, my unpublished masterpiece, was completed just as the Civil Rights Movement expanded from the South to the East Coast. Inspired by the bravery of the student nonviolence crusade, I rushed to join the Brooklyn Congress of Racial Equality while still shuttling my novel on the publishers' circuit. It was an exciting and demanding period. I became totally absorbed and locked away my literary ambitions.

Immersed in the great gumbo of civic, political, religious, and personal activities of the sixties, my character traits became more concentrated and more productive. The encyclopedic approach to learning and living fostered my interweaving of my librarian's view of the world with the rough-and-tumble incidents unfolding in the theater of volunteer civil rights activism. Every picket line, sit-in, and stall-in was far more complicated than surface headlines showed. Without thorough homework and prepa-rations, each crusade could have been lost. Protests of inadequate bus transfers, garbage dumping on the steps of City Hall to demand equal sanitation service, the capture of live rats to dramatize the plight of ten-ants in slum housing, and rent strikes to protest violations—each of these projects spawned many ramifications and a myriad of details needed to be addressed to achieve success. While fellow organizers panicked, I fol-lowed the example of the Dewey Decimal Classification and assumed that any mass of confusion, like the totality of human knowledge, could be carved into smaller units and rendered doable.

In a nonviolent struggle, the pen becomes a vitally important weapon, though the writing itself is not a creative challenge. What is creative is figuring out how to make sure the memos, instructions, leaflets, hand-books, and letters clearly state the demand for the cause's required nego-tiations in such a way that people will pay attention. I discovered that as a generalist and a writer my ability to organize and energize human resources was greatly enhanced. And the sparkplug of commitment to worthy causes, combined with the engine of steady dedication, held all of my assets together. I never had a plot or plan for moving step by step up a political career ladder. I merely responded to the struggle around me and found myself rewarded by those who appreciated my talent.

One other personality trait is worth sharing: the courage to take risks and seize opportunities. I left the generous health plan, pension, and the other fringe benefits offered by my library system employment and joined an antipoverty corporation in formation. It was a daring venture that I believed was necessary. As one of 26 such community action corporations in New York City, we enjoyed such overwhelming success that Mayor John Lindsay asked me to serve as the commissioner of the Community Development Agency with oversight authority for the total citywide pro-gram. At that point chaos had descended on the agency, and racist politi-cians demanded the shut-down of the system of 26 nonprofit corporations with a total of 500 subcontracted delegate agencies employing 5,000 peo-ple. Again, an encyclopedic approach was absolutely necessary for the survival of that enterprise with diversified neighborhoods, ethnic groups, and multiple program missions. With the power of the pen—master plans, handbooks, procedure manuals, fiscal and personnel directives, and so on—we ended the chaos and created the breathing room needed to attack poverty and promote empowerment.

In a six-year period the new agency developed the internal controls and discipline that other units of city government had taken several decades to complete. New African American and Latino leadership emerged from the ranks of the corporations and delegate agencies under the Community Development Agency. When I was sworn in to the New York State Senate in 1974, one year after retiring from the commissioner position, all but one of the 25 minority members of the legislature were former employees or beneficiaries of the NYC Community Action Program.

During my eight years in the State Senate and my 23 years in Congress, my ability to survive challenging elections while still achieving vital goals and objectives for my constituents was constant because of the same application of encyclopedic oversight, writing skills, organization skill, appreciation for strategic and tactical planning, and willingness to take risks in seizing opportunities. Some weaknesses that have not been discussed in this sketch are the lack of an aggressive public relations posture and the lack of enthusiasm for fund raising. Despite these weaknesses I have survived, but I do not recommend that aspiring politicians ignore the need for such talent.

Regardless of the cash-flow problems, in politics what must be remembered are the arguments that I have been trying to unfold here. Using the attributes I have illuminated will result in the creation of certain parameters of calm around you that help you facilitate control and avoid anxiety or panic. A generalist with communications skills is likely to always retain command of his post. Consultants and staff can be hired to fill many gaps; however, the point of this exercise is to alert political aspirants to the not-so-secret fact that there are personal traits and habits that bolster one's advantages. Along with these traits, it is highly desirable to move up to the Congress with a great distillation of the kinds of experiences I have enumerated from lower levels on the ladder.

To compensate and substitute for my lack of a big campaign war chest my community activism has never ceased. My constituents know that I am still responding to the pain of their struggles and that my dedication and commitment are as strong as ever. My opponents have always been shocked when I win against great odds. But the people in the neighborhoods and the streets understand.

Today, there are approximately 650,000 constituents in each congressional district. My district is one of the poorest and most diverse with a very low percentage of college graduates. It is a political unit immersed in the city, state, and federal power decision-making environment. Cross currents from all of these levels of government interact with a myriad of problems ranging from immigration and deportations to food stamps and homelessness. World trade policies that devalue banana production in the Caribbean, for example, hurt a portion of my constituents. Terrorism in Haiti and civil war in Liberia, which increase the number of refugees, are examples of international conditions that routinely had on my agenda. To understand problems and challenges I start with my broad encyclopedic review. To resolve problems my basic communications and management skills are launched into a myriad of battles. Like the practice of medicine, the practice of politics is filled with never-ending challenges.

CHAPTER 23

Reminiscences of the Honorable Peggy A. Quince

PEGGY A. QUINCE

Associate Justice,
Florida Supreme Court,
Tallahassee, Florida

Often as I sit in my office at the Florida Supreme Court, I reflect on the circumstances of my life and marvel at being a member of the state of Florida's highest court. Most of us, when viewing this court and other similar institutions, believe that the people who are selected to these positions must come from backgrounds that include prestige and privilege. I certainly cannot make that claim.

I was born during the winter of 1948 in Norfolk, Virginia, the second of five children from the union of Solomon Quince and Pinkie Howell. My father worked long dawn-to-dusk hours as a stevedore at the Norfolk Naval Base loading and unloading heavy crates of cargo from the holds of ships in order to earn enough money to support his wife and growing family. By the time I reached the second grade, my father was not only working as many hours as he could (overtime paid for many things that we could not otherwise afford), but he was also raising five children as a single dad. Among my earliest memories of my father are those of having him waking us up to get ready for school at 6:00 a.m. as he picked up his lunch pail and got in his car to go to work. For my father, a car was not a luxury but a necessity; otherwise, he would not have been able to go to work. We lived in the rural area of Chesapeake, Virginia (formerly Norfolk County), at least an hour away from the naval base.

The stress of raising five children, coupled with my father's long hours away from home, proved to be too much for my emotionally fragile mother to bear. My parents separated when I was in the second grade. Because of this unhappy circumstance, my father was left to raise the children alone after my mother moved out of the home and to another city. I learned at an early age, through the hands-on experience of caring for my three younger siblings, the meaning of responsibility and the importance of caring for others who are less able to care for themselves. I also learned the quiet satisfaction that comes with putting the welfare of others before the welfare of one's self. Ours was a closely knit and loving family that, with God's help, managed to pull itself through those difficult early years. Under my father's watchful eye and loving guidance, my siblings and I learned the importance and dignity of honest work; faith in God; service to others, especially those less fortunate than ourselves; and the emancipating power of a good education. Although my dad only completed the sixth grade, he often said, "Study hard in school so that later on in life you can work with your mind, and not have to work with your back." This sage advice was imparted by my father to each of his children as we were growing up.

Despite the United States Supreme Court opinion of *Brown v. Board of Education* (347 U. S. 483 [1954]), I attended segregated elementary and high schools until I graduated from Crestwood High School in Chesapeake, Virginia, in 1966 and entered college. Perhaps Crestwood's most well-known graduate is the very talented actor Tim Reid, who graduated several classes before me. I followed my father's sound words of advice and studied hard in school. One of the happiest days in my life was that wonderful spring day in 1966 when I went to my family and proudly showed them my acceptance letter from Howard University. Although I had been accepted to a number of colleges and universities throughout the United States, Howard was my choice because it was a well-respected Black university and was not too far from home. The acceptance letter also included information about the scholarship that I had been awarded. Of course, a scholarship was absolutely necessary because my father could not afford to pay college tuition and room and board.

I entered Howard as a zoology major with the intention of becoming a physician or maybe doing PhD-level research into the causes and (I dared to hope) the eventual cure for sickle-cell anemia. I had witnessed for myself the pain and suffering that terrible disease had visited upon so many people in the Black community and felt the personal calling to help find a cure. I was financially able to pursue my college education thanks in no small measure to a scholarship and an EEOC (Equal Employment and Opportunity Commission) grant from the federal government, which were based on my high SAT and PSAT scores.

To supplement my scholarship funds, I also worked a part-time grave-yard shift at the Government Printing Office (GPO) on Sunday and Monday nights from 10 p.m. to 6 a.m., filling the never-ending orders that people throughout the country had placed for government publications. In addition to my government job with the GPO, I was also hired by one of my professors to type the galley sheets for one of his forthcoming books. That typing course in high school, which I had not wanted to take, certainly proved to be worth the time and effort.

During my undergraduate days, I also found time to join the Alpha Kappa Alpha Sorority, Incorporated, and to do volunteer work with Angel Flight, a service organization of young women associated with the Air Force ROTC (Reserve Officers' Training Corps). Among our many activities, the members of Angel Flight regularly visited and tried our best to cheer up the servicemen hospitalized at the nearby Walter Reed Army Hospital. For the most part, these servicemen had been wounded while fighting in the Vietnam conflict. Many of those wonderful young men were no older than we were. Although I am sure they didn't realize it at the time, by allowing us to come into their lives, however briefly, those brave young soldiers gave back to us as much as we gave to them.

The late 1960s was an exciting time to be in college. The winds of social change blowing across the country were sweeping away generations-old barriers of racial segregation, inequality, and discrimination. A United States Supreme Court intent on bringing social justice to all Americans was slowly, case by case, dismantling the legal architecture that had enabled segregation to thrive for so many years. Dr. Martin Luther King, Jr.'s nonviolent protest movement of civil disobedience, the freedom marches in the Deep South, and the countless other acts of individual heroism by Black and White people alike were empowering Black people everywhere for the first time in American history. The positive changes these events were bringing to the country infused Black America with a theretofore unknown sense of hope and optimism that one day soon we too would enjoy the opportunity to gather and enjoy the fruits of American citizenship as fully and completely as those fruits had been gathered and enjoyed by White America since the day this nation was founded almost 200 years before.

Things that were absolutely unthinkable to my parents' generation, things that were dangerous to people of color less than a decade before, had suddenly become possible in the late 1960s and were even showing promise of becoming so commonplace that someday soon they would not even merit mention. Who today, for example, would even think it worth mentioning that he or she had dined out the previous evening in a restaurant where the customers were a mixture of White people and Black people? As trivial and unremarkable as such an observation would be today, before the mid-1960s such an occurrence would have been of all-consuming interest to people of all races because that sort of thing was simply not done back then, at least not in the South. This sort of racial integration, as inconsequential as it seems today, was either out-right illegal in some states (and therefore not even tried by Black people who knew what was good for them), or the restaurant owner would refuse to serve anybody who was not White. Many public establishments of the time still had signs hanging on their front doors announcing "White Public Only" or more bluntly "No Dogs or Niggers Allowed." "Colored people" such as I were expected to "know their place," and that place was most emphatically *not* seated beside White people. I remember most vividly the fact that my White Jewish doctor had a waiting room for "col-oreds" and a waiting room for "whites."

I can recall to this day the mixed feelings of apprehension and triumph I experienced the first time a small group of my intrepid friends and I sat down at a table in a small Southern White restaurant and were actu-ally served our food and allowed to eat our meal in the same room with White people without being harassed by other customers or arrested by the police! In retrospect, to borrow the words of author James Baldwin, at least for those of my background and before the Civil Rights Movement, America truly was "another country."

It was in large measure the momentous and revolutionary social changes I witnessed throughout this country that inspired me to put aside my earlier ambition of becoming a doctor and instead turn my focus to the study of law. I saw the legal system as the one institution of society that presented the best hope of effectively remedying the countless wrongs of the past that had waited far too long for redress. The basic civil rights that had been withheld from Black people for generations were finally being restored by the Supreme Court and by the various lower courts following its mandates and examples. As I became more socially conscious, brilliant and fearless champions of the cause of freedom and equality, such as Justice Thurgood Marshal and Dr. Martin Luther King, Jr., became not just my heroes but my role models. Let me be candid: I wanted to join the revolution; I wanted to make a difference.

It is impossible for me to describe the soul-numbing emotional devastation the murders of Dr. King and Senator Robert Kennedy visited upon members of our communities. I was no exception. Within a span of two short months the two seemingly indispensable figures in our nation's struggle for civil rights and social justice had been mercilessly cut down by assassins' bullets. After a period of personal mourning, I promised myself that I would not allow the bullets that killed those two men to also kill the dreams and hopes that still lived within me. I resolved in my own small way to continue the legacy of these great persons; the movement would not die with them. For those of us who had glimpsed the promised land spoken of by Dr. King, there was no going back.

I applied and was accepted to the law school in 1972 at the Catholic University of America in Washington, D.C. Catholic University's law school was the first school I attended where I was in the minority. Although the College of Law at Howard was and is an excellent school, I believed it was now time for me to be in a setting that would approximate what I would face in the work world. I knew, especially in the field of law, that I would not be the majority in most workplaces. My first semester of law school taught me that I could compete and compete effectively in the legal arena. I found the study of law, although intellectually challenging, nothing that I could not (with some effort) readily handle.

The study of law imposed a new structure on my thinking and provided me with an analytical framework from which to examine and resolve problems. I found constitutional law to be the most interesting academic subject I studied in law school, followed closely by the study of property law. As luck would have it, while participating in a study group, I met my future husband, Fred LaVerne Buckine. Fred, who is also a lawyer, was without question the best (tangible) thing I got out of law school. He is the devoted and loving father of our two daughters, Peggy and Laura.

While in law school, I joined the Phi Alpha Delta Law Fraternity and the Black American Law Students Association, and I also served in the law school's student government. Although we were told by the administration that it was not a good idea to work while in law school, I worked various part-time jobs nonetheless. I worked during my first year of law school as a computer operator on the evening shift (generally from 3:00 p.m. to 11:00 p.m.) at International Group Plans, an insurance company that underwrote group health insurance plans. During the summer after my first year of law school, I worked at the university's legal services clinic. I worked during the summer after the second year and during my final year of school for the Federal Deposit Insurance Corporation (FDIC), as a law clerk giving advice on how to maximize insurance coverage. After completing law school, I followed the advice that I now give to law students; I did not work until I had studied for and taken the bar examination.

My first job out of law school was as a hearing officer for the Rental Accommodations Office in Washington, D.C. This job entailed hearing and resolving rent-control disputes that arose between tenants and their landlords. I subsequently decided to go home to Virginia to practice law and practiced with several lawyers in Norfolk, Virginia, in the areas of general civil litigation, divorce, real estate law, and some criminal law. I still vividly recall the first criminal case I tried as a private attorney. I remember the disappointment I felt at losing the case before a jury despite my best efforts to free a man who I, like most novice attorneys, believed was innocent. For the next month, I spent every spare moment I had researching and preparing his appeal to the Virginia Supreme Court. I argued the case myself before a three-judge panel, but alas, I lost the appeal. This was my first experience in the area of law that was to eventually become my field of professional expertise—preparing and presenting cases to the appellate courts.

In 1978, my husband and I moved to Florida, where I became an associate of Fred G. Minnis, esquire. Mr. Minnis was an early pioneer in the area of civil rights. Among his many other accomplishments, it was he who filed (and won) the first wage-discrimination lawsuit in Pinellas County, Florida. He also argued the infamous case of *Williams v. State* (110 So. 2d 654 [Fla. 1959]), which allows the state to use similar fact evidence if that evidence is relevant to any issue in the case except that of bad character or propensity. This fine man and dedicated attorney taught me a great deal about the practice of law.

In 1980, I learned through a friend that the Florida Attorney General's Office was actively seeking an appellate attorney to work in its Tampa office. The office was looking for someone who would represent the state of Florida in the various state courts of appeal and in the federal courts up to and including the United States Supreme Court. Although I lost that appeal in Virginia, the research and the writing "appealed" to the academic in me and was an aspect of the law that I found challenging. The chance that I might one day argue a case before the nation's highest court, the court that had been so crucial to the Civil Rights Movement, was irresistible. I applied for the job and was hired (I was later told) based on my earnestness at the job interview and the quality of the brief I had written in my first criminal appeal case. I worked at the Attorney General's Office for 14 years; the last 5 years were as the bureau chief of the Tampa office.

In 1993, I was interested in and encouraged to apply for one of two newly created seats on Florida's Second District Court of Appeal. By that time I had represented the state of Florida in literally hundreds of cases before the Second District, the Florida Supreme Court, the United States District Court for the middle District of Florida, the Eleventh Circuit Court of Appeals, and the United States Supreme Court. I had been an appellate attorney for 13 years, and I believed that I was uniquely qualified to be on the appellate court and would do a good job as an appellate judge. Then Florida governor Lawton Chiles agreed and appointed me to the court. I was retained in office by a vote of the people of Florida in the November election of 1996 for a six-year term.

In 1998, due to the retirement of a sitting justice, a seat on the Florida Supreme Court became open. With my joint appointment by former governor Lawton Chiles and then governor-elect Jeb Bush, I became the first Black woman appointed as a justice to the Florida Supreme Court. Because Governor Lawton Chiles died several days after the appointment was announced, Lieutenant Governor Buddy McKay was sworn in as governor to serve the remaining three weeks of the term. One of Governor McKay's official acts as governor was signing my Commission to Florida's highest court.

As I took my seat on the bench of the Supreme Court for the very first time in January 1999, a bittersweet emotion washed over me because I knew that my father, Solomon Roosevelt Quince, Sr., who had died before I became an appellate court judge, was standing next to God the Father watching the proceeding. I knew that the justice that had been denied him during his lifetime was now reflected in the words JUSTICE Peggy A. Quince.

CHAPTER 24

Dedicate Yourself to Success

LEAH WARD SEARS

Attorney, Schiff Hardin LLP,
Atlanta, Georgia;
Former Chief Justice,
Supreme Court of Georgia,
Atlanta, Georgia

When I was seven or eight years old I knew that one day I would attend college. I sent away for catalogs and brochures and spent long hours looking at the pictures and reading about degree programs and campus life. Some colleges interested me more than others did. Harvard and Yale, for instance, interested me a great deal. But as I read about those schools and looked at their colorful brochures, I couldn't help noticing that none of the students in the pictures looked like me. They were all White males. If there has been a defining moment in my life, that was probably it. I knew that America needed to change, and I wanted to be one of the people who helped bring about necessary changes in American life.

I owe so much to my parents. The deep love, solid support, and constant encouragement I received from them while I was growing up filled me with hope and confidence. My family didn't possess the financial resources I would need, however, to attend a college like Harvard or Yale. Knowing that made me work harder and study longer, because one of my goals was to get the best college education available. All that hard work finally paid off when I earned a full scholarship to Cornell University.

Note: Before Chief Justice Leah Ward Sears retired, she submitted this chapter for publication.

Then, after graduating from Cornell in 1976, I returned to Georgia and earned my law degree at Atlanta's Emory University.

I was drawn to the study of law for a number of reasons. One of my heroes when I was growing up was Thurgood Marshall, who later served on the Supreme Court of the United States. His success as a trial court lawyer in working to bring about important social change in cases like *Brown v. Board of Education* was an inspiration to me. Like Thurgood Marshall, I saw myself arguing important civil rights litigation before the Supreme Court of the United States and working to help America become the free and open society promised in the Constitution and the Bill of Rights.

When I was young, the Civil Rights Movement and the women's movement were actively engaged in working for social change for minorities and women. In those days there were very few African American lawyers, very few women lawyers, and almost no African American women lawyers. This was another reason why I turned to the law. I had something to prove as a woman and as an African American. But after graduating from law school and then passing the bar exam, I didn't go into civil rights litigation. Instead, I joined a large law firm in Atlanta and concentrated my practice on corporate law. Soon, however, I found the paperwork burdensome and tedious. I was spending too much of my time behind a desk and not enough time meeting and working with people.

When an opportunity to serve as a judge on Atlanta's Traffic Court came along two years later, I jumped at the chance. The pay wasn't as good and neither were the perks, but I felt positive about the change. Then three years later I ran for a seat on the Fulton County Superior Court and won a hard-fought election, becoming the youngest person and the first African American woman to serve on a superior court in Georgia. Four years later I was appointed to a seat on the Supreme Court of Georgia, the state's highest appellate court. Not only was I the first woman to serve on the court but I was also the youngest person ever to serve on the Supreme Court of Georgia and only the second African American. In 2005, my 13th year on the Court, I became the first African American woman to serve as chief justice of a state supreme court in the United States.

Unlike the other justices on the Supreme Court of Georgia, I have faced opposition in every election. Some of my political opponents have made unfair claims about me and my record on the bench. Although personal attacks are a common feature of the political campaign process, it is never easy to see myself portrayed in a false light. But even when I was the subject of personal attacks, I have refrained from retaliating. It is not in my nature to make derogatory comments about political opponents or their records. Such comments only serve to reflect adversely on my character. I firmly believe that if you can't say something good about someone, you're better off saying nothing at all.

Success in life can be achieved in many ways. I've always felt that I needed to be more prepared than anyone else. That's one sure way I've found to earn and maintain the respect of my colleagues and peers. When I first came on the Supreme Court at the age of 36, one of the older justices told me that I was "too damn young to be on a court like this!" And he meant it. It wasn't exactly what I wanted to hear, but it served to remind me that I still had something to prove.

I also believe that opportunity alone will not lead to success. Success comes to those who make the most of opportunity when it comes their way. That's why I'm a big believer in asking questions and seeking out answers. I'm always eager to learn something new. After all, success is an ongoing process. To remain successful, you must continue to do those things that led to your success in the first place.

Success can also be measured in many ways. Despite all the time and effort expended pursuing their goals, most truly successful people never lose sight of who they are and where they came from—their roots. Maintaining a good reputation in their community, enjoying the respect of their colleagues, being the kind of person their family and friends can rely on—these are some of the important ways to measure the value of success.

Women—and especially African American women—began the 20th century unable to vote or earn a college degree, and they certainly were not encouraged to become Supreme Court justices. Today, most of the legal barriers to success that women used to face have been dismantled. Women have taken their places alongside men in every walk of life. But it is never enough to set personal goals and achieve them, or to store up treasures here on earth, or to satisfy our own needs and desires. Because just as success can be measured in many ways, it also has many consequences. One consequence of success should be a willingness on our part to give something back, to help ensure the success of someone else. When I think of giving back, I also think of the people who helped me to reach my goals and make the most of the opportunities that came my way. Without the love, aid, and guidance of family, friends, and colleagues, I would not be where I am today.

I also know that being a wife and a mother has enriched my life in many ways. Even though balancing my family's needs with the demands of my profession has not always been easy, the rewards have been great. The success I have enjoyed would not have been possible without the constant love and support of my husband, Haskell Ward, and my children, Addison and Brennan. And that is why I strongly encourage career women and men to strike that same balance in their own lives.

Although there may be no magic formula for achieving success, preparedness, dedication, and a positive outlook will go a long way toward its attainment. Being prepared promotes self-confidence. Your colleagues and peers are much more likely to listen to what you have to say if you can confidently address any concerns they may have about a decision or a course of action you are recommending they take. Success and dedication also go hand in hand. The ability to focus on a given task and see it through to completion are the hallmarks of every success story. Finally, you are far more likely to convince others of your point of view if you bring positive energy to every endeavor. Enthusiasm for your priorities and initiatives can be, and often is, highly contagious.

I want to make one final point about the pursuit of success and its ultimate achievement. When you are young, and this is true for everyone, it is easy to get discouraged or lose interest in your goals when you suffer a temporary setback. You may begin to question the value of all your hard work, and the world may suddenly seem like a cold and uncaring place. But that is exactly when many a success story has gotten its start. Adversity will often bring out the best in people, but only if they never allow temporary setbacks to become permanent ones.

CHAPTER 25

Faith, Hope, Delivery

DIANE E. WATSON

Former U.S. Congresswoman,
D-California, Los Angeles, California

At a very young age, my sister and I would sit at the foot of our maternal grandmother as she spoke of such world-renowned figures as Mohandas Gandhi, Marcus Garvey, Eleanor Roosevelt, and Mary McLeod Bethune as if they were actual relatives. Gandhi's passive resistance to the demeaning oppression of India's occupation by the British had a tremendous impact on her, and it was passed on to us. Marcus Garvey's Back to Africa movement consumed her, given that her own grandmother had been fathered by a slave master. The longing to return to the continent from whence her people had come ran deep within her veins. My grandmother was so taken with Garvey's movement that she would bring her children, including my mother, to hear him whenever he made an appearance in Los Angeles. Grandmother's classmate from the South, Mary McLeod Bethune, had been one of 17 children of former slaves: That gave Grandmother a sense of kinship with this confidant of Eleanor Roosevelt. The First Lady's involvement with the educational needs of young black women so impressed my grandmother that Mrs. Roosevelt was held up to us as a role model. Ms. Bethune's work with the women's movement and the National Council of Negro Women also made a lasting impression. My grandmother took note of Ms. Bethune's memorable speech on the power of education and passed that passion on to her grandchildren. It was never a question of *if* we would go to college but *where* and *how*. Grandmother was as dedicated to education as was her sister, Pauline Slater, the first African American teacher in the Los Angeles Unified School District; their baton was passed to me to carry in continuous pursuit of education. Thus, my leadership quest began with familial direction. There was always an unspoken expectation of success that could only come from the acquisition of a quality education. With this built-in encouragement to set goals and not give up until they were met, the road map was drawn.

My mother, Dorothy O'Neal Watson, was Applicant No. 3 when she registered at the new Los Angeles City College. At age 21 she dropped out, married my father, and devoted herself to raising four children, while instilling within them her dreams of seeking higher education and personal professional achievement. But to the amazement of her friends and family, eventually she returned to college, graduating with my younger sister in the 1970s. She never gave up on her dream.

I envisioned a professional career from the time I entered junior high school and witnessed the White girls at my high school receive corsages, indicating that they were invited to join a collegiate sorority. When asked where they planned to attend college, the answer would be "You-kluh." With rising self-confidence I mocked those girls and said I, too, was going to "You-kluh," not knowing they meant the University of California at Los Angeles! Yet in associating myself with like-minded students, albeit White, and realizing they were destined to go places, I attached myself to their star to advance my pursuit of success.

Leadership skills develop as you advance in influence and authority. I looked for activities where there was a fit and that I enjoyed. The Latin classes I took in high school taught me how to conjugate verbs, to interpret prefixes and suffixes, and to effortlessly define a new word using roots. When you spell well you write well, if you know the rudiments. Joining the Latin Club helped put my knowledge to use.

My college experiences would provide the additional tools I needed, enhancing my conceptual and leadership skills over time. Regardless of the obstacles that stood in my way, I would not take "No!" for an answer and persisted until admitted to UCLA as an education major with a social work minor. Now that I was truly a scholar, my aunt, who had just retired from the U.S. Postal Service, willingly paid the house fees allowing me to stay on campus at Steven's House. There, I joined several campus organizations and was inducted into the Alpha Kappa Alpha sorority. Part of pledging was completing community projects and taking the lead in shaping their outcomes.

In these circumstances, you learn responsibility and become creative and innovative. Problem solving results out of necessity when there is no set path.

Growing up on a block that was integrated when my family moved in allowed us to associate with Asian, Mexican, Greek, and Jewish children. We played together innocently, without any preconceived racial notions. Oh yes, we heard about racial discrimination in the South, but I had little exposure to racist behavior while I was growing up. I was very comfortable among people of other ethnic backgrounds and bore few feelings of victimization or inferiority.

Yet, there were instances when you suspected you were being treated differently. But as the sum total of my experiences, I felt quite well-adjusted because we had been told of our worth and lineage. Therefore, I adopted an attitude that I could achieve against all odds. Living on campus at UCLA's Steven's House, a well-planned interracial setting, was a nurturing and enlightening experience. I quickly learned that, regardless of ethnicity, we had more in common than not. Moreover, it prepared me for those situations I would encounter in the outside world.

After graduation, I taught elementary school and shaped learning experiences that would make a difference in the children's future lives. Your skills are honed whenever you work with children. They let you know very quickly if they think you are faking it and are true critics of your performance. You have to *keep it real*—a lesson well learned!

The stories my paternal uncle told me about his journeys throughout the Orient as a merchant seaman were an intriguing fascination when I was very young. The stories stuck with me and later, on a whim, I put them into action and went off to teach in Okinawa and France! Taking language classes enabled me to make my way around. Merchants were especially considerate when they heard me speak a few words in their language. Eventually, the foreign language background would serve me well when I applied for what I considered the ultimate leadership position: U.S. ambassador.

While serving as a member of the Los Angeles Board of Education, I continued moving toward my goal by working on my master's degree. At the same time, while chairperson of the Educational Development Committee, I worked with the civil rights community on strategies to integrate our schools. Often, that meant leading demonstrations in support of busing and holding informational meetings. We developed a Truth Squad that followed the antibusing crowd wherever they went to disparage our efforts: We brought forth the facts in spite of them. In convening the activist community, I was the link between the school board and those affected by the court desegregation mandate. It was a role I relished because of my position as the sole Black member of the board at that time. It took constant information gathering, contact with concerned parents, and many public appearances to articulate the issues.

This experience became the subject matter of my dissertation for my PhD in education administration. In 1987, I received my doctorate while serving as a California state senator. That required triple duty over a 10-year period, but I learned how to use my time more wisely and make every minute count. When time is of the essence you learn to set priorities. You must take your tasks *more* seriously—but yourself *less* so. It helps to have positive people in your life with whom you engage regularly, and special friends in whom you can confide. On the personal side, I learned never to let my color or sex get in my way; it would be someone else's problem, not mine! Continuous learning, developing an extensive vocabulary, and realizing that appearances matter distinguish you from the crowd. Also, having resources, whether personal or shared, makes a difference in empowering yourself to lead.

Among Black people, leadership evolves from overcoming the societal hardships imposed on you by color. Feelings of inferiority, both imagined and valid, can be diminished by using your support system to build self-esteem, by polishing your personality, and by developing a sense of humor. My spiritual beliefs have given me a faith in the future that seems to get brighter every day. The real test of leadership came when President Clinton appointed me U.S. Ambassador to the Federated States of Micronesia. I had to represent those values and principles upon which democracy is built.

Now that I recently retired as a member of the U.S. House of Representatives, I can look back over the past and realize that it was my support and my religious base that gave me confidence and propelled me to a position where I could provide leadership by influencing policy that lifts the quality of life for all Americans.

As an African American woman who has experienced triumphs that I could not even imagine as a young child, I count my blessings every day for the family, friends, opportunities, and challenges that guided my success. I thank them all—and to God be the glory!

CHAPTER 26

Reaching Out to Your Community Through Public Service

JESSE WHITE

Illinois Secretary of State,
Springfield, Illinois

My name is Jesse White, and I am currently serving my fourth term as Illinois Secretary of State. For almost 40 years, I have been blessed with the opportunity to serve the people of Illinois in many different capacities. However, there is no doubt in my mind that the success I have experienced could not have occurred without strong core values, a solid educational foundation, a positive attitude, and a lot of determination.

I was born in 1934, in Alton, Illinois, the middle child of seven brothers and sisters. Growing up on public aid, and with so many siblings, meant that money was always tight, and we couldn't afford many extras. The lack of material items helped strengthen our family bond, and we frequently went on family picnics and to ball games together. Having a tight family unit helped shape my attitude, and I learned at an early age to strive for excellence in everything I do. As a young man attending Waller High School in Chicago (currently Lincoln Park Academy), I learned to carefully juggle my academics, extracurricular activities, and a part-time job at the local grocery store. I was also a drummer in the band and captain of both the basketball and baseball teams my senior year. It made for a hectic schedule, but it all paid off when I graduated high school in 1952. By keeping my nose to the grindstone and with the help of basketball and baseball scholarships, I prepared for further education at Alabama State College (now Alabama State University). Four years later, I graduated with a bachelor's degree.

Not long after graduation, I signed a contract to play professional baseball with the Chicago Cubs organization. However, less than a week before I was scheduled to report for Spring Training, I was drafted by another organization—the U.S. Army. I served as a paratrooper in the 101st Airborne Division for two years. After being formally discharged, I resumed my professional baseball career with the Chicago Cubs organization and played professional baseball for eight wonderful years.

Based upon my experiences in the military and my home life, I learned to respect other people equally and discovered the intrinsic value of helping others. It wasn't long before I took an active interest in my community and the people living within it. I took special interest in those that were younger and always looked at each child with hope for the future. It is our youth who will become the future leaders of this great country, and I believe we should preserve our most precious resource. This philosophy led me to pursue a teaching career. As a teacher and administrator with the Chicago Public School system, I played an active role in the lives of young people and helped them stay on the right track.

I also realized the need for constructive extracurricular activities for children living in Chicago's Cabrini-Green and Henry Horner public housing communities. The pressures to use drugs, drop out of school, and join gangs are serious issues that can easily overwhelm children who simply have no other options. Therefore, one of my first endeavors was the creation of the Jesse White Tumbling Team. Tumbling has always been a passion of mine, and this team provided a positive alternative for at-risk children. Since I created the team, no matter what job or office I held, I have steadfastly continued my involvement with the tumblers and am proud of the more than 13,000 young men and women who have performed with the team over the past 51 years. At last count, only 99 have gotten themselves into trouble with the law.

After years of working with Chicago youth, I decided that I could assist a broader spectrum of people in a larger setting by running for state representative in the Eighth Legislative District (formerly the 13th Legislative District) of the Illinois General Assembly. I won this office in

1975 and became a voice for one of the most culturally, economically, and racially diverse districts in Illinois. For 16 wonderful years, I worked toward legislation that would help not only my local community but also the entire state. During my tenure, I introduced and supported legislation that fought crime, improved education, provided affordable housing, and helped senior citizens. It took a lot of energy to continue my current job as a teacher and juggle all of my obligations and new duties, but I made it work. It was a combination of determination, confidence, and a genuine enthusiasm for the work that kept me motivated and allowed me to excel.

In 1992, I decided to make a transition from being a legislator to an administrator. I successfully ran for the office of Cook County recorder of deeds and officially hung up my legislative hat. As recorder of deeds, I was exposed to a whole new world of management and accountability. I was directly responsible for more than 270 employees and a budget of more than $13 million. With service in mind, I brought innovation to the office and generated more than $145 million in revenues and processed more than 4.5 million documents, which were both all-time highs. I was able to streamline the office and increase efficiency through the application of new business practices and automation. It felt good to know that my hard work was producing tangible results for the people of Cook County. I enjoyed public service and was fortunate enough to win reelection to a second term in 1996.

In all of my years, I have never been one to settle in. I look at each hour as an opportunity to accomplish something great, to strive for excellence. When the opportunity to run for secretary of state presented itself, I accepted the challenge. In November 1998, I won my first statewide office by a margin of more than 450,000 votes and was elected the 37th Illinois secretary of state. In November 2002, I was reelected Illinois secretary of state, winning by more than 1.3 million votes and winning all 102 counties in the state of Illinois. In November 2006, I was reelected to a third term, having received 63 percent of the vote statewide. The secretary of state's office is the largest and most diverse office of its kind in the nation, providing more direct services to the people of Illinois than any other public agency. This is the perfect arena for me to truly serve all of the people of Illinois.

During my time in office as secretary of state, I have worked to bring integrity and innovation to the office and to make our highways as safe as possible. I have been a strong advocate on traffic safety issues. In 2007, I initiated teen driver safety legislation giving Illinois one of the top-ranked graduated driver licensing programs in the country. Since the law took effect in 2008, teen driving deaths in Illinois dropped by 56 percent.

I have also worked to crack down on DUI, partnering with Mothers Against Drunk Driving (MADD) on key DUI legislation. Effective January 1, 2009, the new law requires all first-time DUI offenders who wish to obtain driving relief to install a breath alcohol ignition interlock device on their vehicles. MADD called this one of the most important pieces of DUI legislation passed in Illinois in several years.

My administration has also worked to improve truck safety and the commercial driver's license (CDL) licensing process. In my first year in office, I initiated a comprehensive highway safety package to tighten up the rules and regulations of the CDL licensing process. I implemented a key policy change, beginning May 1, 2008, in which out-of-state CDL holders moving to Illinois must take and pass the written and road tests before they are issued an Illinois CDL. Illinois was the first state in the nation to require these tests for licensed CDL holders moving from another state. The policy change has received praise from law enforcement and trucking industry representatives.

Additionally, I have been committed to improving customer services through streamlined operations and the innovative use of technology. This has resulted in shorter than ever wait times at driver licensing facilities as more customers take advantage of new, technology-based transactions that the office has developed to better serve the public. Over the past few years Internet transactions have more than doubled in my office. In 2006, internet transactions accounted for more than $41 million. In 2009, these transactions accounted for more than $87 million.

Having had a sister who years ago received a kidney transplant, I understand the life-saving importance of organ and tissue donation. Thus, I initiated legislation creating the First Person Consent Organ/Tissue Donor Registry, which makes a person's decision to donate legally binding. Since 2006, more than 5.4 million people have signed up for the registry.

As many may recall, in 1999, I inherited an office under a cloud of corruption from George Ryan. I immediately pledged to restore integrity and eliminate all forms of institutionalized corruption and wrongdoing. Some key efforts included establishing a code of conduct for employees; setting strict fundraising policies that prohibit employee contributions; hiring Jim Burns, former U.S. attorney for the Northern District of Illinois, as inspector general; strengthening the inspector general's office; and initiating legislation to make the position of inspector general permanent with broad powers to root out corruption.

I feel both honored and privileged to again have the opportunity to serve in the capacity of secretary of state. I have had a chance to see and do many wonderful things in my life. I have taken with me the knowledge from each past experience and am more determined than ever to be the best secretary of state that Illinois has ever enjoyed. Finally, I believe that when you go through this world and become successful, you should give something back.

Conclusion

Congratulations Reader! You have reached the end of your journey with us. What an exciting, inspiring ride! Now that you have experienced *Voices of Historical and Contemporary Black American Pioneers*, we hope you have a greater respect for the struggles and successes that Black American pioneers, past and present, experienced in pursuit of freedom and equal opportunities. We hope this journey has transformed you, in terms of how *you* might make a difference, by targeting your talents and academic interests toward areas in which Black Americans are historically underrepresented, as well as fields more traditionally associated with Black American culture. As the pioneers in this literary vehicle show, the success of Black Americans in all professions and career fields has been extraordinary, capturing their persistence, concentrated determination, and resilience to achieve goals and dreams that others said were impossible.

We also hope you have absorbed the abundance of information about the life stories and careers of Black American pioneers found throughout all four volumes. Can you imagine America without the remarkable contributions of Black people? With research and worthwhile effort, one can discover and transmit much about the contributions of Blacks to America and to the world. Remember your heritage. Never forget what Black pioneers in America endured and achieved for freedom. You are here today, standing on their shoulders. Do not disappoint them or yourself.

For, in studying these remarkable Black men and women, we recognized that, despite movement toward higher ground, racial prejudice and discrimination are alive and well. As a nation, we must be diligent in our efforts to eradicate discrimination wherever it raises its ugly head. As Dr. Martin Luther King, Jr. reminds us in "I Have a Dream," we will be able to create a society where every individual, regardless of color, can realize the American dream. " [T]hey will not be judged by the color of their skin but by the content of their character" (King 1993, 101). King's vision of people living together in a nonviolent society was the springboard of our inspiration for this project.

Such inspiration is carried on today. With the phenomenal accomplishment of Barack Obama's ascension to the heights of this country as the 44th president of the United States, Black Americans are even more inspired to reach as far as their vision and dreams will take them. As we celebrate our president, let us remember not only how far we have come but also how far we need to go. Slavery seems so long ago; in the history of the world, however, such suffering happened in the blink of an eye. Since the abolition of slavery, through the 20th century and into the 21st century, Black Americans have made tremendous contributions to America and the world. One can only imagine how many more inventions, discoveries, and advancements Black Americans could have made had it not been for slavery. More miraculous achievements remain to be gained.

We owe a great deal of gratitude to the historical Black American pioneers upon whose shoulders we stand. It is probably best said by scholar Benjamin E. Mays, who wrote:

> We, today, stand on the shoulders of our predecessors, historical Black American pioneers, who have gone before us. We, as their successors, contemporary Black American pioneers, must catch the torch of freedom and liberty passed on to us by our ancestors. We cannot lose this battle. (Mays and Colston 2002)

We hope *Voices of Historical and Contemporary Black American Pioneers* will help you forge your own path while honoring the contributions of the pioneers. One way to begin acknowledging and repaying the debt we all owe the pioneers is by paying it forward, lending a helping hand, and making a commitment to make a difference by using your time and financial resources, no matter how large or how small, to make someone's path a little easier; to help build up a neighbor, a friend, or even a stranger (Hyde 2000).

We have faith that this vehicle will inspire you, the future generation of Black Americans, to achieve even more extraordinary successes in all professions, fields of study, and careers. Be proud. Be inspired. Be courageous. Make your mark. Shine a light in the dark. Live the legacy of the ancestors and the pioneers as you build your own. Let *Voices of Historical and Contemporary Black American Pioneers* be your light and guide for years and generations to come. Take your destiny into your own hands. For with faith in self, perseverance, diligence, love, and trust in God's wisdom, there is no goal you cannot achieve.

Vernon L. Farmer, Editor
Evelyn Shepherd-Wynn, Associate Editor

References

Hyde, C. R. 2000. *Paying It Forward: A Novel*. New York: Simon and Schuster.

King, C. S. 1993. *The Martin Luther King, Jr., Companion*. New York: St. Martin's Press.

Mays, B. E., and F. C. Colston. 2002. *Dr. Benjamin E. Mays: Representative Speeches of a Great American Scholar*. Lanham, MD: University Press of America.

Afterword

GUION S. "GUY" BLUFORD, JR.

Colonel, U.S. Air Force (Retired);
Former NASA Astronaut;
President of the Aerospace Technology
Group, North Olmsted, Ohio

Becoming an aeronautical engineer was in the stars for me. If my high school counselor had had her way, however, I would have pursued a career that required less training, aptitude, and altitude. Yet I knew that I could achieve my dream, and I was willing to make the necessary sacrifices. I pursued my passion, and because I did, today, I am known worldwide as the first Black astronaut to fly into space. One of the life lessons of *Voices of Historical and Contemporary Black American Pioneers* is that you should listen to your own heartbeat, follow your dreams, and pursue the profession or career that you desire, no matter how difficult. In this collection, Vernon L. Farmer and Evelyn Shepherd-Wynn bring together the career histories of historical and contemporary Black American pioneers whose achievements, in spite of many adversities, are beyond exceptional. In fact, as you have seen, many became the first in their chosen professions or career fields.

In *Voices of Historical and Contemporary Black American Pioneers*, Farmer and Shepherd-Wynn have methodologically researched the literature, with the goal of providing a pathway toward educating and inspiring readers—Black youth, especially—to pursue their chosen professions or career fields. The constellation of authors whose works are collected here have accomplished this goal. The chapters allow the reader to hear contemporary Black American pioneers tell their stories in their own voices, giving life to this multivolume set. What sets this work apart from other publications is that it brings together the extraordinary achievements of historical and contemporary Black American pioneers in a single collection.

Readers of *Voices of Historical and Contemporary Black American Pioneers* will acquire a wealth of information that can be applied to everyday life and professional success. As you travel along an established trail that Black American pioneers blazed, use your passion to propel you forward, following the trail, or, better yet, blazing new trails, for generations to come. The universe is yours.

About the Editors

Vernon L. Farmer is a professor of educational leadership in the College of Education at Grambling State University. He is a former head of the department and previously served as acting assistant vice president for academic affairs and dean of the Graduate School. He earned his AB, AM, and PhD at the University of Michigan. He studied for the PhD at Michigan's Distinguished Center for the Study of Higher Education. Among Farmer's scholarly works are *Selected Models of Developmental Education Programs in Higher Education, The Black Student's Guide to Graduate and Professional School Success, Meeting the Challenge of Cultural Diversity in Higher Education in the New Millennium*, and *Teaching Culturally Diverse College Students in a Pluralistic Society*.

Evelyn Shepherd-Wynn is an assistant professor of English in the College of Arts and Sciences at Grambling State University. She is a former associate dean and currently interim dean for the college. She earned a BS in English from Grambling State University and an MA in English from Louisiana Tech University. She earned a doctorate of education (EdD) with a major in developmental education at Grambling State University. This unique major is the first of its kind offered in the nation. Wynn's publications include *Teaching Culturally Diverse College Students in a Pluralistic Society* and a number of book chapters. She is currently pursuing her PhD in English literature.

Illustration Credits

The editors and publishers gratefully acknowledge permission for use of the following material:

Index

Note: Page numbers for main entries are in **bold.** Page numbers for photographs are in *italics.*